Nostradamus

by

Tom Jones

DORRANCE PUBLISHING CO., INC.
PITTSBURGH, PENNSYLVANIA 15222

Dorrance Publishing Co., Inc.
701 Smithfield Street
Pittsburgh, PA 15222
Visit our website at *www.dorrancebookstore.com*

ISBN: 978-1-4349-1823-9
eISBN: 978-1-4349-1743-0

Nostradamus
Century I

Nostradamus

Century I

1.   "Being seated by night in secret study, *alone* resting on the brass stool: a slight flame coming forth from the solitude, *that* which is not believed in vain is made to succeed." Being seated by night, as under cover of darkness, a sign of wickedness, in secret study, evil deeds wanting to be hidden, alone or without the council of God, resting on the brass stool, as the Delphic Oracle used, producing his prophetic works: A slight flame of falsely inspired revelation coming forth from the solitude of man's wisdom, the truth which is not believed is preached in vain, in a perverted gospel and made to succeed with converts.

2.   "With rod in hand set in the midst of Branchus, *with* the water he wets both limb and foot: *fearful*, voice trembling through his sleeves: *divine* splendor. The divine seats himself nearby." With the rod or pen in hand set in the midst of Branchus, as the laurel branch used by the ancient oracles on their pen as a sign of honor and fame; with the water or ink, he wets both limb and foot of the pen. Acting fearful with his voice trembling, it is a trick as if a magician pulls something through his sleeves, pretending the divine splendor of God is present, seating Himself nearby.

3.   "When the litter is overturned by the whirlwind, and faces will be covered by their cloaks, *the* republic will be vexed by new people, *then* whites and reds will judge in contrary ways." When the Catholic Church, exalted on the litter, is overturned by the whirlwind of the reformation, and faces of shame will be covered by the cloak of perverted religion, the republic of France will be vexed by new people of Spanish forces, invited to fight against the Protestants. This is when the whites and reds, French white scarves and Spanish indicated by Red scarves, will judge in contrary ways of perverted Catholicism.

4.   "In the world there will be one *monarch who* will not long be in peace or alive: Then the fishing bark will be lost, *it* will be ruled to its greater detriment." The Catholic Church was as one monarch in the world, there being no other Christian faiths, but it will not long be in peace or alive. Then the fishing bark or fishing vessel, indicating the church, will be lost as it is ruled to its greater detriment, away from the truth.

5.   "They will be driven away without much fighting. They will be very much harried in the country: town and city will have a greater debate; Carcassonne and Narbonne will have their hearts tried." The Catholic Church will be driven by false teachings away from the truth without much fighting. The church will be harried in the country as some of the cities become Protestant. These towns and cities have a greater debate as the French cities, represented by Carcassonne and Narbonne, turning to Protestantism, having their hearts tried as the French and Spanish Catholics bring resistance.

6.   "The eye of Ravenna will be forsaken. When the wings give way at its feet: The two of Bresse will have made arrangements in Turin and Vercelli, which the Gauls will trample." The eye of prophecy at Ravenna, Italy, which implies church teachings are forsaken by Protestants. The wings of the Catholic witness gives way where it interferes with the Christian walk. The purged and wicked Catholics of Bresse, France, keep their allegiance with the Catholic faith as they make arrangements in Turin and Vercelli, Italy, representing historical beginnings and tradition, which the Gauls or Protestant invaders will trample.

7.   "The arrival late, the execution completed, *the* wind contrary, the letters seized en route: The conspirators fourteen of a sect, *the* enterprises by the wise Red-Haired One." The late arrival of Theodosius as the last Roman emperor completed an execution order that Ambrose hand over his cathedral church to the emperor. The wind was contrary against this order, or letters, as they were seized en route, not reaching their destination of fulfillment. The Catholic Church to go through seven church ages, later splitting into Roman Catholic and Greek Orthodox, makes up fourteen of a sect at this time. The order was disobeyed by Bishop Ambrose, the wise Red-Haired One.

8.   "How many times will you be taken, solar city, *changing* the barbarian and vain laws: Your evil approaches: you will be more tributary, *the* great 'Adria' will recover your veins." How many more times will the solar city or Catholic Church be taken, captured by false teaching derived by changing the barbarian and vain laws of heathen religion. Because of the Catholic approach of compromise, the church will be more tributary, depending on the converts to regulate church doctrine, similar to the great "Adria" regaining its independence or recovering the Italian veins that were once unified.

9.   "From the Orient will come the Punic heart *to* vex Adria and the heirs of Romulus, *accompanied* by the Libyan fleet, Malta trembling and the neighboring isles empty." From the Orient, Persia will attack, coming

with the Punic heart or treacherous Carthaginian spirit, to vex Adria or Venice and the heirs of Romulus, the other Italian states, accompanied by the Libyan fleet as the Moslems also attacked from the south, Malta trembling from the siege protecting the inhabitants from the neighboring islands left empty.

10.   **"The serpent conveyed in the iron cage *where* the seven children of the *king* are taken: Their progenitors will come out from their underworld below, *before* dying seeing of their offspring death and cries."** The serpent or Catholic Church is conveyed or carried through in the iron cage of the Roman Empire where the seven children or church ages of the king, or Catholic Church, are taken through. Their progenitors or offspring will come out from their underworld below of perverted teachings, before dying to each succeeding age, seeing of their offspring death and cries as they further stray from truth.

11.   **"The motion of sense, heart, feet, and hands *will* be in accord. Naples, Leon, Sicily: swords, fires, waters, then the noble Romans submerged, killed dead because of a weak brain."** The sanity and physical makeup of Italy will be in accord, Naples, Leon, Sicily united in the Roman Empire: then swords, fires, waters as the state system of governments divides the country. Then the noble or proud Romans are submerged, killed, dead, as the French conquer Italy, because of their weak brain, leadership divided in the states.

12.   **"In a short time a false, frail brute will lead, elevated quickly from low to high: Then in an instant disloyal and labile, he who will have the government of Verona."** During a short time, Charles V, false and uncaring, brute in his power and conquests, and fragile in his shaky position and responsibilities, will lead, elevated quickly from low to high, inheriting his empire and conquering the French in Italy. Then at the end of his reign, in an instant, disloyal as he abdicates and becomes labile concerning his empire, he who will have through conquest, the government of Verona, Italy.

13.   **"The exiles because of anger and intestine hatred *will* bring a great conspiracy to bear against the *king*: Secretly, they will place enemies as a threat. And his own old ones against them sedition."** The exiles or Protestant states in Austria, because of anger and hatred of government policy and laws, will bring a great conspiracy to bear against Charles V, secretly placing enemies, like the French, as a threat to distract him, and his own old ones who advise the king, including his relatives, against them sedition to rebel.

14.   **"From the slavish people songs, chants, and requests, *for* princes and lords in the prisons: In the future such by headless idiots will be received as divine utterances."** The Slavs were the heathen who brought with them songs, chants, and requests to influence the Catholic princes and lords in the prisons of perverted doctrines. Later on, these songs, chants, and requests would be received as divine utterance from God, by those headless idiots not following and seeking God.

15. "Mars menaces us with his warlike force, *seventy* times will he cause blood to flow: Rise and fall for the clergy *and* more for those who will want to hear nothing from them." Mars is the Roman god of war representing the Catholic Church, which was menacing and warlike. Seventy is the number of years given to man and represents the lifetime of the church where blood flowed as she persecuted the saints. The church rose to its peak until the reformation, when she began to fall. After the reformation, there was even more insanity and chaos in the church, for those who didn't want to hear the truth.

16. "The (false) joined with the pond towards Sagittarius *at* the high point of its ascendant, *plague*, famine, death by military hand, *the* age advances its revival." The false or wicked are joined with the pond, symbolic place of torment, towards Sagittarius, the ninth sign of the Zodiac, representing the ninth age, after the seven church ages and the millennial age, at the high point of its exaltation, indicating the White Throne Judgement where God's Word is clearly revealed, bringing judgment like plague, famine, death by military hand or the sword of the Word. The age advances with its revival for the saved, too.

17. "For *forty* years the rainbow will not appear, *for forty* years it will be seen every day: The parched earth will wax more dry, *and* great floods will accompany its appearance." For forty years or one generation, the rainbow of God's covenant will not appear for the wicked; for forty years years it will be seen every day by the saved: The parched earth judging the wicked will wax more dry as they separate further from God, and the great floods of God's blessings will accompany the saved with its appearance.

18. "Because of the Gaulic discord and negligence *a* passage will be opened to Mahomet: The land and sea of Siena soaked in blood, the Phocaean port covered with sails and ships." Because of the Gaulic or French discord of losing to Austria in Italy, and French negligence not making wise decisions, a passage, through alliance, will be opened to Mahomet to invade. The land and sea of Siena indicates Italy as the battlefield again; this time, however, the Phocaean port, indicating French ports, will be covered with sails and ships not joining in the fight.

19. "When the serpents will come to encompass the altar. The Trojan blood will be vexed by the Spaniards: Because of them a great number will be made to suffer for it, *the* chief flees, hidden in the marshes." When the Serpents or Habsburg Empire will come to encompass the altar, representing the Italian possessions with the Papal states, the Trojan blood or French will be vexed by the Spaniards, Spain having been added to the Habsburg Empire. Because of the Habsburgs, a great number of French will be made to suffer in warfare. The chief, Frances II, flees back to France, hidden or protected behind the marshes or heavily defended borders.

20. "Tours, Orleans, Blois, Angers, Reims and Nantes, Cities vexed through sudden change: Tents will be pitched by those of foreign tongues, *rivers*, darts at Rennes trembling of land and sea." Tours,

Orleans, Blois, Angers, Reims, and Nantes are French cities vexed through the sudden change of defeat in Italy. Tents will be pitched by the armies of foreign tongues from Austria and Spain. Now, the rivers are as darts at Rennes as the French are trembling on land and sea on the defensive.

21. **"Deep white clay nourishes the rock, *which* from an abyss will go forth milky, *needlessly* troubled they will not dare touch it, *unaware* that the earth at the bottom is clayish."** The deep white clay of the Catholic faith nourishes the rock representing Spain, which, from an abyss of disagreement, will go forth milky in warfare. Needlessly troubled by the Protestant move in France, they will not dare touch Spain with continued fighting, unaware that the earth of the Spanish faith at the bottom being clayish or Catholic would support the rock of Spain from moving in battle against French Catholics as they fight the French Protestants in their country.

22. **"That which will live without having any sense, its artifice will come to be fatally injured: For Autun, Chalon, Langres, and the second Sens, hail and ice will cause much evil."** France will live as a nation without having any sense; its artifice or Catholic guile will be fatally injured by the reformation: France represented by the cities Autun, Chalon, Langres, and the second Sens, also a word meaning sense. Hail and ice of fighting, the Protestants will cause much evil or damage.

23. **"In the third month the Sun rising, *the* Boar and Leopard on the field of Mars to fight: The tired Leopard raises its eye to the heavens, *sees* an Eagle playing around the Sun."** In the third month or spring, the Sun, representing England, is rising to power; the Boar, France, and the Leopard, or Habsburg Empire, are on the field of Mars, representing Italy, where the fighting took place, Mars being the Greek god of war. The tired or aging leopard representing Charles V, the Habsburg king, with his eye raised to the heavens, sees an Eagle, American Colonies, playing, as in its youth, around the Sun or England.

24. **"At the new city contemplating a condemnation, *the* bird of prey comes to offer itself to the heavens: After victory pardon to captives, Cremona and Mantua will have suffered great evils."** At the new city, Naples, representing Italy, contemplating a condemnation of more battles on her soil, the bird of prey or American Colonies comes to offer itself to the heavens, England being the rising power located in the heavens: after victory with its colonial interests, England pardons or forgets about the captives or once attractive and still weak lands of Italy, Cremona and Mantua representing Italy, having suffered great evils or injury from wars.

25. **"Lost, found, hidden for so long a time, *the* pastor will be honored as a demigod: Before the Moon finishes its full period He will be dishonored by other winds."** The Catholic Church claimed to find new truths that had been lost and hidden for so long a time. The pastor or Pope will be honored as a demigod as he adds new doctrines and teachings to the faith. Before the Moon, representing the Catholic Church, finishes the full period of its life, it will be dishonored by other winds of fighting the Protestants.

26. **"The great one of the lightning falls in the daytime, Evil predicted by the bearer of demands: According to the prediction another falls in the nighttime. Conflict at Reims, London, Tuscan plague."** The great lightning of the reformation crashes in the daytime of revival, evil of fighting predicted by the bearer of demands, the Catholic Church demanding one Christian faith. According to the prediction of the Catholic doctrine, another Protestant sinner falls in the nighttime of wickedness, supposedly. Conflict with the Protestants was at Reims, France, and London, England, with Tuscan, Italy represented with plagues from desolation.

27. **"Under the oak tree of Guienne struck from the sky. Not far from there is the treasure hidden: He who for long centuries had been gathered,** *found* **he will perish, his eye put out by a spring."** Under the oak tree of the Catholic Church of Guienne, indicating France, struck from the sky, the reformation came like lightning striking. Not far from the church is the treasure of doctrines hidden or incorporated in Catholicism. The church which for long centuries gathered in unity, found it will perish, his eye of prophecy and leadership put out by the spring or shower of the reformation move.

28. **"The tower of Bouc will fear the Barbarian foist,** *then* **much later, the Hesperian bark: Cattle, people, chattels, both cause great waste, Bull and Balance, what a mortal quarrel!"** The tower of Bouc in France is a watchtower, as the early generations kept watch against the invasions of the barbarians. Later, it was the Hesperian bark that brought fear. The Greeks called Rome the western land or Hesperia, so the Catholic Church is indicated. Both cause great waste to cattle, people, and chattels. The barbarians did it through battle indicated by the Bull, and the church in its later history did it by craft, indicated by the Balance.

29. **"When the terrestrial and aquatic fish** *will* **be put upon the beach by a strong wave,** *its* **form strange, attractive, and frightful,** *by* **sea the enemies very soon at the walls."** The Vikings came in their ships, the terrestrial men riding in the aquatic ships. The ships will be put on the beach by a strong wave of fighting warriors. The manner of attack is strange, unlike other armies, attractive, being very noticeable, and frightful as they instill fear in their victims. Coming by sea, they can reach the city walls very quickly, traveling up the rivers.

30. **"Because of the stormy seas, the strange ship** *will* **approach an unknown port,** *not* **withstanding the signals from the branch of palm. After death, pillage: good advice given late."** The stormy seas of life's struggles for survival cause the strange ship of the Catholic Church to approach a port of a newly discovered group of people. These people having signaled for peace with the branch of palm discover they are being killed and pillaged, as they are caught up in false teachings. Offering themselves in peace didn't avoid ruin after all.

31. **"The wars in Gaul will last for many years,** *beyond* **the course of the monarch of Castulo: Uncertain victory will crown three great ones, the Eagle, Cock, Moon, Lion, Sun engraved."** Wars in France will last many years beyond the course of Charles V, the monarch of Spain, a part of the Habsburg Empire. The Eagle, United States, the Cock-Moon, France, and Lion-Sun, England, are the three great nations crowned with uncertain victory, since all the kingdoms of the world are eventually brought down and God establishes His Kingdom on earth.

32. **"The great empire will soon be transferred *to* a little place which will very soon come to grow: A very lowly place in a petty country *in* the middle of which he will come to lay down his sceptre."** This is when England became a world leader gradually taking over as France began to slip down. England is lowly because it depends upon trade to survive; it is petty because of its business nature, with nothing else to fall back on. The sceptre of world dominion was passed from France to England.

33. **"Near a great bridge of a spacious plain, *the* great Lion with Imperial forces, He will cause a felling outside the austere city, Because of fear the gates will be opened to him."** The great bridge is shipping lanes of the ocean, where England dominated as the great Lion with her Imperial fleet of ships. England will cause a felling, taking world dominion away, outside the austere city, Paris, indicating embittered France. Because she feared war, the gates of the bridge of world dominion will be open to England.

34. **"The bird of prey flying to the left side, *before* the conflict preparation made by the French: One will take it for good, another for ambiguous or inauspicious, the weak party will hold it as a good omen."** The Colonies in America rebelling is indicated where the bird flies to the left or negative side. The French side with the Colonies and give them support against the English, the French taking the conflict as a good omen of England weakening. However, England kept control of the shipping lanes and didn't feel she would be weakened. France is the weak party hoping the Revolutionary War would give some advantage to them.

35. **"The young lion will overcome the old one *on* the field of battle in single combat: He will put out his eyes in a cage of gold: Two fleets one, then to die a cruel death."** England, the young lion, overcomes the old lion in single combat as they competed over world domination. France sits in her cage of gold, feeling confident, but loses her vision of victory, as if two fleets became one in combat and France lost, drowning in the ocean, a cruel death for her shipping trade.

36. **"Too late the monarch will repent *of* not having put to death his adversary: But he will come to consent to a much greater thing, *that* of killing off all his blood."** Too late France repents of overconfidence. She could have taken action against England during the war with the Colonies. But France will have to admit to a much greater thing, killing off French Protestants and causing her own people to emigrate out of the country, which is killing off her own blood.

37. **"Shortly before the Sun sets, Battle is given a great people in doubt: Ruined, the marine port makes no reply, Bridge and sepulchre in two strange places."** Shortly before England loses her world domination, as the sun before it sets, battle is given a great people in the United States whose success was doubtful. However, England, the marine port, is ruined in defeat, not able to make a reply. It is strange for a bridge to be the shipping lanes and the sepulchre to be England, an island in the ocean, not on a large land mass.

38. **"The Sun and the Eagle will appear as victor, *the* vanquished is reassured with a vain reply: With hue and cry they will not cease arming, *revenge*, because of death peace made right on schedule."** England and the United States will appear as victor, because England remains friendly after her losses. The vanquished is France, who lost her domination, and was bitter about it. France reassures herself with the vain reply saying they will ever be arming to protect their world empire. This gives her a feeling of revenge for England's defeat but soon peace with the United States.

39. **"By night the highest one strangled in bed *because* the blond elect had tarried too long. The Empire enslaved by three in substitution, *put* to death with document and packet unread."** Night is a time of sleep, France not being alert, when she was strangled in bed. France considered herself the elect all Catholic nation, but tarried too long to regain trade dominion. The trade empire was captured by the English, three islands, taking France's place, in substitution. France figured on inheriting the empire back from England, but this will or document was left unread, still in the packet.

40. **"The false trumpet concealing madness *will* bear Byzantium a change of laws: From Egypt there will go forth one who wants the withdrawal of Edicts debasing the quality of coins."** The Vatican was the false trumpet trying to conceal the madness of compromise to heathen changing church laws. Byzantium, the Orthodox Catholic Church, was presented these changes. Egypt was under the Byzantium rule and complained about the devaluation of church teachings in France with their new edicts.

41. **"City besieged, and assaulted by night. Few escaped: conflict not far from the sea: On the return of her son a woman fainting from joy. Poison and letters hidden in the fold."** France is a city besieged and assaulted by night, as a judgment meted out like a Vikings' attack. Few can escape a surprise attack which can be carried out easily when the city is near the sea. A son who got released returns, and a woman faints from joy to see her son. However, the enemy had given him poison and letters which would bring even more terror as he would die and the letters would be discovered.

42. **"The tenth of the Calends of April of Gothic count *revived* again by wicked folk: The fire put out, diabolic assembly *searching* for the bones of the Demon of Psellus."** April 10 was a special day for magical evocations, according to the heathen way of figuring, the wicked reviving the observance of this day, France being implied. The fire of truth is put out so the devilish assembly can dig through the ashes in search of the heathen teachings. Psellus had written on how to evoke demons.

43. **"Before the change of empire occurs, *a* very marvelous event will take place: The field moved, the pillar of porphyry *placed*, transferred onto the knotty rock."** Before France loses world dominance with its empire, a marvelous event will take place. The field representing prosperity leaves France. The pillar of porphyry, a purple stone, indicates the country to have world dominion. These are transferred onto the knotty rock, symbolic of England. This rocky terrain would seem an unlikely place for putting a field.

44. **"In short sacrifices will be resumed, Transgressors will be put to martyrdom: No longer will there be monks, abbots, or novices: Honey will be much more expensive than wax."** Soon after the shake-up of the reformation, Catholic France will backslide, resuming the sacrifices of heathen practices. Protestant transgressors are forced to leave the country or be killed, this being a martyrdom. The holy men among the monks, abbots, and novices will not remain as they convert to the new move of God in the reformation. Then the burning of wax for candles will be in less demand, so honey becomes more expensive than the wax.

45. **"Founder of sects much grief to the accuser: Beast in the theater, the pantomine prepared: The inventor exalted by the ancient fact, *the* world confused and schismatic because of sects."** Luther and the other reformers were much grief to the Catholic Church, which stood as the accuser. However, the beast, representing the Catholic Church, is in the theater, where the pantomine exposes sins of the church. The inventor is exalted by God with blessings, because of the ancient truths witnessed. Confused and schismatic from reformation changes, the world goes through a shake-up, with new sects forming.

46. **"Very near Auch, Lectoure and Mirande Great fire will fall from the sky for three nights: A very stupendous and marvelous event will occur: Very soon after the earth will tremble."** Very near France, represented by the three cities, the great fire or revival will take place, lasting for three nights, three church ages where grace has left and judgment is begun for the Catholic Church. The reformation move of God is very stupendous and marvelous. Soon after it starts, the witness of the Word of God brings the earth to tremble under conviction and judgments.

47. **"The sermons from the Lake of Geneva annoying, *from* days they will grow into weeks, *then* months, then years, then all will fail, *the* magistrates will damn their useless laws."** Calvin with his sermons at Geneva had the greatest influence, annoying the Catholic Church, which at first ignored the reformation, thinking that it would be put down in time. However, the days grew into weeks, months, then years; then the Catholic Church considered that all failed. Then the magistrates damned the useless laws of the Catholic Church and turned their cities to the better Protestant stand.

48. **"Twenty years of the reign of the Moon passed, Seven thousand years another will hold its monarchy: When the Sun will take its tired days *then* is accomplished and finished my prophecy."** France and the Catholic Church both represent the Moon, as a fallen witness to the faith after their time of grace ended halfway through the forty years given for a generation. Seven thousand years from Adam, Jesus holds the monarchy with the saints. This time of the White Throne Judgement will also involve the Sun, symbolized by the purged church which slept one thousand years. Nostradamus's prophecies will be fully revealed to all the saints by this time, accomplished and finished.

49.   "Very much before such intrigues *those* of the East by virtue of the Moon: The year 1700 they will cause great ones to be carried off, *almost* subjugating the 'Aquillon' corner." Very much in the forefront are the intrigues concerning the Italian lands to the east, because of France's focus on them. By 1700, the Italian lands will be the reason great nations are carried off or ruined, almost affecting the whole "Aquillon" corner, or Europe.

50.   "Of the Aquatic triplicity there will be born One who will make of Thursday his holiday: His fame, praise, rule and power will grow, *by* land and sea a tempest to the East." England is made up of three parts: England, Scotland, and Ireland and is the mother country of the United States. Thursday is the U.S. holiday, when the nation gives thanks to God for His blessings, Thanksgiving Day. Fame, praise, rule and power came as the U.S. grew to dominate the world, by land and sea a tempest or agitation to the rest of the world east of her.

51.   "Jupiter and Saturn in the head of Aries, Eternal God, what changes! Then for a long age his wicked time returns, Gaul and Italy, what disturbance." Jupiter is an Italian god showing Italy sowing seeds of the early Catholic doctrines, Saturn being a seed-sowing God. The head of Aries shows this to be the first church age, Aries being the first sign of the Zodiac. "Eternal God, what changes" indicates the reformation with its new witness of truths. After a long age with the reformation, the Catholic Church returns to its wicked prominence, represented by both France and Italy, in disturbance of judgment.

52.   "The two wicked ones conjoined in Scorpio, *the* Grand Seignior murdered in his hall: Plague to the Church by the King newly joined, Europe low and northerly." France conquers Italy so they are together briefly to represent the church in its last judgment, Scorpio being the eighth sign of the Zodiac to represent the age following the seven church ages. The Grand Seignior represents the Pope murdered in the hall or church, symbolic of judgment or plague to the church in its last newly joined condition and shown when Charles V overran Italy. The countries represented are Italy, low, and France, northerly, in Europe.

53.   "Alas! A great people will one see tormented *and* the holy law in utter ruin, *other* laws throughout all Christendom, *when* a new mine of gold and silver is discovered." In despair, the Catholic Church is now seen in torment with their dogma and doctrine, which they consider holy, going into complete ruin. The true laws of the Bible are made available with the revivals of reformation and a new mine of gold and silver discovered, the silver of William Branham's ministry and gold of Thomas.

54.   "Two revolutions made by the wicked scythe bearer, *change* made in realm and centuries: The movable sign so intrusive in its place to the

two equal and like-minded." The two revolutions indicate two life periods as though the Catholic Church, or the wicked scythe bearer, Saturn, died and later resurrected with a larger realm and in a later century. Libra, the movable sign is the seventh sign of the Zodiac; the Catholic Church moving into the seventh church age becoming intrusive or important in its place among the churches; the Catholic teachings of both periods being equal and like-minded.

55. "**Under the climate opposite to the Babylonian *there* will be great effusion of blood, *the* unrighteous will be on land and sea, in air and sky, *sects*, famine, realms, plagues, confusion.**" The climate represents the condition opposite because it is on the same level as the Babylonian, the church taking people into captivity. Effusion of blood shows that this leads to spiritual death for many. The unrighteous on land and sea, as well as in air and sky, shows the period of this end time where air travel exists. The different sects have a famine for the word and their realms have plagues of judgments for rejecting God.

56. "**You will see great change made soon and late, *extreme* horrors and vengeances. Because as the Moon is conducted by its angel, *the* Sun is approaching its inclinations.**" A great change occurs soon when the wickedness of the Catholic Church or Moon is in the fifth church age or reformation, and suddenly the sun rises with the reformation and outshines the moon, causing it horror. Great change is made late when the Catholic Church is resurrected in the seventh church age and outshown by the coming of the Lord in the last revival, which is vengeance of final judgments. This is because as Satan conducts the wickedness of the Catholic Church, or Moon, the coming of the Lord conducts the reformation and later revivals of the Sun.

57. "**Through great dissension the earth will tremble. Harmony broken lifting its head to heaven: The bloody mouth will swim in the blood, *on* the ground the face anointed with milk and honey.**" Disagreement among the churches makes the earth tremble, their harmony broken as pride lifts its head to heaven. Those who profess murder and judgment will swim in the blood themselves. Those who keep humble, as on the ground, will see the blessings of God with milk and honey.

58. "**The belly cut, it will be born with two heads *and* four arms: several years it will live intact: The day on which Aquileia will celebrate its feasts, Fossano, Turin, the chief of Ferrara will follow.**" It was an unnatural birth since the church was away from God having two heads, doctrines of early history and later history. It will live intact for several years through the seventh church age. Aquileia, shortlived city in early Italy, represents the early church, its special feast days still followed by Turin of Fassano, Turin being chief over Ferrara, showing the Catholic Church dominating over the Protestant churches.

59. "**The exiles transported to the isles, *at* the advent of a more cruel monarch, *will* be murdered, and burnt two *who* had not been sparing with their speech.**" The Catholic Church, former and latter, are the exiles transported into judgment at the advent of Jesus, reigning in judgment, as though cruel or merciless. The two reigns of the church are murdered and burned, murdered first when the reformation began, and later burned by the wrath of God at His coming, or last outpouring of revival entering the Millennium. The Catholic Church hadn't been sparing in its doctrines of deceit.

60. **"An Emperor will be born near Italy, one who will cost his Empire a high price: They will say that from the sort of people who surround him He is to be found less prince than butcher."** The emperor born is Charles V. Holy Roman Emperor, born near Italy, his empire just about surrounding Italy. He will cost his Empire a high price with wars against France and Moslems. Because of the seditions in his government, he seems to be less of a prince or leader than a butcher, causing the people to divide up and go against him.

61. **"The miserable unhappy republic *will* be ruined by the new magistrate: Their great accumulation in wicked exile *will* cause the 'Suevi' to tear up their great contract."** Switzerland is a miserable unhappy republic ruined by the new magistrate who banished Calvin and his followers. This great accumulation sent in wicked exile will cause the Suevi or Swiss to repent and tear up their great contract with Catholicism, inviting Calvin back to their country, instead.

62. **"Alas! What a great loss will letters suffer, *before* the cycle of Latona is completed: Fire, great deluge more through ignorant rulers *than* will be seen made up for a long time."** Letters are the diplomacy of the Catholic Church as she suffered loss trying to keep control, until her cycle or lifespan is completed. Fire and deluge of judgments occur because of the ignorance of the wicked, separated from God. This great deluge of final judgment to the church won't be seen for a long time, since it is a type of the judgment after the Millennium.

63. **"The scourges passed the world shrinks, *for* a long time peace and populated lands: One will travel safely by air, land, sea and wave, *then* the wars stirred up anew."** The scourges of judgment gone past, the world population is decreased going into the Millennium where there is a long time of peace and populated lands without all the plagues and wars, as before. Travel can be done in safety with the wars over, going by air, land, sea, and wave. Then the wars are stirred up anew during the White Throne Judgement after the Millennium.

64. **"They will think they have seen the Sun at night *when* they will see the pig half-man: Noise, song, battle, fighting in the sky perceived, *and* one will hear brute beasts talking."** Those who slept for a thousand years will then resurrect and figure they have seen the Sun at night when they actually see the moon or pig half-man, representing an adulterated witness of the Word. This follows with noise and song of perverted witness and battle, fighting in the sky, indicating aircraft are still in use during this judgment time. The brute beasts of man's doctrines are heard talking as they proclaim the perverted witness.

65.   "Child without hands never was so great a thunderbolt seen: The royal child wounded at the game of tennis. On the hill fractures: lightning going to grind: Three under the oaks trussed up in the middle." The full and clear witness is seen as a great thunderbolt, the noise shock of it seeming to take the arms right off the person with a perverted witness. Considering themselves royal children of God, they find themselves wounded, their pride hurt, even at a game of tennis. Lightning on the hill fractures the sky as it goes to grind, meting out judgment; the trinity faith in three gods, a type of perverted teachings, is tied up and made helpless.

66.   "He who then will bear the news, He will shortly after come to rest. Viviers, Tournon, Montferrand, and Pradelles. Hail and storms will make them sigh." Those who will bear the good news of the full word of God will shortly find rest and peace of mind, while the wicked, indicated by a type of these cities of France, will experience hail and storms of judgment to make them sigh in grief.

67.   "The great famine that I sense approaching, *often* turning, then becoming universal, *so* great and long that one will come to pull out roots from woods, and babe from breast." The great time of judgment at the end of the Millennium is like a great famine. A person can sense it coming to various places and then becoming universal. The intensity is so great and long the people resort to eating roots for food and taking babies from their mother's breast, lest they both starve.

68.   "Oh, what a horrible and miserable torment, *three* innocent ones whom one will come to deliver. Poison suspected, poorly guarded betrayal: Delivered to horror by drunken executioners." Some of those who slept for a thousand years awake to a horrible and miserable torment of judgment. The three seemingly innocent ones are the gods of perverted teaching, delivered to destruction. They suspect their perverted teachings have been betrayed and poisoned by the "true" doctrine of God, those witnesses of truth called drunken executioners.

69.   "The great round mountain of seven stades, *after* peace, war, famine, flood, *it* will roll far sinking great countries, *even* the ancient ones, and of great foundation." Mt. Vesuvius is a round mountain in Italy, about seven stades high, representing seven church ages with the Catholic Church. After the Millennial peace, it symbolically erupts, typing the last judgment with war, famine, flood, as before it buried Pompeii and Herculaneum. The mountain of God's judgment does more than bury two cities, though; it rolls far sinking great countries. It involves the resurrected of past nations, even ancient nations, and of great foundation.

70.   "Rain, famine, war in Persia not over, *the* too great faith will betray the monarch, *finished* there begun in Gaul: Secret sign for one to be moderate." Persia is one of the ancient countries whose wicked are resurrected for judgment, because of their too great faith, away from the truth, betraying the monarch towards the way of death. The White Throne Judgement finishes things there after the Millennium, the judgments that began in Gaul with the

reformation. The wicked signal the righteous to be moderate or secretive with their witness, which judges them.

71.   "The marine tower thrice taken and retaken by Spaniards, Barbarians, and Ligurians: Marseilles and Aix, Arles by those of Pisa. Devastation, fire, sword, Avignon pillaged by Turinese." The marine tower of Bouc is located near Marseilles and Aix, and Arles, and indicates France. France was taken by three religious groups: the Moslem Spaniards, the Barbarians with their beliefs, and the Catholics two times, represented by the Italians or Ligurians. Italian Pisa first conquered Marseilles, Aix, and Arles with the Catholic faith. Italian Catholic Turinese retook Avignon symbolically, representing France, later, like the resurrecting Catholic Church.

72.   "The inhabitants of Marseilles completely changed, flight and pursuit up to near Lyons. Narbonne, Toulouse wronged by Bordeaux: Killed and captives nearly a million." People of Marseilles are forced to leave as a new group moves in; flight indicates the inhabitants escape as the other group pursues them to near Lyons. Two other cities are wronged by Bordeaux with a million killed and captive, indicating a type of the wicked at the last judgment, on a larger scale than with these French cities.

73.   "France because of negligence assailed on five sides, Tunis, Algiers stirred up by Persians: Leon, Seville, Barcelona having failed, *for* the Venetians there will be no Fleet." French Charles VIII attacked the five Italian states after bribing Spain and the Habsburgs to neglect defending them, resulting in Francis I gaining complete control a few years later. Moslem Tunis and Algiers attack Italian possessions from the south, directed by the Persians who attack from the east towards Venice. The Spanish Moslems indicated by Leon, Seville, and Barcelona, were pushed back in yet earlier history. France asked the Persians to help them fight the Austrians in Italy, so she didn't send her own fleet to Venice.

74.   "After having tarried they will wander into Epirus: The great relief will come towards Antioch, *the* black frizzled hair will strive strongly for the Empire: Bronzebeard will roast him on a spit." Charles V delayed fighting the Moslems, since he was also fighting the French to the West, but his army will finally wander into Epirus, northwestern Greece, after years of fighting. His army was fighting against, or heading towards, Antioch, the Moslem stronghold. Suleiman represents the Moslems with the black frizzled hair, striving strongly for the empire, but Charles V pushed back the Moslems to roast him on a spit, so to speak.

75.   "The tyrant of Siena will occupy Savona: The fort won he will hold the marine fleet: The two armies for the march of Ancona, *because* of terror the chief examines his conscience about it." Francis I of France was the ruler or tyrant of Siena who will occupy Savona. Charles V won the fort there and stopped the French marine fleet, Savona being a port city. The two armies of Charles, including Austria and Spain, march to Ancona and take the rest of Italy. Because of the terror and bloodshed of fighting, with his Spanish

soldiers helping him, Charles assigns control of Italy to Spain, his conscience showing his own inability at ruling in Spain.

76.   "**With a name so wild will he be brought forth *that* the three sisters will have the name for destiny: Then he will lead a great people by tongue and deed, *more* than any other will he have fame and renown.**" The three sisters—Austria, Netherlands, and Spain—will be known as Habsburgs, even though ruled by different men later in history, the French fighting them still fearing their strong ties. Charles led a great people with the size of his empire and conquests, and he proclaimed defense of Christianity from the Moslems. Charles V had the full attention of all Europe as the nations feared his power.

77.   "**Between two seas he will erect a promontory He who will then die by the bite of a horse: His own Neptune will fold the black sail, *through* Gibraltar and the fleet near Rocheval.**" Italy is between two seas, a promontory erected or taken by the French. However, the French there will die by the bite of a horse as Charles V sends his army and conquers by land invasion, or by horse. The Habsburgs own Neptune, god of the seas; folds the black sail up, this representing bad luck and not necessary. They controlled the seas through Gibraltar, and their fleet can now sail near Le Rochevelle, France, easily.

78.   "**He will be born of an old chief with dulled senses, *degenerating* in knowledge and in arms: The Chief of France feared by his sister, *fields* divided, granted to the troops.**" Charles V will be heir to the Holy Roman Empire through Maximilian, his grandfather, whose reign was with dulled senses, the empire degenerating in knowledge to govern and in arms of defense. The chief of France, Charles VIII, was feared by Austria's sister, Spain, as the Spanish lost their Italian possessions to France.

79.   "**Bazas, Lectoure, Condom, Auch, Agen *moved* by laws, quarrel, and monopoly: For Bordeaux Toulouse Bayonne will ruin: Wishing to renew their bull-sacrifice.**" France, represented by these five cities, is disturbed or moved by religious laws and quarreling and Catholic monopoly. Then the cities divide, France represented by three cities this time, going into ruin, wishing to renew their old faith of Catholicism, similar to the Jews wanting to go back to the bull sacrifice rather than take Christianity.

80.   "**From the sixth bright celestial splendor *it* will come to thunder very fiercely in Burgundy: Then of a very hideous beast will be born a monster. March, April, May, June great tearing and clipping.**" Five thousand five hundred years from the fall of Adam, the reformation returning of the Lord will come to thunder very fiercely in France. Then the Catholic Church will change from a hideous beast into a monster as March, April, May, June of the first church ages finish their time of grace and take the church into its judgment of great tearing and clipping (First Book of Adam and Eve, Chapter 38, *Lost Books of the Bible and the Forgotten Books of Eden.*).

81.   "**Nine will be set aside from the human flock, *removed* from judgment and counsel: Their fate will be determined on departure, K., Th., L., dead, banished, astray.**" Nine men are set aside by God and kept

holy to accomplish His work of the seven church ages. They are removed from judgment and council of man, since the Lord keeps them and instructs them. The fate of three will be determined after their departure. Knox and his teachings were killed off in Britain. Thomas and his writings are banished. Luther was considered astray from the Catholic Church.

82. **"When the columns of wood trembling greatly, *led* by the south wind, covered with red ochre: A very great assembly will empty outside, Vienna and the land of Austria will tremble."** The columns of wood is Austria; the forest trembling greatly because of the forest fire directed by the south wind, or France, covering the sky with sparks of red ochre. France got complete control of Italy after defeating Austria at Marignano. Then Austria trembled in anger and emptied its army into Italy in a counterattack.

83. **"The strange nation will divide spoils, Saturn in Mars his aspect furious: Horrible slaughter of the Tuscans and Latins, Greeks, who will desire to strike."** The strange nation, Austria, will divide the spoils as Charles V sent his army to war. Saturn shows Austria in its golden age of glory now in Mars or at war, Mars being the god of war, her fury kindled. The Greeks under Moslem rule will desire to strike, but will be pushed back with a longer war lasting all of Charles's reign.

84. **"The Moon hidden in deep shadows, *her* brother passes with a rusty color: The great one hidden for a long time under the eclipses, Iron will cool in the bloody wound."** The glory of France becomes as the Moon, hidden in deep shadows as her brother, the Sun, outshines her passing, representing Austria emerging in triumph over France. France is hidden for a long time in the shadows and in the solar eclipse just as the Catholic Church or Moon is outshown by the reformation Sun. The iron sword of the Sun cools or dims as it passes into the Moon for the eclipse, indicating the conflict.

85. **"Because of the lady's reply, the King troubled: Ambassadors will take their lives in their hands: The great one doubly will imitate her brothers, Two who will die through anger, hatred and envy."** Because of France's response, after her defeat by Austria, Charles V was troubled. France sent ambassadors to the Moslem enemy, disregarding the risk to Christians. France, the great one, will try again, or doubly, to win against Austria in more fighting over the years, imitating her brothers Austria and Moslems in fighting. Two will die or lose out: France and the Moslems, as they fought Austria through anger, hatred, and envy.

86. **"The great Queen when she shall see herself vanquished *will* act with an excess of masculine courage: On horseback, she will pass over the river entirely naked, *pursued* by the sword: it will mark an outrage to faith."** France, the great queen, when she sees herself defeated in the long battles with the Habsburgs, which includes Spain, will then act with excess manly courage, out of character. Nakedness was a show of defeat as she crossed the river, the sword of the reformers pursuing her, and asked Spain to help her. The reformation marked an outrage to the Catholic faith.

87. **"Volcanic fire from the center of the earth *will* cause trembling around the new city: Two great rocks will make war for a long time. Then Arethusa will redden a new river."** Volcanic fire indicates wars and fighting from the Habsburgs, who were from the center of the earth with their strength, causing trembling around Naples, representing Italy. The two great rocks making war for a long time represent France continuing to fight after losing Italy, and the Moslems continuing to fight, though retreating. Then Arethusa, a Greek god who was changed into a stream, and under the sea emerging as a fountain, represents the new river of the volcano of fighting erupting as the reformation establishes itself more in Austria.

88. **"The divine sickness will surprise the great Prince *shortly* before he will have married a woman, His support and credit will suddenly become slim, Counsel will perish for the shaven head."** Epilepsy, the divine sickness, indicates the unsteady political thinking of Charles V shortly before he abdicated the throne and moved into a monastery, dedicating himself to the church like a marriage. Because of enemy influences, his support and credit suddenly became slim, his counselors leaving him as they think their head or leader is torn down.

89. **"All those from Lerida will be in the Moselle, *putting* to death all those by the Loire and Seine: Marine relief will come near the high wall *when* the Spaniards open every vein."** In France, the fighting turns to the Protestants as those from Lerida will be thrown into the Moselle River, putting them to death by the Loire and Seine Rivers, too. Invited help comes from the Spanish who send their fleet near the French high wall, which once held them back. They open every vein or river entering France as they come to kill off the Protestants.

90. **"Bordeaux, Poitiers at the sound of the tocsin, *with* a great fleet one will go as far as Langon, *their* north wind will be against the Gauls, *when* a hideous monster will be born near Orgon."** The French fight the Protestants in Bordeaux. Poitiers and with the great Spanish fleet will go as far as Langon. The north wind of the French Protestant move will be against France, when the hideous monster of the new Catholic era is born near Orgon, neighborhood of Nostradamus, the French Catholics turning from his Christian views.

91. **"The Gods will make it appear to the mortals *that* they will be the authors of the great conflict: Sword and lance before the sky is seen serene, *so* that there will be a greater affliction towards the left hand."** The false gods of doctrines in the Catholic Church make the followers believe that the church requires them to battle against the Protestants. These gods say sword and lance of conflict must take place before the sky can be seen serene and peaceful. The greater defeat or affliction should go to the wicked, or Protestants, in their opinion.

92. **"Under one peace will be proclaimed everywhere, *but* not long after pillage and rebellion, *because* of a refusal town, land and sea encroached upon, *dead* and captives one third of a million."** Under the

one Catholic Church, peace is proclaimed everywhere within their doctrines, but not long after the Catholics pillage the Protestants who are in rebellion. Because of their refusal, town, land, and sea is encroached upon by the Catholic defenders, with dead and captives being one third of a million, pointing to the future time of spiritual dead and captives resulting from Catholic teachings, blinding them from truth, preventing them from knowing salvation.

93. **"The land of Italy will tremble near the mountains, Lion and Cock not too well confederated, *in* place of fear they will help each other, *alone* Castulo and the Celts moderate."** French controlled Italy was conquered by Charles V, the trembling of fighting done mostly near the mountains in northern Italy. The Lion (Sun), or England, is not well confederated with the Cock (Moon) or France, but because they fear the strength of Charles V, they form the league of Cognac to help each other. Staying alone, Castulo representing Charles V, refused to ally with the Celts or Henry VIII to carve up France, but moderated to keep it intact.

94. **"At port Selin, the tyrant put to death Liberty nevertheless not recovered: The new Mars because of vengeance and remorse, the lady honored through force of terror."** Near port Selin, in northern Italy, now Genoa, close to Pavia, the reign of the tyrant is put to death as Austria defeated Francis I of France, and took him captive. Liberty wasn't recovered, though, because of the new Mars, or renewed fighting between Austria and France, where Francis I tries to get vengeance for the remorse of defeat. France takes care of its honor through force of terror, lasting many years fighting against Austria.

95. **"A twin child found before the monastery One of the heroic blood of an ancient monk: His fame, renown and power through sect and tongue *such* that one will say the perfect twin has been well raised."** Austrian Charles V was as a twin child, also known as Charles I of Spain. He was elected as Holy Roman Emperor, putting him before the religious order succeeding his grandfather, Emperor Maximilian. His fame, renown, and power was mostly in Austria, such that one would say the healthy of the twins was well raised.

96. **"He who will have charge of destroying *temples* and sects changed through fantasy: He will come to do more harm to rocks than to living people *because* of the din in his ears of a polished tongue."** Charles V was leading in the fight against Protestantism and against the Moslem threat, two faiths changed or away from Catholicism, through man's fantasy, supposedly. When he abdicated the throne, he got to where he did more harm to stones than to living people, or became politically harmless because of the polished tongue of his many enemies, within as well as outside the country, forcing him out of his office or reign.

97. **"That which fire and sword did not know how to accomplish, *the* smooth tongue in council will come to achieve: Through repose, a dream, the King will be made to meditate, *the* enemy more in fire and military**

blood." Fire and sword of wars could not defeat Charles V and his army, but the smooth tongue in council did make him abdicate. As if in a dream, the King is made to believe that the enemy is more in defeat than he really is.

98.   "**The chief who will have led an infinite people** *far* **from skies of their own, of customs and tongue strange: Five thousand finished in Crete and Thessaly,** *the* **chief fleeing saved in a marine barn.**" The chief, Charles V, who will have led an infinite people, or large army, far from their own skies of customs and tongue in the Empire strange or diverse, five thousand finished as far into Greece as Crete and Thessaly before Charles fled or abdicated the throne, and saved the rest of his life in a marine or watered farm or monastery.

99.   "**The great monarch who will make company** *with* **two Kings united by friendship: Oh, what a sigh will the great host make,** *children* **around Narbonne, what a pity.**" The great monarch, the Lord, will make company with two kings, two times revealing Himself, once through the ministry of Enoch and the second through the ministry of Thomas, united in friendship or united in agreement of truth. Oh, what a sigh will the great host of the wicked make, these children around Narbonne, France, the nation symbolic of the wicked; what a pity that they refused truth and goodness, as Charles V fights against them, a type of Thomas.

100.   "**For a long time a gray bird will be seen in the sky Near Dole and Tuscan land: Holding in its beak a verdant sprig,** *soon* **the great one will die and the war will end.**" For a long time, even going into the Millennium, a gray bird, or dove, symbolic of peace as proclaimed by the Catholic Church, will be seen in the sky still hanging onto its position near Dole, France, and Tuscan land, indicating Italy, the two representing the last resurrected revival period of the church, where it is holding in its beak a verdant sprig of false promises. Soon the great one will die and the war will end, the son of perdition revealed in its perverted teachings. This also happened with France as she kept the verdant sprig of Catholic teachings, but soon the great church and country will die, and the war will end as the Protestants flee the country.

PARALLEL

95.   The writings of Thomas are found before the church. He is from the heroic blood of an ancient monk, being Enoch returned to taste of death. According to his fame, renown and power in his second ministry, it will be such that one will say the perfect or healthier twin has been well raised, the second ministry with Enoch's return being perfect or greater in the comparison.

96.   Thomas, who will have the calling to minister judgment through God's Word, destroying temples and sects that have perverted the truth through man's fantasy, will come to do more harm to rocks of wrong decision or revelation, than to living people, because of the din in his ears arousing him to go against the polished tongue of error.

97.   Fire and sword of worldly wisdom was not able to teach Thomas, but the smooth tongue or still small voice of the Holy Ghost in council will come to accomplish it. Through repose, resting in the Lord, the King, Thomas as a king and priest in Christ, will be made to meditate a dream or vision of God's fullness. The enemy and the wicked are seen more in fire and military blood of judgments.

98.   The chief, representing the prophet, will have led an infinite people of the saved arriving from other centuries and skies or countries of their own, of different customs and tongue. As Charles V during his reign fought against the Moslems moving them back from Crete and Thessaly, the ministry of Thomas will fight with the sword of truth against perverted religions in his ministry. The prophet's ministry fleeing from sin in the world is saved in a marine barn or a ship, the ship of Zion.

Nostradamus
Century II

Nostradamus

Century II

1.   "**Towards Aquitaine from the British Isles *by* great invasions through these themselves. Rains, frosts will make the soil uneven, Port Selyn will make mighty invasions.**" Towards Aquitain in south France, from the British Isles bordering to their north, there will be great invasions by the French themselves to possess Italy. Rains and frosts making the soil uneven indicates wars causing changes in boundaries, as Port Selyn, indicating the Moslems, is making mighty invasions expanding the Turkish Empire, too.

2.   "**The blue head will strike upon the white head *as* much evil as France has done for their advantage. Dead at the sail-yard the great one hung on the branch, when seized from his own the king saying how much.**" The blue head, Charles V, blue showing royalty like a new believer, will strike upon the white head, Francis I, white being self-righteous purity, as much evil as France has done for their own benefit capturing Italy. "Dead at the sail-yard, the great one hung on the branch," symbolizes the capture of Francis I as he is taken from his own and forced to say how much to concede for his release.

3.   "**Because of the solar heat on the sea *of* Euboea the fishes half cooked: The inhabitants will come to cut them, *when* the biscuit will fail Rhodes and Genoa.**" Because of the solar heat of Habsburgs attacking on the sea of **Euboea**, Moslem territory, the fishes of the allied French and Turks are half cooked from Moslem defeats. The inhabitants of Italy now, the Habsburgs, will come to cut then in warfare when the biscuit will fail to sustain Rhodes or Moslems, and Genoa or the French, as from a siege.

4.   **From Monaco to near Sicily *the* entire coast will remain deserted: There will remain there no suburb, city or town *not* pillaged and robbed by Barbarians.**" From Monaco to near Sicily, the entire west coast of Italy

will remain deserted of Moslems after the Habsburgs recapture the country. No suburb, city, or town not pillaged and robbed with the Moslem captivity as these barbarians or non-Christians had dominated in Italy.

5. **"That from in the fish, including iron and letter, out will go one who will then make war, He will have his fleet well rowed by sea, *appearing* near Latin Land."** That from within the fish, the Pisces sign being two fish, indicating the French and Turk alliance, including the iron of warfare to be done by the Turks and the letter of support that the French promise to supply, out will go one, the Turks, who will then make war, he who will have his fleet well rowed at sea, appearing at Latin Land, or Italy.

6. **"Near the gates and within two cities There will be two scourges the like of which was never seen, *famine* within plague, people put out by steel, *crying* to the great immortal God for relief."** Near the gates of Italy are the French and within Italy the Moslems fighting, as two cities allied to make two scourges and never the like of it was ever seen, like famine within plague, the people, Habsburg occupants, are put out by steel of the Moslem sword, the Habsburgs like the saints crying to the great immortal God for relief when shaken.

7. **"Amongst several transported to the isles, one to be born with two teeth in his mouth They will die of famine the trees stripped, *for* them a new King issues a new edict."** Among the several armies transported to the isles of Italy, one to be born, Suleiman, with two teeth in his mouth, being the Turk army with its French ally nearby, Italy will be dying of famine as its resources are taken by the Turks after capturing Italy from the Habsburgs. For Italy, a new king, Suleiman, issues a new edict of Moslem laws.

8. **"Temples consecrated in the original Roman manner, *they* will reject the awkward foundations, *taking* their first and humane laws, *driving* away, though not entirely, the cult of saints."** From the temples consecrated in the early Roman or Christian manner, the Moslems will reject these awkward foundations, instead engaging in their own elementary and humane Moslem laws, driving away, though not entirely, the Christian sect of the saints.

9. **"Nine years the lean one will hold the realm in peace, *then* he will fall into a very bloody thirst: Because of him a great people will die without faith and law killed by one far more good-natured."** Nine years the lean one, Frances I, will hold the realm, Italy in peace, or without serious opposition. Then, or during the nine years, he will fall into a very bloody thirst of greed, renewing the Italian wars. Because of him instigating more wars, a great people without true faith, indicating the Christian French, and without law, indicating later allied with the Turks, will die, killed by one far more good natured, Charles V, who holds true to God's Word.

10. **"Before long they will be subdued, *we* will expect a very sinister century, *the* realm of the masked and solitary ones much changed, *few* will be found who want to be in their place."** Before long, they will all be subdued by Charles V; we will expect a very sinister century of warfare like the

former hundred years war. The realm of the masked ones, Moslems, and solitary ones, French, keeping to themselves even though allied, will be much changed by defeats, because of the Habsburg counter attacks so that few will be found who want to be in their place.

11. **"The nearest son of the elder will attain *very* great height as far as the reign of the privileged: Everyone will fear his fierce glory. But his children will be thrown out of the realm."** The nearest son, Suleiman I, of the elder Francis I, related by alliance, will attain very great height as far as the reign of the privileged. Everyone will fear his fierce glory as he wages war capturing Italy, but his children will be thrown out of the realm as later in history the Moslems are pushed out from their conquered territories.

12. **"Eyes closed shall be open by antique fantasy. The garb of the lonely will be put to naught: The great monarch will punish their frenzy, *ravishing* the treasure from before the temples."** People with eyes closed, being sinners, shall have them opened to God by the old fantasy of the Moslem faith, the garb of the solitary or Christain religion of the French solitary ones, like Catholicism with their monks being solitary, shall be abolished. The great monarch, Suleiman, shall punish their madness of perverted Christianity as he ravished the treasure in front of their temples.

13. **"The body without soul no longer to be at sacrifice: Day of death put for birthday: The divine spirit will make the soul happy. Seeing the Word in its eternity."** The body without soul, or sinful life, will no longer be sacrificed or put to death, the day of death put for the birthday as the saved walk in newness of life. Instead, it will be the divine spirit who will make the soul happy, as the believer sees the Word in its eternity through the Moslem faith.

14. **"At Tours, Gien, guarded, eyes will be searching, *discovering* from afar her serene Highness: She and her suite will enter the port, *combat*, thrust, sovereign power."** At Tours, Gien, indicating France, her fearful or guarded eyes searching and discovering from afar, not participating in the fighting though allied with the Moslems, seeing the serene Highness, the Habsburgs, representing the believer with the peace that passes all understanding. Charles V and his army, like Jesus followed by His army of angels, will enter the port in Italy with the combat thrust of the new counter offensive.

15. **"Shortly before the monarch is assassinated, Castor and Pollux in the ship, bearded star: The public treasure emptied by land and sea. Pisa, Asti, Perrar, Turin land under interdict."** Shortly before the monarch Suleiman is assassinated, indicating his retreat from Italy, Castor and Pollux, sons of Zeus, enter into the ship, like the double annointing of God's fullness entering into the believer, because of the bearded star, Enoch, publisher of these revelations, Charles V also reinforced to double strength: the public treasure of Italy emptied by land and sea by Moslems: Pisa, Asti, Ferrera, and Turin being Italy under Moslem interdict.

16.   **Naples, Palermo, Sicily, Syracuse, New Tyrants, celestial lightning fires: Force from Londres, Ghent, Brussels and Susa, Great slaughter, triumph leads to festivities."** Naples, Palermo, Sicily, Syracuse, indicate Italy, where new tyrants, France allied to the Moslems, cause lightnings of celestial fires with fighting and burning. The force of espionage is used by Landres, indicating France, against Ghent, Brussels, and Susa, indicating Habsburgs, causing great slaughter by rebellions, triumph leading to festivities for the French.

17.   **"The field of the temple of the pure virgin, *not* far from Elne and the Pyrenees mountains: The great passage is hidden in the trunk, *to* the north rivers overflown and vines battered."** The Habsburg country with the temple (person) of the pure virgin (believer), not far from Elne and the Pyrenees mountains bordering France, the great passage by espionage has documents hidden in the trunk of the spy passing to the north. Austria, where rivers are overflown and vines are battered, symbolizing rebellions created.

18.   **New and sudden, impetuous rain will suddenly halt two armies. Celestial stone, fires make the sea stony. The death of seven by land and sea sudden."** A new and sudden, impetuous rain will be the Habsburg counter attack that will suddenly halt two armies, the Moslems in Italy allied with the French. Celestial stone or hail, and fires of lightning bolts in the sky describe this counter attack as a storm making the sea rough, the death or defeat of seven, like the termination of the seven church ages at the end time by land and by sea in spiritual warfare will be sudden, as with the Moslems and French.

19.   **"Newcomers, place built without defense. Place occupied then uninhabitable: Meadows, houses, fields, towns to take at pleasure. Famine, plague, war, extensive land arable."** The newcomers, or Habsburgs, will return to recapture Italy and build the place without defense, the attitude of the saints who put their trust in God to be their defense instead of their own means. Italy is occupied by them again, where it was not habitable, being held by the Moslems, before: the meadows, houses, fields, towns are theirs to take at pleasure, the famine and plague of war leaving the extensive land of Italy arable to them again.

20.   **"Brothers and sisters captive in diverse places will find themselves passing near the monarch: Contemplating them his branches attentive, displeasing to see the marks on chin, forehead, and nose."** Christian brothers and sisters captured by the Moslems are held in diverse places in slavery, finding themselves passing before the Moslem monarch, as he looks upon them, contemplating them attentively as if they are his offspring or branches, it being displeasing to see the marks on chin, forehead, and nose of the more rebellious ones.

21.   **"The ambassador sent by biremes. Halfway repelled by unknown ones: From the salt four triremes will come, reinforced in Euboea bound with ropes and chains."** The ambassador, Charles V, being like the saint as ambassador for Christ, is sent by biremes, or small ships, showing power for witnessing. Halfway, indicating the ability to drive out the French, but not to

keep possession of Italy. Charles V is repelled by unknown ones, the Moslems secretly allied to the French, but from the salt or ocean, Charles V comes reinforced with four triremes, increased power, as the saint reinforced by God's Word; in Euboea, the Moslems bound up with ropes and chains of defeat.

22. **"The imprudent army of Europe will depart, *uniting* itself near the submerged isle: The weak fleet will bend the phalanx, *at* the navel of the world a greater voice substituted."** The imprudent army of Europe, the defeated French, will depart out of Italy, later uniting itself near the island, Sicily, submerged or unseen because of secret alliance with Moslems, the French fleet will in this way bend the phalanx of the Moslem army at the navel of the world. Italy, as the greater voice of allied strength, is substituted for the single force of just the French army, before defeated.

23. **"Palace fowl, by the bird chased out, *very* soon after the prince has arrived: Although the enemy is repelled beyond the river, *outside* seized, the trick upheld by the unremitting bird."** The palace fowl of the French in Italy are chased out by the bird of the Habsburg counter attack very soon after the prince, Francis I has arrived in full power with his army. Although the Habsburgs had been repelled beyond the river or out of Italy, Francis I, being outside his own country is siezed, the counter attack trick successful by the unremitting Habsburgs.

24. **"Beasts ferocious from hunger will swim across rivers: The greater part of the army will be against the Hister, *the* great one will cause him to be dragged in an iron cage, *when* the German child will be cautious for nothing."** Beasts, indicating the Habsburg countries, ferocious from hunger, will swim across rivers: the greater part of the Habsburg army was kept back against the Ister or Danube, but the great one, Habsburgs, will cause him, Francis I, to be dragged in an iron cage, indicating his capture, when the German child, Charles V, will be cautious for nothing in his counter attack.

25. **"The foreign guard will betray the fortress, hope and shadow of a higher marriage: Guard deceived, fort seized in the press, Loire, Saona, Rhone, Garonne, by death outraged."** The foreign guard or Habsburg army will betray the fortress of the French who had hopes for and even the shadow, through military successes, for a higher marriage with Italy being their possession. However, the French guard was deceived with their easy triumph when the French fort was seized in the press by the Habsburg counter offensive, leaving the French, indicated by Loire, Saone, Rhone, Garonne, with the outrage of death, or defeat.

26. **"Because of the favor that the city will show *to* the great one who will soon lose the field of battle, *then* into the Po position, the Ticino will overflow *with* blood, fires, deaths, flooded by the long-edged blow."** Because of the favor of deceitful encouragement that the city easily captured in Italy will show to the great one, Frances I, who will soon lose the field of battle; then into the Po position, the Ticino, tributary to the Po River, will overflow with blood fires and deaths of warfare, flooding by the cutting blow of the Habsburg counter attack.

27.   "The divine word will be struck from the sky, one who cannot proceed any further: The secret closed up with the revelation, *such* that they will march over and ahead." This divine word of God, like a sword, will be struck from the sky as with the witness of a believer, symbolized by Charles V, so that he, Francis I, cannot proceed any further in conquest, similar to Satan's perversions trying to conquer the world: the revelation of the hidden secret of God's Truth, such that one will march over and ahead with it in victory as Charles V did.

28.   "The penultimate of the surname of the Prophet will have Diana for his day and rest: He will wander far because of a furious head. In delivering a great people from imposition." The last but for one being of the name of the prophet, indicating the Mohammedans, will have the moon goddess Diana, symbolic of the Moslem faith, or the reflected light instead of the direct Christian sunlight of God's Word, for his day of rest with salvation. The Turks wander far conquering, because of Suleiman, their furious head, in delivering a great people from imposition of the Christian faith.

29.   "The Easterner will leave his seat, *to* pass the Apennine mountains to see Gaul: He will transpierce the sky, the waters, and the snow, *and* everyone will be struck with his rod." The Easterner, Suleiman I, will leave his seat in Turkey, to pass the Apennine Mountains of Italy to see Gaul in alliance: like the wicked he will penetrate in warfare the sky of the believer with the rod of chastisement, the waters or saved being purged, and the snow or wicked experiencing judgment, and everyone will be struck with his rod because of weak Habsburg resistance.

30.   "One who the infernal gods of Hannibal *will* cause to be reborn, terror of mankind Never more horror nor worse of days, in the past than will come to the Romans through Babel." Suleiman I is one who will cause the infernal or warlike gods of Hannibal, Moslem faith, to begin a terror of mankind from the Moslem faith becoming perverted: never more horror nor worse of days in the past will come to the Romans, Italy, from Babel, indicating the Moslem take over.

31.   "In Campania the Capuan (River) will do so much *that* one will see only fields covered by waters: Ahead after the long rain One will see nothing green except the trees." In Campania, Italy, the city Capua on the Vulturno River, suggesting the Capuan River, will have so much flooding that one will see only fields covered by waters, this being the capture of Italy by the Moslems. Ahead after this long rain or warfare, one will see nothing green except the trees stranding above the flood waters, indicating the destruction.

32.   "Milk, blood, frogs prepared in Dalmatia. Conflict given, plague near Treglia: A great cry will sound through Slavonia: Then a monster will be born near and within Ravenna." Milk, indicating the saints, blood, indicating the purged, and frogs, indicating the wicked, will be prepared like a brew in Dalmatia with conflict given by the Moslems, plague of fighting also near Treglia, central Italy and a great cry of battle will be heard through all

Slovakia, another part of the Turkish conquest. This is when the Moslem monster revived in near countries and within Ravenna or Italy.

33. **"Through the torrent which descends from Verona its entry will then be guided to the Po, *a* great wreck and no less in the Garonne, *when* those of Genoa march against their country."** Through the torrent of Habsburgs attacking, which descends from Verona, Italy, his entry by then guided as if by the Po River will cause great shipwreck of defeat, and no less in the Garonne, indicating allied France, when the Habsburgs, coming from Genoa, northern Italy, will march against their Moslem held country of Italy.

34. **"The senseless ire of the furious combat will cause steel to be flashed at the table by brothers: To part them death, wound, and curiously, the fierce duel will come to harm France."** The senseless hatred of furious combat will cause the Habsburg and French brothers, both Christian nations, to flash their swords at the table of their meeting in Italy to part them death and wound in warfare, and curiously, the fierce duel will come to harm France by Moslem loss of Italy.

35. **"The fire by night will take hold in two lodgings, *several* within suffocated and roasted. It will happen near two rivers as one: Sun, Sagittarius, and Capricorn all will be reduced."** Fire of judgment by night, or against the wicked, will take hold in two lodgings, typed by France and Turks, and typed by Catholics and Protestants, several within, like the wicked are suffocated and roasted in judgment. It will happen near two rivers as if one, indicating the increased strength of the Habsburg army like a flood. The sun shining in the eighth Millennial judgment, Sagittarius the ninth sign and ninth Millennium, and Capricorn, the tenth, at which time the wicked will be reduced in judgment.

36. **"The letters of the great Prophet will be valued, they will come to fall into the hands of the tyrant: His enterprises will be to cheat their King, but his plunderings will very soon trouble him."** The great prophet, indicating Suleimam I, whose letters will be valued, will come into the hands of the tyrant, Francis I, in allegiance. His Moslem enterprises will be to cheat their king, Francis I, but the Moslem plunderings will very soon trouble him, the French retrieving many of the captured Christian slaves, later.

37. **"Of that great number that one will send *to* relieve those besieged in the fort, *plague* and famine both will devour them, *except* seventy who will be destroyed."** Of that great number that one, Suleiman I, will send into Italy to fight to relieve the French who are staying back in their own country, like besieged in their fort, plague and famine of difficulties will devour them like the final judgment, except for seventy representing earlier prejudgment in the gentile ages, which are ruined or ended at the coming of the Lord, like the Habsburgs attacking the Moslems.

38. **"The condemned will be a great number *when* the monarchs will be reconciled: But for one of them such a bad impediment will arise *that* they will be joined together but loosely."** The condemned, like the wicked, will be a great number when the monarchs, France and Turks, will he reconciled in alliance. But for one of them, the Moslems, such a bad impediment will arise from Christian captives being held in slavery, that the two allied will be joined together but loosely.

39. **"One year before the Italian conflict, Germans, Gauls, Spaniards to the fort: The republican schoolhouse will fall, *there*, except for a few, they will be choked dead."** One year before the Italian conflict involving France in Italy, the German Habsburgs, Gauls or French, and Spanish Habsburgs go to the fort or prepare for the war, the republican schoolhouse or France will fall when, except for a few who escape, they will be choked dead in defeat, this being a type of the lesser judgment, or prejudgment during the church ages.

40. **"Shortly afterwards, without a very long interval. By sea and land a great uproar will be raised: Naval battle will be very much greater, fires, animals, those who will cause greater insult."** Shortly afterwards, without a very long interval from the Habsburg Italian triumph, by sea and land a great tumult of battle will be raised again. Naval battle against the Habsburgs will be much greater, and the fires and beasts in the land, being the Moslem army as if riding horses and holding torches, will make a greater insult in warfare than France did earlier.

41. **"The great star will burn for seven days, *the* cloud will cause two suns to appear: The big mastiff will howl all night *when* the great pontiff will change country."** The great star of the gentile dispensation will burn for seven days or seven church ages, then the cloud of the Lord's coming will cause two suns to appear, being the double portion or fullness of God's Word (the sun appearing larger through the clouds like two suns.). The big mastiff or dog, indicating the Catholic Church, will howl all night in judgment when the great pontiff will change country, like the French allying with the Turks, and later Catholic to Protestants.

42. **"Cock, dogs, and cats will be satiated with blood *and* from the wound of the tyrant found dead, *at* the bed of another legs and arms broken, He who wouldn't have fear to die a cruel death."** Cock, France, allied with the Turks, like dogs and cats fighting, will be satiated with blood, and from the wound of the tyrant, or Habsburgs, they are found dead in defeat, France at the bed of another, the Turks, with legs and arms broken, France not being afraid to die a cruel death, like a sinner who has his conscience seared.

43. **"During the appearance of the bearded star, *the* three great princes will be made enemies: Struck from the sky, peace earth quaking, Po, Tiber overflowing, serpent placed upon the shore."** During the appearance of the bearded star, Charles V, the three great princes, Francis I, Suleiman I, and Charles V, will be made enemies: struck from the sky will be the lightning counter attack of Charles V, peace on the earth shaking, Po, Tiber, rivers in Italy overflowing in this judgment like serpent rivers placed upon the shore, out of their channels.

44. "**The Eagle thrusting around the tents *will* be chased from there by other birds: When the noise of cymbals, trumpets, and bells *will* restore the senses of the senseless lady.**" The eagle, indicating the standard thrusting in the wind around the tents of the Moslem army, will be chased from Italy by other birds, the reinforced Habsburgs, when the noise of cymbals, trumpets, and bells of warfare will finally restore the senses of the senseless lady or Habsburgs, like the great shaking to the saints so they will desire God's new revelations.

45. "**Too much the heavens weep for the Hermaphrodite begotten, *near* the heavens human blood shed: Because of death too late a great people re-created, late and soon the awaited relief comes.**" Too much the heavens, indicating the saints, weep in chastisement because of the hermaphrodite begotten being the Catholic and Protestant churches united at the end time: near the heavens, indicating the saved, human blood of purging is shed: because of death in sin, it is too late for a great people re-created, late with the resurrected wicked and soon with the perverted churches as the awaited relief of judgment comes.

46. "**After great trouble for humanity, a greater one is prepared The Great Mover renews the ages: Rain, blood, milk, famine, steel, and plague, *in* the heavens fire seen, a long spark running.**" After great trouble or tribulation for humanity a greater one, the saints, are prepared, the Great Mover, the Lord, renews the ages with rain of blessings mixed with blood of judgments, milk of blessings mixed with famine of judgments, the steel or sword of God's Word mixed with plague to the rebellious as in the heavens of the righteous the fire of truth is seen as lightning.

47. "**The great old enemy mourning dies of poison. The sovereigns subjugated in infinite numbers: Stones raining, hidden under the fleece, *from* death articles are cited in vain.**" The great old enemy, World Council of Churches, dies by defeat from poison, perverting the faith, similar to the sovereigns, France and Moslems, subjugated in infinite numbers in defeat: the hailstones raining judgments hidden under the fleece or clouds of Christ's return, from death or sin the articles of the faith are cited in vain by Catholic and Protestant.

48. "**The great force which will pass the mountains. Saturn in Sagittarius Mars turning from the fish: Poison hidden under the heads of salmon. Their war-chief hung with cord.**" The great force of the wicked passes the mountains as in retreat when Saturn, the false seed sower, is in Sagittarius, the ninth millennium, where Mars of judgement is turning from the fish or wicked, judgement being completed, poison hidden under the heads of salmon, being perverted teachings accepted by the wicked, as their war chief, Satan is being hung with cord of defeat.

49. "**The advisers of the foremost monopoly, *the* conquerors seduced for Malta: Rhodes, Byzantium for them exposing their pole: Land will fail the pursuers in flight.**" The advisors of the foremost monopoly, French and Moslems, are the conquerors, seduced by greed for Malta or Italy. Rhodes and Byzantium, the Turks, for them exposing their pole by applying their army in battle, the land, Italy, will fail the pursuers, French and Moslems being in retreat.

50.   "When those of Hainaut, of Ghent and of Brussels *will* see the siege laid in front by Langres: Behind their flanks there will be cruel wars, *the* ancient wound will do worse than enemies." When those Habsburgs of Hainaut, Ghent, and Brussels will see the siege by Langres or France laid in front of them, from behind the flanks of the battle line there will be painful quarrels as the ancient wound of grievances is aroused by French spies among the Habsburgs, doing more damage making rebellions, than enemies could do with armies fighting.

51.   "The blood of the just will commit a fault at Landes, Burnt through lightning of twenty threes the sixes: The ancient lady will fall from her high place. Several of the same sects will be killed." The blood of the just, like the Habsburgs, will be the fault of Landes, being France, like the Catholic Church burnt through lightning of twenty threes, the sixes or 666, Satan's mark. The ancient lady, the Catholic Church, will fall from her high place of self exaltation and many of the same sect, Protestant Christians, will be killed from perverting the faith.

52.   "For several nights the earth will tremble: In the spring two efforts in pursuit: Corinth, Ephesus will row from the seas: War stirred up by two valiant in combat." For several nights, just before the great tribulation of judgments waiting the wicked, the earth will tremble: in the spring with two efforts of the French and Moslems in pursuit of conquest: Corinth, Ephesus or Moslems will row from the seas, as war is stirred up by the two allied valiant in combat.

53.   "The great plague of the maritime city *will* not cease until there be avenged the death *from* the just blood, condemned for a price without crime, of the great lady unwronged by pretense." The great plague of warfare by the maritime city France, will not cease until there be avenged the death, or defeat, from the just blood or Habsburgs, condemned for the price of possessing Italy, though it was no crime, by the great lady France who was actually unwronged by pretense.

54.   "Because of people strange, and distant from the Romans *their* great city of water much troubled: Maid handless, domain too different, Chief taken, lock not having been picked." Because of Habsburgs, a people strange, and from the Romans or French distant, their great French city seeking after water of conquest is much troubled, the French maid handless or powerless with her domain too different after losing Italy, the chief, Francis I, taken by the Habsburgs, the lock of French army security not having been picked illegally.

55.   "In the conflict the great one who was worth little *at* his last will perform a marvelous deed: While Adria will see what was lacking, *during* the banquet the proud one stabbed." In the conflict, the great one, France, who was worth little at his last attempt against the Habsburgs, performs a

marvelous deed allying with the Turks. While Adria, Italy, under Habsburg rule, will see what France was lacking by its defeat to the Habsburgs, during the banquet or victory party, the proud Habsburg victor is stabbed by Moslem invasion into Italy.

56. **"One whom neither plague nor steel knew how to finish, Death on the summit of the hills struck from the sky: The abbot will die when he will see ruined Those of the wreck wishing to seize the rock."** Habsburgs, who plague and sword of the French couldn't finish, to them death of defeat on the summit of the hills from Moslems invading Italy, striking like lightning from the sky: the abbot, symbolizing the Catholic faith in Italy will die when he will see ruined those of the wreck or defeated Italy, wishing to seize the rock of St. Peter instead of the Moslem faith.

57. **"Before the conflict the great wall will fall, the great one to death, death too sudden lamented, Born imperfect: the greater part will swim: Near the river the land stained with blood."** In the conflict, the great wall of French and Moslems will fall, the great one to death, death of judgment too sudden and lamented by their thinking, born imperfect in this allegiance, the greater part being two armies now, will swim away in defeat, near the river the land is stained with blood from Habsburg counter attack, like rivers that flooded.

58. **"With neither foot nor hand because of sharp and strong teeth *from* the crowd at the fort of the port and the elder born: Near the portal treachery proceeds, Moon shining, little great one led off."** Habsburgs with neither foot nor hand because of sharp and strong teeth from the Moslem throng at the fort of the Italian port and the elder born or allied French: near the portal leading into Italy treachery of the Moslem attack proceeds, moon shining symbolic of Moslem success as the little great one or Habsburgs chastised, in defeat are led off retreating.

59. **"Gallic fleet through support of the great guard *of* the great Neptune and his trident soldiers, Provence reddened to sustain a great band: Mars more at Narbonne, because of javelins and darts."** Gallic or French fleet through allied support for the great guard of the great Neptune and his trident soldiers, the Moslem army, Provence or France is reddened, draining its blood to sustain the great Moslem band, Mars or warfare felt more at Narbonne, or France, because of javelins and darts of war supplies provided to the Moslem army.

60. **"The Punic faith broken in the East, Ganges, Jordan, and Rhone, Loire, and Tagus will change: When the hunger of the mule will be satiated, Fleet scattered, blood and bodies will swim."** The Punic or Moslem faith in the East breaks forth with fighting, Ganges, Jordon Moslems, and Rhone, Loire, French, and Tagus or Spanish Habsburgs occupying Italy, change places, when the mule, hybrid like the two allied, will from hunger of greed be satiated, recapturing Italy, the Habsburg fleet scattered with blood and bodies swimming from the fighting.

61.   "Agen, Tamins, Gironde, and La Rochelle: O blood of the Trojan: killed at the port by an arrow *beyond* the river the ladder raised against the fort, *points* to fire great murder on the breach." Agen, Tamins, Gironde, and La Rochelle, indicate France, O blood of the Trojan, French, killed by the arrow, by war supplies draining their resources beyond the river leading out of France for Moslems fighting in Italy where the ladder is raised against the Habsburg fort, points or directs to fire great murder on the breach of Habsburg defenders.

62.   "Mabus then will soon die, there will come Of people and beasts a horrible rout: Then quite a blow of vengeance one will see, Blood by stealth, thirst, hunger when the comet will pursue." Mabus (Etampes) near Paris shows France soon after dead in defeat, when there will come from people and beasts of the Habsburgs a horrible rout of the Moslem defenders in Italy. When quite a blow of vengeance with counter attack one will see, blood of warfare coming by Habsburg stealth using thirst and hunger of siege as when Haley's comet, type of the Habsburgs, will pursue in 1986 with more manna of the Lord's returning.

63.   "The Gauls Ausonia will subjugate very little, Po, Marne and Seine Parma will make drunk: He who will prepare the great wall against them, He will lose his life from the least at the wall." The Gaul or French Ausonia, Bordeaux being where Ausonius, a Latin poet favored by Nostradamus, was born, in France subjugating very little. Po, Marne, and Seine, France, are who Parma, Italy, will make drunk with desire. France will prepare the great wall of the Moslem army against the Habsburgs, but France will lose his life by defeat from the least at the wall or from the routed Habsburgs counter attacking.

64.   "The people of Geneva drying up with hunger, with thirst, Hope at hand will come to fail: On the point of trembling will be the law of him of the Cevennes, Fleet at the great port cannot be received." The people of Geneva, France, dry up with hunger and thirst, hope near at hand coming to fail by Habsburg counter attack. On the point of trembling will be the law of the Cevennes, France, symbolizing the doctrines of the Catholic Church, the Moslem fleet at the great French port not to be received, allegiance no longer needed because of defeat.

65.   "Le Parc inclines toward great calamity *to* be done through Hesperia and Insubria: The fire in the ship, plague and captivity, Mercury in Sagittarius Saturn will fade." Le Parc (Paris) is France inclining toward great calamity to be done through defeat in Italy, Hesperia to the Turks and Insubria or Milan to the French. The fire in the ship of their allegiance giving plague to France and captivity to the Moslem army like later when Mercury the messenger god indicating God's Word witnessed in Sagittarius, the ninth Millennium, when Saturn the god of harvest will fade, its job done throughout the eighth Millennium.

66.   "Through great dangers the captive escaped: In a short time great his fortune changed. In the palace the people trapped, *through* good omen

the city besieged." Through great dangers the captive Habsburgs in Italy escaped the Moslems: in a short time great, the Habsburg fortune changed through counter attack. In the palace or in France the people are trapped with their alliance, through good omen of Habsburg success the French city is besieged, their hope of victory destroyed from afar.

67. **"The blond one will come to compromise the fork-nosed one *through* the duel and will chase him out: The exiles within he will have delivered, committing the strongest to the marine places."** The blond one or Francis I will support the Moslems in Italy to fight the fork-nosed Charles V in the duel of warfare and chase him out of Italy. The exiles or Habsburgs captured within, he, the Moslems will have delivered as slaves, committing or imprisoning the strongest or most loyal Habsburgs to the marine places or Islands.

68. **"The efforts of Aquilon will be great: The gate on the ocean will be open, the kingdom on the Isle will be restored: Londres will tremble discovered by sail."** The efforts of Aquilon or the Habsburg north country will then be great in counter attack. The gate to the ocean or Italy will be opened when the Habsburgs get victory. The kingdom above the Isle of Sicily, or Italy, will be restored to the Habsburgs. Landes, or France, will tremble, their sail discovered sending supplies to the Moslems.

69. **"The Gallic king through his Celtic right arm seeing the discord of the great monarch: He will cause his sceptre to flourish over the three parts, against the cloak of the great Hierarchy."** The Gallic King, Francis I, through his Celtic right arm alliance, seeing the discord of leadership in the great Habsburg monarchy, he will cause the French sceptre to flourish over the three parts of the Habsburg empire including Austria, Spain, and Italy, against the cloak, indicating running retreat of the great Habsburg hierarchy out of Italy.

70. **"The dart from the sky will make its extension, Deaths in speaking: execution. The stone in the shaft, the proud nation surrendered, *contention*, human monster, purge expiation."** The French dart of warfare from the sky will make its extension in Italy, a type of the Catholic Counter Reformation with spiritual deaths in speaking perverted doctrine causing a great execution of souls. The stone in the French catapult causes the proud Habsburg nation to surrender, like the Catholic contention, a human monster with its purging atonement by getting rid of Protestants in earlier history.

71. **"The exiles into Sicily will arrive *to* deliver from hunger the foreign nation: At daybreak the Celts will fail them: Life remains by reason: the King joins."** The exiles from the true faith, like the French, will arrive in Sicily or Italy, to deliver the foreign nation France from hunger of its greed: at daybreak of the Reformation the French or Celts, like the Catholic Church, will fail them: Life or subsistence for France remains by reason, the King states, similar to the Catholic Church perverting the faith with man's reasonings.

72. **"Celtic army vexed in Italy *on* all sides conflict and great loss: Romans fled, O Gaul repelled: Near the Ticino, Rubicon uncertain battle."** The Celtic, French, army was vexed in Italy where on all sides came the counter attack with the French taking great loss. The Romans, as the French called themselves, fled, O Gaul repelled out of Italy when near the Ticino, the battle of Pavia, the Rubicon or uncertain fateful battle occurred.

73. **"To Lake Pucino from the shore of Lake Garda, *taking* from the Lake of Geneva to the port of L'Orgulon: Born with three arms the predicted warlike image, *through* three crowns to the great Endymion."** To the Lake Pucino, northeastern Italy, from the shore of Lake Garda, near Rome, and capturing from Lake Geneva to the Portoguaro, northeastern Italy, the French are like the Catholic Church with three arms of the trinity faith perverted to three crowns of three gods leading to the great Endymion in the church's sleep of death.

74. **"From Suez, from Autun they will come as far as the Rhone *to* pass beyond towards the Pyrenees mountains: The nation to leave the March of Ancona: By land and sea it will be followed by great suites."** From Sens and from Autun, of France, coming as far as the Rhone in north Italy, only to pass further towards the Pyrenees Mountains, southern France, in defeat, the French nation to leave from the March of Ancona, eastern Italy, where by land and sea this defeat will be followed by the great allied suites of French and Moslems.

75. **"The voice of the rare bird heard, *on* the pipe of the chimney: So high will the bushel of wheat rise, *that* man will be eating his fellow man."** The voice of the unusual bird, allied French and Moslems, will be heard upon the pipe of the chimney stack, the wind making noises. So high the bushel of wheat rises indicating God's Word, the Bread of Life, being scarcely preached in the Catholic Church, that man of other men will be cannibal, which is partaking of man's doctrine in the church.

76. **"Lightning in Burgundy will make an unfavorable case, *one* which could never have been done by skill. Sexton made lame by their senate will make the affair known to the enemies."** Lighting of warfare from Burgundy, France performs a portentous deed of attacking Italy, which by France's own skill could never have been done again. From their senate, the sexton, or clergy is made lame, in making known to the Moslem enemies the affair of being allied.

77. **"Hurled back through bows, burning pitch and by fires: Cries, howls heard at midnight: Within they are placed on the broken ramparts. The traitors fled by the underground passages."** The Habsburgs are hurled back through bows, burning pitch, and by fires: cries, howls of this tribulation and shaking time are heard at midnight, like the end time when the Bride Groom, Jesus, appears: within the Moslems are placed on the broken ramparts, the Habsburg traitors from the fort having fled by the underground escape passages.

78. **"The great Neptune of the deep of the sea With Punic race and Gallic blood mixed. The Isles bled, because of the tardy rowing: More harm will it do him than the ill-concealed secret."** The great Neptune, of the deep of the sea, indicating great strength, from the Punic race and Gallic blood mixed in Moslem and French alliance, the Islands indicating Italy in blood of warfare through the later rowing of the Moslem attack fleet, more harm will it do Italy with the Christians enslaved, than the Habsburg occupation representing the believer with his poorly concealed secret of the true faith.

79. **"The beard frizzled and black through skill *will* subjugate the cruel and proud people: The great Chyren will remove from far away *all* those captured by the banner of Selin."** The "Black frizzled beard," as Don John was known, a son of Charles V, will through skill subdue the cruel and proud Turks, as at the battle of Lepanto. The great Chyren or Henry II of France, during these same years of Don John, will set free the Christian captives held from earlier Habsburg fighting against the Turkish banner of Selin I, similar to freeing prisoners of the perverted faith of Catholic and Protestants.

80. **"After the conflict by eloquence of the wounded one For a short time a soft rest is contrived: The great ones are not to be allowed deliverance at all: They are restored by the enemies at the proper time."** After the conflict by the eloquence of the Habsburgs, wounded by retreat, for a short time he contrives for himself a feigned rest like the Christian who is wise not to always argue, the point of one not allowing the great ones, French and Moslems, a deliverance of total victory: they are restored back to fighting the Habsburg enemies only at the proper time for Habsburg advantage.

81. **"Through fire from the sky the city almost burned: The urn threatens Deucalion again: Sardinia vexed by the Punic foist, after Libra will leave her Phaethon."** Through fire from the sky, the Moslems attacking, the city almost burned, the urn of total defeat threatening another Deucalion, or destructive flood, Sardinia, or Italy vexed by the Punic foist in the invasion, after which Libra, seventh sign, designating the Millennium, will leave her Phaethon or the churches, slain, as when the Habsburgs gradually drove back the Moslems.

82. **"Through Hunger the prey will make the wolf prisoner, the aggressor then in extreme distress. The born heir from before is the last, the great one does not escape in the middle of the crowd."** Through hunger by the siege, the former prey or Habsburgs make the wolf or Moslems prisoner, the Moslem aggressor then in extreme distress like at the great tribulation of final judgment. Habsburgs who are the born heir of Italy from before the Moslem take over, are the last owner of Italy, the great one Moslems do not escape in the middle of the crowd, a type of the final judgment, with no escape.

83. **"The large trade of a great Lyons changed, the greater part turns to pristine ruin *prey* to the soldiers reaping by pillage: Through the Jura mountain and Suevia drizzle."** The large trade or abundance of a great Lyons

France, is changed, the greater part with its alliance turning to pristine or old ruins, being prey to the Habsburg soldiers reaping by pillage through the Jura mountains, in southeast France, and Suevia, Switzerland with the long drizzle of Habsburg fighting.

84. **"Amid Campania, Siena, Florence, Tuscany, *six* months nine days without a drop of rain: The strange tongue in the Dalmatian land, *shall* pursue after, moreover devastating the entire land."** Amid Campania, Siena, Florence and Tuscany in Italy, held by Moslems, six months nine days without a drop of rain, like 70 years life span of the wicked resurrected living in the judgment day, the strange tongue of the Habsburgs in Dalmatian land will overrun against the Moslems, devastating the whole country.

85. **"The old full beard under the severe statute Made at Lyon over the Celtic banner: The little great one perseveres too far: Noise of arms in the sky: Ligurian sea red."** The old full beard, France, under the severe statute or limitation agreement with the Habsburgs made at Lyon, or France, over the Celtic banner or French army with surrender terms: the little great one, Habsburgs, too far persevere against the allied Moslems, noise of arms in the sky is warfare as the Ligurian sea, near Genoa, France, is made red with blood from the Moslems retreating.

86. **"Wreck for the fleet near the Adriatic Sea: The land trembles shaken against, from the wind placed on land: Egypt trembles Mahometan increase, *the* Herald surrendering himself is appointed to cry out."** Wreck of the Moslem fleet near the Adriatic off east Italy, as the land trembles from the Habsburg counter attack, shaking as from hurricane winds placed upon the land. Egypt trembles with the Mahometan increase, Moslems retreating into their country. The Herald, surrendering himself is the Moslems defeated at Italy earlier and now entering Egypt crying out as though from judgment.

87. **"After there will come from the outermost countries A German Prince, upon the golden throne: The servitude and waters met, the lady serves, her time no longer adored."** After there will come from the remote Habsburg countries, a German prince, Charles V, upon the golden throne, gold symbolizing the saints who entered into God's fullness of His Word. The servitude and waters, French and Moslem, met in battle with the Habsburgs, the lady France or Catholic Church serving in a perverted Christianity with her time no longer adored.

88. **The circuit of the great ruinous deed, the seventh name of the fifth will be: Of a third greater the stranger warlike: Mouton, Paris, Aix will not guarantee."** The circuit or type of the great ruinous deed of the Habsburg counter offensive, the seventh name, Enoch, like the fifth, Charles V, will be, of a third one, the Moslems, type of the Protestants, joining the French to make a greater effort, the stranger being of another faith, is warlike in capturing Italy, however, Mouton, Paris, and Aix, or France, like the Catholic Church, will not be guaranteed safe from judgment.

89. "One day the two great masters will be friends, their great power will he seen increased: The new land will be at its high peak, to the bloody one the number is told." One day the two great masters, France and Turks, will be friends, their great power is seen increased, at first pushing back the Habsburgs out of Italy, the new land conquered bringing them to their highest peak, to the bloody one, Habsburgs, who were driven out, the number left in his army is recounted as they regroup for counter attack, like the believer stumbling but not completely falling down.

90. "Through life and death the realm of Hungary changed: The law will be more harsh than service: Their great city cries out with howls and laments, Castor and Pollux enemies in the arena." Through life and death of warfare, the realm of Hungary changes, captured by the Moslems: the law of the Islam faith will be more harsh by making slaves than service of the Christian faith was before: their great city, Budapest, cries out with howls and laments with its capture, Castor and Pollux like Habsburgs and Turks, enemies in the arena of Hungary, as they take their turns to rule.

91. "At sunrise one will see a great fire, Noise and light extending towards Aquilon: Within the circle death and one will hear cries, through steel, fire, famine, death awaiting them." Sunrise in the east, indicating the Moslems origin, one will see a great fire of battle, the noise and light of warfare tending more towards Aquilon, the north country in Hungary: within the circle of siege, death by defeat and one will hear cries from the initial Habsburg retreat, through steel fire, famine, of later counter attack, death by defeat awaits the Moslems, too.

92. "Fire color of gold from the sky seen on earth: Heir struck from on high, marvelous deed done: Great human murder: the nephew of the great one taken, Death spectacular the proud one disappears." Fire the color gold, like the fullness of Jesus, from the sky seen on earth: the Heir like Charles V striking from on high as in northerly Hungary with the counter attack, a marvelous deed done like the judgment: Great human murder by defeating the Moslems: Moslems being like a nephew of the great one France by alliance, deaths of French and Moslems spectacular as the proud ones disappear in war defeats.

93. "Very near the Tiber presses death: Shortly before great inundation: The chief of the ship taken, thrown into the bilge: Castle, palace in conflagration." Very near the Tiber River, close to Pavia, presses death of defeat for the Habsburgs: shortly before this a great inundation of Moslems swept through Italy: the chief of the ship taken and thrown into the bilge, symbolic of the Habsburg loss of Italy: the castle of Italy being a palace in conflagration or disorder, like the great awakening time of the saints when they go through a shaking time.

94. "Great Po, great evil will be received through Gauls, Vain terror from the maritime Lion: People will pass by the sea in infinite numbers, without a quarter of a million escaping." Great Po, or Italy, great evil of conflict will be received through Gauls, or French, sending in the Turk allies, it being a vain or fruitless terror from the maritime Lion of France: people of the Moslem army will pass through the sea to Italy in infinite numbers, without a quarter of a million escaping from the Habsburg counter attack.

95.　**"The populous places will be uninhabitable: to obtain fields there will be great discord: Realms delivered to prudent incapable ones: Then for the great brothers dissension and death."** The populous places in Italy will be deserted as the inhabitants are taken away in slavery: to obtain fields there will be great discord as realms are delivered to the prudent Moslem victors who weren't capable managers, then for the great brothers, France and Moslems, death of defeat from the Habsburg counter attack and dissension between allies, too.

96.　**"Burning torch will be seen in the sky at night Near the end and beginning of the Rhone: Famine, steel: the relief provided late, Persia turns to invade Macedonia."** Burning torch of the Moslem army encampments will be seen in the sky at night, near the end and beginning of the Rhone River or in eastern France: famine and steel of Moslems attacking Italy: when the relief or Turkish army is provided late as with the wicked when they are resurrected at the final judgment, Persia or Moslems turn to invade Macedonia as they begin their new campaigns.

97.　**"Roman pontiff beware of approaching *the* city that two rivers flow through, *near* there your blood will come to spurt, *you* and yours when the rose will flourish."** Roman Pontiff, beware of approaching to the city of New Jerusalem, being the saints, that two rivers water, like the double anointing of God's fullness. Near to there with the Moslems like France's earlier defeat at Pavia, your blood will come to spurt in judgment, you and yours, Catholic and Protestants, when the Rose of Sharon, Jesus, will flourish in His reign.

98.　**"The one whose face is splattered with the blood Of the victim nearly sacrificed: Jupiter in Leon, omen through presage: To be put to death then for the bride."** The French whose face is splattered from before with the blood of the Habsburg army, the victim nearly sacrificed in warfare: Jupiter, Zeus being the Reformation in Leo, the fifth church age with Luther being an omen or sign of prediction through presage or previous experience: the Catholic Church like the French to be put to death of defeat then at the end time as justice for the sake of the bride or saints.

99.　**"Roman land as the omen interpreted *will* be vexed too much by the Gallic people: But the Celtic nation will fear the hour, the fleet has been pushed too far by Moreas."** Roman land, or Italy under Moslem rule, as the omen or prediction is interpreted, will be vexed too much by the Gallic people or French allied with the Turk army, but the Celtic nation, France, will fear the hour Boreas, the north wind, or Habsburgs will push the Moslems southward too far and beyond Italy, this being a type of their final judgment.

100.　**"Within the isles a very horrible uproar. One will hear only a party of war, so great will be the insult of the plunderers That they will come to be joined in the great league."** Within the isles near Italy a horrible uproar by the French driven out of the country, nothing one can't hear but a warlike solicitation or talk of revenge, so great will be the insult of the Habsburg plunderers now possessing Italy, that the French and Moslems will come to be joined together in the great league, like the Catholic and Protestant churches in the World Council of Churches at the end time.

Nostradamus
Century III

Nostradamus

Century III

1.   "After combat and naval battle, the great Neptune in his highest belfry: Red adversary will become pale with fear, Putting the great Ocean in dread." After combat and naval battle the great Neptune, Moslems, in his highest belfry of glory: Red adversary or Spain will become pale with fear indicating their defeat in Italy, Spain being part of the Habsburg Empire, Putting the great Ocean, which conveyed the Moslems, in dread as with chastisement to the saints at the end time.

2.   "The divine Word will give to the substance, including heaven, earth, gold hidden in the mystic deed: Body, soul, spirit having all power, as much under its feet as the Heavenly see." The divine Word revealed to man will give to the substance, including the Saints seated together in heavenly places in Christ, and earth including the saved, gold of the fullness hidden in the mystic deed of God's Word. Body, soul, spirit having all power as much under his fleshly feet as is under his heavenly seat.

3.   "Mars and Mercury, and silver joined together, towards the south extreme drought: In the depths of Asia one will say the earth trembles, Corinth, Ephesus then in perplexity." Mars of warfare where Mercury (France) and the moon (Turks) are joined together in alliance, towards the south indicating Italy there is extreme drought indicating judgment by warfare: In the depths of Asia, indicating the Turks, one will say the earth trembles as Corinth and Ephesus are in perplexity showing Moslem defeats from fighting the Habsburgs.

4.   "When they will be close the lunar ones will fail, from one another not greatly distant, Cold, dryness danger towards the frontiers. Even where the oracle has its beginning." When the Habsburgs counter attacking will be close the Lunar ones or Moslems will fail in defeats, from the one and

the other not greatly distant, which describes the siege, Cold, dryness, danger from increased resistance towards the frontiers of Moslem borders Even where the oracle has had its beginning indicating Moslem retreat back to Greece.

5.   **"Near, far the failure of the two great luminaries Which will occur between April and March. Oh, what a loss! But two great good-natured ones by land and sea will relieve all parts."** Near and far is the failure, by defeats, of the two great luminaries, Moslems and France, which will occur between April and March, wars usually resuming in the spring. Oh, what a loss to Habsburgs in Italy. But two great good natured ones, Spain and Austria by land and sea will relieve all parts Moslems captured.

6.   **"Within the closed temple the lightning will enter, the citizens within their fort injured: Horses, cattle, men, the wave will touch the wall, through famine, drought, under the weakest armed."** Within the closed temple, Italy under Moslem religion, the lightning of Habsburg Christianity will enter recapturing Italy. The citizens, or Moslems, within their fort injured in defeat: Horses, cattle, men of Moslems and their possessions the Habsburg wave of onslaught will touch at the wall, through famine and drought of siege on the weaker armed Moslems.

7.   **"The fugitives, fire from the sky on the pikes: Conflict near the ravens frolicking, from land they cry for aid and heavenly relief, when the combatants will be near the walls."** The Habsburg fugitives return like fire from the sky on the pikes of the mountains; conflict of counter attack near to the frolicking ravens, Moslem and French. From land the Moslems cry for French supplies and even as hypocrites will cry to heaven for relief, when the Habsburg combatants will be near the walls in siege.

8.   **"Those of Cambrais joined with their neighbors will come to ravage almost Spain; *peoples* gathered in Guiene and Limousin *will* be in league and will bear them company."** Those of Cambrai, indicating the French, joined with their neighbors the Turks in alliance, will come to almost ravage Spain by defeating the Spanish government in Italy; French peoples gathered in Guienne and Limousin or France will be in league by alliance and will bear the Moslems company providing them supplies in the capturing of Italy.

9.   **"Bordeaux, Rouen and La Rochelle joined will hold around the great Ocean sea, Angles, Bretons and the Flemings allied will chase them as far as Roanne."** Bordeaux, Rouen and La Rochelle, or France, joined in alliance, will hold around the great Ocean or Mediterranean. Angles, Bretons and the Flemings, referring back to Roman times of Barbarian invasions, now indicate the northern Habsburgs allied and chasing the French, who consider themselves Roman, as far as the Roanne located on the upper Loire in France.

10.   **"Greater calamity of blood and famine, Seven times it approaches the marine shore; Monaco from hunger, place captured, captivity, *the* great one led crunching in a metaled cage."** Greater calamity of blood and famine or judgments, Seven church age times approaches the marine shore of Italy symbolizing the Catholic Church; Monaco, annexed to France in 1793,

indicated France the place captured and later in captivity, as if from hunger of siege with Moslems, the great one, France, like the Catholic Church led crunching his teeth in the metaled cage defeated.

11. **"The arms fight from the sky a long time, the tree in the middle of the city fallen: Sacred bough clipped, steel, in the face the firebrand, then the monarch of Adria fallen."** The arms fight from the sky a long time as arrows used in a siege, the Moslem tree fallen in defeat: The sacred Moslem bough is clipped, by steel of sword and in the face the firebrand of Habsburg counter attack. Then the Moslem monarch of Adria or Venice falls.

12. **"Because of the swelling of the Ebro, Po, Tagus, Tiber and Rhone And because of the pond of Geneva and Arezzo, the two great chiefs and cities of the Garonne, Taken, dead, drowned: human booty divided."** Because of the swelling warfare involving Ebro-Spanish, Po and Tagus-Italy, and Tiber-France, and because of the pond of Geneva, France again taking Arezzo or Italy, the two great chiefs, France and Moslems and cities of Garonne or French supplies, Italy in taken, dead, drowned: human booty or slaves divided among the Moslems.

13. **"Through lighting in the arch gold and silver melted, of two captives one will eat the other: The greatest one of the city stretched out, when submerged the fleet will swim."** When Moslem lightning is in the arch or Italy, Habsburg gold and silver is melted for war supplies, of two captives, French and Moslems in retreat, the Moslems will consume French war supplies: The greatest one or Moslems ruling the Italian city will be stretched out, when submerged by secret alliance, the French fleet will swim.

14. **"Through the branch of the valiant personage Of lowest France: for the father unhappiness Honors, riches, travail in his old age, for having believed the advice of a sample man."** Through the Moslem branch of the valiant personage of lowest France, indicating their unequal alliance: for the father or France unhappiness, allied like a father and son, Honors, riches from capturing Italy lead to travail for France in his old age, for having believed the advice of a foolish man, Suleiman tricking France in the alliance.

15. **"The realm will change in heart, vigor and glory, in all points having its adversary opposed: Then through death France an infancy will subjugate, a great Regent will then be more contrary."** The realm of Italy will change in heart, vigor, and glory during Moslem rule in Italy. In all points having its Moslem adversary opposed: Then through death of defeat for France, an infancy, the Habsburgs, will subjugate Italy, A great Regent or France will then be more opposed by Habsburgs for having allied with the Moslems.

16. **"An Angles prince Mars in his heavenly heart will want to pursue his prosperous fortune, of the two duels one will pierce his gall: Hated by him well loved by his mother."** A Barbaric Angles prince, indicating Charles V, with Mars of warfare in his heavenly heart, as the Christian seated in heavenly places in Christ, will want to pursue his prosperous fortune recapturing Italy, of the two duels one, the Moslems, will pierce his gall:

Moslems hated by the Habsburgs and loved by his mother France, through alliance.

17. "**Mount Aventine will be seen to burn at night: The sky very suddenly dark in Flanders. When the monarch will chase his nephew, then Church people will commit scandals.**" Mount Aventine one of the seven hills of Rome indicates the Catholic Church burning in the night of judgment, the sky very suddenly dark in Habsburg Flanders as the French spies cause rebellions: When the French Monarch will follow his Moslem nephew through alliance, then church people will commit scandals as France did to the Habsburgs.

18. "**After the rather long rain of milk, in several places in Reims the sky touched: Alas, what a bloody murder is prepared near them, Fathers and sons Kings will not dare approach.**" After the long rain of milk or prosperity, in several places in Reims or France the sky is touched as by lightning of Habsburg counter attack: Alas, what a bloody murder of warfare is prepared near them in Italy, Fathers and sons like allies of the opposing forces other Kings will not dare approach to intervene.

19. "**In Lucca it will come to rain blood and milk, Shortly before a change of praetor: Great Plague and war, famine and drought will be made visible Far away where their prince and rector will die.**" In Lucca or Italy it will rain blood and milk from Habsburg counter attack shortly before the change of the praetor where Habsburgs take over Italy, Great plague and war, Famine and drought through Habsburg capture of Italy will be seen far away from where their Moslem prince and French rector will finally die in defeat.

20. "**Through the regions of the great river Guadalquivir Far from Iberia to the Kingdom of Granada Crosses beaten back by the Mahometan peoples One of Cordova will betray his country.**" Through the Italian regions ruled by the great river Guadalquivir or Spain, being far from Iberia or Spain to the Italian Kingdom governed by Grenada or Spain. Crosses of Christianity are beaten back by the Moslems invading Italy and banishing Christianity. The Spanish of Cordoba or Spain will betray their country through defeat in Italy.

21. "**In the Conca by the Adriatic Sea there will appear a horrible fish, with face human and its end aquatic, which will be taken without the hook.**" In the Conca River by the Adriatic sea there will appear a horrible fish indicating the Moslem invaders With face human and its other end aquatic, similar to a manatee symbolizing the Moslems attacking with their fleet, which shall be taken or defeated by Habsburg counter attack through siege like catching the fish without the hook.

22. "**Six days the attack made before the city: Battle will be given strong and harsh: Troyes will surrender it, and to them pardon: The rest to fire and to bloody slicing and cutting.**" Six days, as in a siege, the attack is made before the Moslem held city or Italy by the Habsburgs: Battle will be given strong and harsh against the Moslems: Troyes or France will surrender

Italy to the Moslems and pardon them: The remainder Habsburgs go to fire and bloody slicing and cutting with counter attack.

23. **"If, France, you pass beyond the Ligurian Sea, You will see yourself shut up in islands and seas: Mahomet against you, more so the Adriatic Sea: You will gnaw the bones of horses and asses."** If France, you pass beyond the Ligurian Sea towards Italy, you will see yourself besieged in Islands and seas by Habsburgs counter attack: Mahomet or Moslems will be against you France, through trickery, and more so the Habsburgs in the Adriatic sea: You will gnaw the bones of horses and asses because of the Habsburg siege.

24. **"Great confusion in the enterprise, loss of people, countless treasure: You ought not to extend further there. France, let what I say be remembered."** Great confusion from the French and Moslem enterprise to recapture and keep Italy, Loss of people killed in battle from the Moslem army and countless French treasure spent for war supplies: You ought not to extend into Italy again. France, try only to remember these Habsburg words they did speak after your earlier defeat.

25. **"He who will attain to the kingdom of Navarre when Sicily and Naples will be joined: He will hold Bigorre and Landes through Foix and Oloron from one who will be too closely allied with Spain."** Francis I who will attain the Italian Kingdom under Navarre or France, when Sicily and Naples or Italy will be joined with France: Francis I will hold Bigorre and Landes through Foix and Oloron, or France in Secret Moslem alliance hidden from the Habsburgs who will be too closely allied with Spain, being part of the Habsburg Empire.

26. **"They will raise up idols of Kings and Princes, soothsayers and empty prophets elevated: Born, victim of gold, and azure, dazzling, the soothsayers will be interpreted."** The Moslems will raise up idols of men from their kings and princes, augurers and hollow elevated soothsayers having perverted the Moslem faith and government: The horn proclaiming God's Word in truth now fallen victim to gold and dazzling blue decorations, the entrails of dead animals will be interpreted by soothsayers as being truth from God.

27. **"Libyan Prince powerful in the West will come to inspire very much French with Arabian. Learned in letters condescending he will Translate the Arabian language into French."** Libyan prince, implying Moslem Suleiman I, powerful in the West through alliance with France, will come to very much inspire the French with a possibility to rule Italy again. Learned in letters, indicating the cleverness of the Moslems, Suleiman I will condescend to translate the Arabian language into French or appear compromising and friendly with the French ally.

28. **"Of land weak and parentage poor, through thrusting and peace he will attain to the empire. For a long time a young female to reign, Never has one so bad come upon the kingdom."** From the Italian land weak and under poor Spanish control, through thrusting and peace Suleiman I will attain to this empire. For a long time a young female, France, like the end time

Catholic Church, will reign over Italy by alliance with the Turks. Never has one so bad come upon the Italian kingdom as these allied rulers.

29. **"The two nephews brought up in diverse places: Naval battle, land, fathers fallen: They will come to be elevated very high in making war To avenge the injury, enemies succumbed."** The two nephews, France and Turks related by alliance, brought up or originating in diverse places: Naval battle, land of Italy under Habsburg fathers, or rulers, fallen in defeat: They will elevate very high in their pride in making war to avenge the injury of France's earlier defeat, Spanish enemies succumbed surrendering Italy to the Moslems.

30. **"He who during the struggle with steel in the deed of war will have carried off the prize from one greater than he: By night six will carry the grudge to his bed, without armor he will be surprised suddenly."** France who during the struggle with steel and in deed of war will have carried off the prize Italy from the Habsburgs, one greater than itself: By night Habsburg siege, will carry the grudge of revenge to France's bed, without armor there France will be surprised suddenly as their Moslem ally loses Italy.

31. **"On the fields of Media, of Arabia and of Armenia Two great armies will assemble thrice: The host near the bank of the Araxes, they will fall in the land of the great Suleiman."** On the Moslem held Italian fields of Media, Arabia, and of Armenia, Two great armies France and Habsburgs will assemble thrice with French defeat, then Habsburg defeat and finally Moslem and French defeat: The Habsburg host near Cape Araxam with the battle of Lepanto, the Turks will fall in the land of the great Suleiman.

32. **"The great tomb of the people of Aquitaine will approach near to Tuscany. When Mars will be in the corner of Germany and in the land of the Mantuan people."** The great tomb or defeat of the people of Aquitaine or France, will approach near from Tuscany or Italy by the Moslem defeat there, when Mars of warfare or Habsburg counter attack will be near the corner of Germany And in the land of the Mantuan people or Italians, to fight against the Moslem defenders there.

33. **"In the city where the wolf will enter, Very near there will the enemies be: Foreign army will spoil a great country. The friends will pass at the walls and Alps."** In the city, representing Italy, where the Moslem wolf will enter, very near there will be the Habsburg enemies preparing for counter attack: The foreign Moslem army will spoil a great country of Italy banishing Christianity and making its people slaves. The Habsburg friends will pass from the walls of defense and the Alps in retreat.

34. **"When the Eclipse of the Sun will then be, the monster will be seen in full day: Quite otherwise will one interpret it, High price unguarded: none will have foreseen it."** When the Eclipse of the sun will then be at the Lord's return, the Monster or Satan symbolized by the French and Moslems in Italy, will be seen in full day: Quite otherwise will one interpret it, High price unguarded like growing church expenses or Moslem supply lines cut off: none will have foreseen these.

35. **"From the deepest part of western Europe, A young child will be born of poor people, He who by his tongue will seduce a great troop: His fame will increase towards the realm of the East."** From the deepest part of western Europe, or France, A young child, Suleiman will be born of poor people or France which was weakened by earlier defeat. Suleiman who by his tongue or trickery in the alliance will seduce a great troop, France: Suleiman's fame will increase towards the realm of the East after capturing Italy.

36. **"Buried apoplectic not dead, He will be found to have his hands eaten: When the city will condemn the heretic, He who it seemed to them had changed their laws."** Buried but not dead apoplectic, being the once defeated French, will be found to have his hands eaten as if by rats in the grave like impairment found in the end-time Catholic Church: When the city, Paris, representing France will condemn the Moslem heretics, who it seemed to them had changed their laws of allied agreement.

37. **"The speech delivered before the attack, Milan taken by the Eagle through deceptive ambushes. Ancient wall driven in by cannon, through fire and blood few given quarter."** The Habsburg speech or complaint delivered to the Moslems before they began their surprise counter attack against them, Milan or Italy taken by the Eagle or Habsburgs through deceptive ambushes while the Moslems were unprepared: Ancient wall of fortifications in Italy driven in by Habsburg cannons, through fire and blood of warfare few Moslems given quarter.

38. **"The Gallic people and a foreign nation Beyond the mountains, dead, captured and killed. In the contrary month and near vintage time. Through the Lords drawn up in accord."** The Gallic French people and a foreign nation, the Turks, Beyond the mountains in Italy, dead, captured, and killed showing their defeat: In the month or like the time of great shaking near the vintage time or end time coming of the Lord, through the Lords, France and Moslems, drawn up in accord of alliance.

39. **"The seven in three months in agreement to subjugate the Apennine Alps: But the tempest and cowardly Ligurian, destroys them in sudden ruins."** The seven or Catholic Church of seven church ages and the Protestants in three months or church ages, in agreement like France and Moslems allied to subjugate the Apennine Alps or Italy: But the tempest of Habsburg counter attack and cowardly Ligurian or Moslems in Italy, Destroys the French and Moslems in sudden ruin of defeat.

40. **"The great theater will come to be set up again: The dice cast and the snares already laid. Too much the first one will come to tire in the death knell, Prostrated by arches already a long time split."** The great theater of warfare will come to be set up again by France: The dice cast and the snares already laid for the attack to recapture Italy. Too much the first one, France will come to tire in the death knell, Prostrated by arches already a long time broken from her earlier defeat by Habsburgs.

41. **"Hunchback will be elected by the council, a more hideous monster not seen on earth, the willing blow will put out his eye: The**

traitor to the King received as faithful." Hunchback, or Turks, in the perverted Moslem faith, will be elected by the French council, A more hideous monster by alliance not seen on earth, the willing blow of the Turks will put out the French eye, since the Moslems dominated Italy: The Moslem traitor against the French king was earlier received as faithful by France.

42. **The child will be born with two teeth in his mouth, *stones* will fall during the rain in Tuscany: A few years after there will be neither wheat nor barley, to satiate those who will faint from hunger."** The Habsburg child will be born with two teeth in his mouth like double strength of reinforcements, Hail stones will fall during the stormy rain of warfare in Tuscany or Italy: A few years after the Habsburg siege begins there will be neither wheat nor barley, to satiate the Moslem defenders who will faint from hunger.

43. **"People from around the Tarn, Lot and Garonne Beware of crossing the Apennine mountains: Your tomb being near Rome and Ancoma. The black frizzled beard will have a trophy set up."** People from around the Tarn, Lot, and Garonne, indicating France, Beware of your Moslem allies passing the Apennine mountains to capture Italy. The French tomb of death by Moslem defeat being near Rome and Ancona, or Italy, the Black frizzled beard Don John will later set up a trophy with victory at Lepanto against the Turks.

44. **"When the animal domesticated by man After great pains and leaps will come to speak: The lightning to the rod will be very harmful, Taken from earth and suspended in the air."** When the animal or Turks seemingly domesticated by French alliance, after great pains and leaps capturing Italy from Habsburg possession, will come to speak his laws and Moslem faith: The Moslem lightning is harmful to the rod, taking the current from earth and suspending it in the air, like hurting France by Moslems enslaving Christians.

45. **"The five strangers entered in the temple, *their* blood will come to pollute the land: To the Toulosans it will be a very hard example of one who will come to exterminate their laws."** The five strangers are France, then Habsburgs, then France and Moslems allied, then Habsburgs again entered into the temple symbolic of Italy, their blood will come to pollute the land of Italy with wars: To the Toulousans or French, it will be a very hard example from the Moslems who will come to exterminate Christian laws.

46. **"The sky (of Plancus's city) forebodes to us through clear signs and fixed stars, that the time of its sudden change is approaching, neither for its good, nor for its evils."** The sky of Lyons representing France and Catholicism is warning through clear signs of past losses during the Reformation and through fixed stars of seven church age messengers preaching, that the time of sudden change with judgments is approaching, not for its good or for its evils, Catholicism being a lukewarm mixture of both.

47. **"The old monarch chased out of his realm will go to the East asking for its help: For fear of the crosses he will fold his banner: By**

Mitylene he will go through port and by land." The old monarch. France, chased out of his realm of Italy will go to the East to King Suleiman I for help: For fear of the crosses of European Christianity the Turks will fold the Moslem banner to ally with France: By Mitylene, Greece, the Turks will go through port and by land approaching to invade Italy.

48.   "Seven hundred captives bound roughly, Lots drawn for the half to be murdered. The hope at hand will come very promptly But not as soon as the fifteenth death." Seven hundred captives or seven church ages bound roughly like prisoners captured in Italy, lots drawn for half to be murdered. Hope of rescue will come very promptly with Habsburg counter attack, but not as soon as the fifteenth death, or termination of the three Protestant church ages, five being the number of grace.

49.   "Gallic realm, you will be much changed: To a foreign place is the empire transferred: You will be set up amidst other customs and laws: Rouen and Chartres will do much of the worst to you." Gallic realm of Italy, your existence will be much changed: To a foreign place or to the Turks is the empire of Italy transferred, Italy will be set up amidst other customs and laws of the Moslem faith: Rouen and Chartres or France, by being allied to the Moslem victors, will do their worst to Italy.

50.   "The republic of the great city will not want to consent to the great severity: King summoned by trumpet to go out, the ladder at the wall, the city will repent." The republic of the great city Paris, or France, will not want to consent to the great severity of the Moslem plans ruling Italy: King Suleiman summoned by trumpet of warfare to go out and capture Italy, the ladder at the wall pillaging there and taking slaves, the city or France will repent of its alliance.

51.   "Paris conspires to commit a great murder Blois will cause it to be fully carried out. Those of Orleans will want to replace their chief, Angers, Troyes, Langres will commit a misdeed against them." Paris conspires with the Turks to commit a great murder capturing Italy, Blois or France will cause it to be fully carried out providing war supplies: Those of Orleans or France later will want to replace Italy's Moslem chief, Angers, Troyes, Langres, or France will commit a misdeed against the Moslems by freeing some Christian slaves.

52.   "In Campania there will be a very long rain, in Apulia very great drought. The cock will see the Eagle, its wing poorly finished, By the Lion will it be put into extremity." In Campania or Italy will be a very long rain and in Apulla another area of Italy very great drought, these diverse conditions indicating the great end time tribulation. The cock, France, will see the Eagles, Habsburgs, its wings badly finished or damaged, By the Lion or Turks the Habsburgs will be put into difficulty retreating.

53.   "When the greatest one will carry off the prize of Nuremberg, of Augsburg, and those of Bale Through Cologne the chief of Frankfort retaken They will cross through Flanders right into Gaul." When the greatest one or Turks will carry off the prize of Italy capturing it from

Nuremberg, from Augsburg, and those of Bale, being the Habsburgs, through Cologne the French spies pass, the chief of Frankfort Charles V is retaken by conspiracies. French spies will Cross through Flanders out of Habsburg lands returning to Gaul or France.

54. **"One of the greatest ones will flee to Spain Which will thereafter come to bleed in a long wound: Armies passing over the high mountains, Devastating all, and then to reign in peace."** One of the greatest ones, Spanish Habsburgs will flee Italy in retreat back to Spain which will thereafter come to bleed in defeat from the great wound against them: The Moslem armies passing over the high mountains of Italy, Devastating all the inhabitants in conquest and then to reign there with peace according to their Moslem laws.

55. **"In the year that one eye will reign in France, the Court will be in very unpleasant trouble: The great one of Blois will kill his friend: The realm placed in harm and double doubt."** In the year that one eye will reign in France, because of Moslem alliance, the French court will be in very unpleasant trouble: The great one of Blois, indicating France, will kill his Moslem friend by slowing supplies: The realm of Italy placed in harm of warfare and double doubt, through Moslem government and religion imposed.

56. **"Montauban, Nimes, Avignon, and Beziers, Plague, thunder and hail in the wake of Mars: From Paris bridge, Lyons wall, Montpellier, after six hundreds and seven score three pairs."** Montauban, Nimes, Avignon and Beziers indicate France, in Plague from thunder and hail of tribulation after Mars or war: From Paris a bridge of friendship to the Turks, Lyons and Montpellier or a French wall of resistance to Habsburgs. After six thousand years from Adam and seven catholic church ages paired to three Protestant Church ages.

57. **"Seven times will you see Brittany change, steeped in blood in 290 years: France at no point supporting Germany. Aries doubts his Bastarnian pole."** Seven times of Catholic Church ages you will see Brittany, or France, symbolizing the Catholic Church, change to judgment, steeped in blood allied with 290 years or three Protestant church ages; France at no point supporting Germanic Habsburgs. Aries ruling in the east is about Moslems who doubt Polish or Habsburg's pole or strength to defend Italy.

58. **"Near the Rhine from the Horic mountains will be born a great one of people come too late, one who will defend Sarmatia and the Pannonians, so that one will not know what became of him."** Near the Rhine from the Noric mountains indicates Austria where Charles V will be born a great one of the Habsburgs coming too late after Moslem capture of Italy, Charles V being one who will defend Sarmatia or Poland and the Pannonians or Hungarians from the Moslems, so that one will not know what became of the Moslems.

59. **"Cruel empire seized by the third, the greater part of his blood he will put to death: Through senile death for him the fourth struck, for**

dread that the blood through the blood be not dead." The cruel Spanish Habsburg Empire of Italy seized by the third or Moslem army, the greater part of Habsburg blood the Moslems will put to death in defeat: Through senile death by siege for the Moslems, the forth Habsburg army struck for dread lest the Spanish blood by the Moslem blood forever be dead from defeat.

60.   "Throughout all Asia great banishment, even in Mysia, Lycia, and Pamphilia. Blood will be shed because of the absolution Of a young black one filled with felony." Throughout all Asia great banishment of Christians by the warring Moslems, Even in Mysia, Lycia and Pamphilia, or Moslem lands, because of intolerant religious beliefs. Blood will be shed with fighting in Italy by the Turks because of the absolution with alliance to the French and a young black one, Suleiman I, filled with felony of aggression.

61.   "The great band and sect of crusaders will arise from Mesopotamia: Owing to the nearby river of the light company that such law will remain for the enemy." The great band of the Moslem army and the sect of crusaders or French ally will arise from Mesopotamia as the Moslems attack the Habsburgs in Italy: Owing to the nearby river or France, the light French company that brings war supplies, that such Moslem law will remain in Italy for the Moslem enemy ruling there.

62.   "Near the Douro by the closed Tyrian Sea, He will come to pierce the great Pyrenees mountain. One hand shorter and his view hidden, He will conduct his intrigues at Carcassonne." Near the Douro River on Spain's border by the closed Tyrian Sea or Bay of Biscay   , discovered by the Tyrian colonizers France will come to pierce the Great Pyrenees Mountains. France's one hand shorter as handicapped by earlier defeat and his view or appearance hidden by secrecy, France will conduct its intrigues at Carcassonne against Spain.

63.   "The Roman power will be thoroughly abased, following in the footsteps of its great neighbor: Hidden civil hatreds and debates will delay their follies for the buffoon." The Roman power which France called itself, will be thoroughly abased, following in the footsteps of its great Moslem neighbor or ally, being defeated in Italy by the Habsburgs counter attack: Hidden or forgotten civil hatreds and debates among the Habsburgs aroused by French spies will delay the French and Moslems becoming follies for the buffoons.

64.   "The chief of Persia will replenish great Olchades. The trireme fleet against the Mahometan people from Parthia and Media, and the Cyclades pillaged: Long quiet at the gray Ionian port." The chief of Persia or Moslems being defeated will repay great Olchades or Cartagena, indicating Spain, the trireme fleet or enforced Habsburgs counter attacked against the Mahometan people of Parthia and Media: And pillaging the Moslem Cyclades captured spoils of war: Long quiet at the great Ionian port as commerce ceases from desolation of Moslem defeat.

65.   "When the sepulchre of the great Roman is found. The day after a pontiff will be elected. Scarcely will he not be proved by the Senate

poisoned, his blood in the sacred chalice." When the sepulcher of the great Roman, or France representing the Catholic Church, is found. The day after this happens a Catholic pontiff will be elected in usual succession: By the Catholic senate of Cardinals will the pontiff barely not be proved poisoned with his blood or mortal doctrine in the sacred chalice at the altar.

66. **"The great Bailiff of Orleans put to death will be by one of blood revengeful: Of death deserved he will not die, nor by chance: he made captive poorly by his feet and hands."** The great Bailiff of Orleans indicating France, put to death by earlier defeat in Italy, will be by one of blood, warning Moslems, revengeful against the Habsburgs in Italy: Of death deserved from the capture Francis I, France will not die, nor by chance. By his hands and feet, poorly Francis I is held captive by Habsburgs.

67. **"A new sect of Philosophers Despising death, gold, honors and riches will not be bordering upon the German mountains: To follow them they will have support and crowds."** A new sect of philosophers indicating the end time saints despising death, gold, honors and riches like the buffeted Habsburgs, will not be bordered or crowded against the German mountains, as they brought a counter attack on the Moslems: Following after the saints will be support and crowds through greater power of God's fullness reinforcing their witness.

68. **"Leaderless people of Spain and Italy Dead, overcome within the Peninsula: Their director betrayed by irresponsible folly, Swimming in blood everywhere in the latitude."** Leaderless people of Spain and Italy describe the losing of power and control by the Spanish ruling Italy and being dead or overcome in the Peninsula by Moslem aggressors: Their Spanish dictator betrayed by irresponsible folly, as the saints initially refuse God's fullness, swimming in blood of defeat everywhere in the latitude of Italy and Spain.

69. **"The great army led by a young man, It will come to surrender itself into the hands of the enemies. But the old one born to the half-pig, He will cause Chalon and Macon to be friends."** The great army led by a young man indicating the Spanish under Charles V will come to surrender itself into the hands of the Moslem enemies: But the old one, Suleiman I, born to the half-pig, or Moslem faith symbolized by the half moon, will cause Chalon and Macon or France to be friends with him in alliance.

70. **"The great Brittany including Angers will come to be flooded very high by waters The new League of Ausonia will make war. So that they will come to strive against them."** The great province of Brittany including Angers located in France represents France which will be flooded very high by waters representing the Habsburgs counter attack. The new French and Moslem league in Ausonia or Italy will make war driving out the Habsburgs. So that the Habsburgs will come to strive against them again in counter attack.

71. **"Those in the isles long besieged will take vigor and force against their enemies: Those outside dead overcome by hunger. They will be put in greater hunger than ever before."** Those Moslems in the isles long

besieged by the Habsburgs will take vigor and force from French supplies against their enemies: Those French outside are dead, overcome by hunger from sending support to the Moslems. They will be put in greater hunger than ever before, since they were already weakened by earlier defeat in Italy.

72.   "The good old man buried quite alive. Near the great river through false suspicion: The new old man ennobled by riches. Captured on the road all his gold for ransom." The good old man or Habsburgs are buried by Moslem victory in Italy, though the Habsburgs were still quite alive, near the great river Pavia was the Moslem false suspicion of Habsburg surrender: The new reinforced old man or Habsburgs, ennobled by riches captured on the road of counter attack, retaking all his gold for ransom.

73.   "When the cripple will arrive into the realm, for his competitor he will have a near bastard. He and the realm will become so very trimmed. That before he recovers, it will be too late." When the cripple of Habsburgs after losing Italy, will arrive into the Italian realm counter attacking, for His competitor he will have a near bastard, the Moslems. The Habsburgs and the Italian realm will become so very trimmed by the quick Moslem advance that before they recover themselves, it will be too late to defend Italy.

74.   "Naples, Florence, Faenza, and Imola. They will be on terms of such disagreement That to comply with the wretches of Nola They complain of property taken by its mocking chief." Naples, Florence, Faenza and Imola, representing Italy under Moslem rule will be on such disagreeing terms against the Habsburgs who are at an initial disadvantage, that in order to better comply with the Moslem wretches in Nola or Italy and not encourage further aggression, only resist by complaining of property taken by its mocking Moslem chief.

75.   "Pau, Verona, Vicenza, Saragossa, from distant swords lands wet with blood: Very great plague will come with the great scab, Relief near, and the remedies very far." Pau or France, Verona and Vicenza or Italy, and Saragossa, or Spain, from distant swords of Austria and Moslems, lands wet with blood: Very great plague will come with the great scab to France and Spain supplying the opposing armies, Relief through supplies near and the remedies of victory very far as the fighting drags on.

76.   "In Germany will be born diverse sects, Coming very near happy paganism. The heart captive and returns small. They will return to paying the true tithe." In Germany will be born divers sects indicating the Protestant churches. Coming very near happy paganism which describes the joy of a closer walk with God, though the Catholics labeled them pagan, the heart captive to God and a small church revenue, Protestants will return to paying the true tithe, which is more than just money.

77.   "The third climate included under Aries The year 1727 in October, the king of Persia captured by those of Egypt: Conflict, death, loss, to the cross great shame." The third climate, lands of Emvan, Tauris, and Hamadan included under Aries or the first owner, the Persians, the year 1727 in October, the Christian King of Persia captured by those of Egypt indicating the

Moslems when conflict, death of warfare brought loss of these lands, to the cross great shame as Moslems given new lands.

78. **"The chief of Scotland, with six of Germany By people of the Eastern seamen captive: Crossing through Gibraltar and Spain, at present in Persia for the fearful new King."** The chief of Scotland indicating Charles V, with six of Germany symbolizing the Habsburg empire, by people of the Eastern seamen captive, indicating their loss of Italy to the Moslems: Spanish Habsburgs who crossed from Gibraltar and Spain to govern in Italy, at present are captive to be slaves for the fearful new Moslem kingking.

79. **"The order fatal and everlasting in the chains will come to wind through consistent command: The chain of Marseilles will be broken: The city taken, the enemy at the same time."** The fatal and everlasting order indicating the Moslems in the chains of prison by defeats will come to turn about into tighter bonds through the consistent commands of Habsburg strategy: The chain of Marseilles, indicating French in alliance will be broken. The Italian city taken by Habsburgs, the allied French energy beaten at the same time.

80. **"The worthy one laid bare the Anglois realm, the adviser through anger put to the fire: His adherents will go so low to efface themselves that the bastard will be half received."** The worthy one or Habsburgs laid bare the realm of Angers or France defeating them. The Moslem adviser through anger of Habsburg counter attack put to the fire: His French adherent or ally will go so low to hide himself in his wicked intentions that the bastard or Moslems will be half received in the alliance.

81. **"The great shameless, audacious brawler, He will be elected governor of the army: The boldness of his contention, the bridge broken, the city faint from fear."** The great brawler, Suleiman I, without shame and audacious, will be elected governor of the attacking army by their French ally as the Moslems invade Italy: With the boldness of his fighting contention, the Italian bridge under Habsburgs broken, the Italian city faint from fear.

82. **"Frejus, Antibes, towns around Mice, they will be strongly immense by sea and by land; the locusts by land and sea the wind propitious. Captured, dead, bound, pillaged without law of war."** Frejus, Antibes towns around Nice, indicate France supporting their Moslem ally will be strongly immense by sea and land: The Moslems invade Italy by land and sea like locusts with a propitious or favorable wind or alliance behind them, Captured, dead, bound, pillaged the Habsburgs are defeated in Italy, the Moslems fighting without law of war.

83. **"The long hairs of Celtic Gaul Accompanied by foreign nations, they will make captive the people of Aquitaine. For succumbing to their designs."** The long hairs of Celtic Gaul, like the later Louis XVIII (Pointing to end time Catholic and Protestant alliance) indicate France accompanied by foreign nations of the Turkish Empire, the Moslems will make France captive by taking advantage of allied people of Aquitaine or France, for succumbing to their designs or craft aimed at Moslem rule in Italy.

84. "The great city will be thoroughly desolated, of the inhabitants not a single one will remain there: Wall, women, temple and virgin violated, through sword, fire, plague, cannon people will die." The great city, indicating Italy, will be thoroughly desolated by the Moslems. Of the inhabitants not a single one remains as they are taken away into slavery: Wall, women, temple and virgin violated by the Moslems contrary to laws of warfare, through sword, fire, plague, cannon of Moslems, the people will die indicating their total defeat.

85. "The city taken through deceit and guile, Taken in by means of a vain new trick: Assault supplied by the Robine near the Aude, He and all dead by having thoroughly deceived." The city or Italy taken by the Moslems through deceit and guile by means of a vain new trick: Assault of the Moslems is supplied at the Robine near the Aude, indicating the French rivers. Habsburgs and all of the inhabitants of Italy dead or defeated by the Moslems and French by having thoroughly deceived them.

86. "A chief of Ausonia will go to Spain by sea, he will make a stop in Marseilles: Before his death he will linger a long time. After his death one will see a great marvel." The Spanish Habsburg chief leaving Italy, escaping to Spain by sea. He will stop in Marsilles, France. Before Spain's death by retreat is over, he will linger a long time being curious about France's noninvolvement in the fighting: After his death, finally getting back to Spain, one will see a great marvel of counter attack develop.

87. "Gallic fleet, do not approach Corsica, less Sardinia, you will rue it: Every one of you will die frustrated of the help of the cape: You will swim in blood, captive you will not believe me." Gallic fleet do not approach Corsica, much less Sardinia, to supply the Moslems, you will regret it. Every one of you will die frustrated in defeat for the support given to Moslems on the cape of Italy: You will swim in blood of defeat, being captive to Moslem alliance you will not believe the Spanish warning.

88. "From Barcelona a very great army by sea, all Marseilles will tremble with terror: Isles seized help shut off by sea, your traitor will swim on land." From Barcelona, indicating Spain, a very great army appears by sea with Habsburg counter offensives, all Marseilles or France will tremble with terror: Isles near Italy siezed by the blockades so help is shut off by sea, France's Moslem traitor will swim on land like a fish out of water, symbolizing Moslems weakened by Habsburg siege.

89. "At that time Cyprus will be deprived of its help from those of the Aegean Sea: Old ones slaughtered: but by speeches and supplications their King enticed, Queen insulted more." At that time, Cyprus will be deprived of its French help or supplies from those French in the Aegean Sea: "Old ones slaughtered," indicates French and Moslem losses: But by Habsburg speeches and supplications during the siege, their Moslem king is enticed to surrender, the Queen or French ally is then more insulted by loss.

90. "The great Satyr and Tiger of Syrcania, contribution presented to those of the ocean: A fleet's chief will set out from Carmania, one who

will take land for the Tyrren Phocaean." The great Satyr or France and Tiger of Hyrcania or Moslems, indicates the alliance, French contribution presented by war supplies to those of the Ocean or Moslems: A fleet's chief, Suleiman I, will set out from Carmania indicating Moslem origins, who will take land by capturing Italy for the Tyrren Phocaean, being Bordeaux representing the French partner.

91.   "The tree which had long been dead and withered, in one night it will come to grow green again: The Crosian King sick, Prince with club foot, feared by his enemies he will make his sail bound." The tree representing France long dead withered by defeat, in one night will come to grow green allying with Moslems: The Cronian or old king sick being weakened France and the prince or Moslems, handicapped with club foot, feared by their enemies because of their alliance, they make their sail bound with new combined strength.

92.   "The world near the last period, Saturn will come back again late. Empire transferred towards the dark nation, the eye plucked out by the Coshawk at Harbonne." The world near the last Millennial period when Saturn or the old man, France, will come back again late symbolized by the Catholic revival at the end time: The Italian empire transferred towards the dark Moslem nation, the eye of greed plucked out at Harbonne or France, because the Hawk or Moslems controled all of Italy.

93.   "In Avignon the chief of the whole empire will make a stop on the way to desolated Paris: Tricast will hold the anger of Hannibal: Lyons will be poorly consoled for the change." In Avignon or France, the Moslem chief of the whole Italian empire will make a stop on his way through desolated Paris or France: Tricast or Troyes represents France, who will hold anger at Hannibal or Moslems: Lyons or France will be poorly consoled for the change brought about by warfare giving Moslems control of Italy.

94.   "For five hundred more years one will take notice of him Who was the ornament of his time: Then suddenly great light will be supplied, which for this period will render them very satisfied." For five hundred more years after the start of the Reformation one will take notice of the Catholic Church agonizing in judgment though she was the ornament of her time, the only Christian church: Then suddenly great light starting with the Reformation for this Protestant period will render the believer very satisfied.

95.   "The Moorish law will be seen to decline: After another much more seductive: Dnieper first will come to give way: Through pardons and tongue another more attractive." The Moorish or Moslem law will be seen to decline: After another, the Habsburgs, being much more seductive in warfare: Dnieper river or Russian lands under Moslem rule will be first to give way during the Habsburg counter offensives: When through pardons and tongue the Habsburgs like the fullness of end time saints are more attractive.

96.   "The Chief of Fossano will have his throat cut by the leader of the bloodhound and greyhound. The deed executed by those of the Tarpeian Rock, Saturn in Leo February 13." The chief of Fossano, Duke de Berry,

symbolizing the Catholic Church will have his throat cut by the leader of the bloodhound and greyhound like Luther leading the Protestants: The deed executed like Protestants at the Tarpeian Rock executing Roman criminals, Saturn the aged Catholic Church in Leo the fifth Reformation church age, February 13 Duke de Berry dying.

97. "New law to occupy the new land *towards* Syria, Judea, and Palestine: The great barbarian empire to decay. Before the Moon completes its cycle." New law of Moslem faith and government to occupy the newly conquered Italian land towards Syria, Judea and Palestine, or Turkish rule: The great barbarian or Turkish empire will decay in later defeats, before the Moon or Moslems complete their cycle, finishing in 1576, like Moslems first capturing territory and later retreating during Habsburg counter attacks.

98.   "Two royal brothers will wage war so fiercely That between them the war will be so mortal That both will occupy the strong places: Their great quarrel will fill realm and life." Two royal brothers, France and Turks, will wage war so fiercely against the Habsburgs in Italy that between the two, having combined their strength, the war will be so very mortal or deadly that both will occupy the Italian strong places, their great quarrel of fighting will fill the realm of Italy and change its life.

99.   "In the grassy fields of Alleins and Vernegues of the Luberon range near the Durance. The conflict will be very sharp for both armies, Mesopotamia will fall in France." In the grassy fields of Alleins and Vernegues of the Luberon Range near the Durance River all indicating French involvement by alliance. The conflict will be sharp and sudden for the two armies with sudden Moslem takeover and sudden counter attack of Habsburgs, Mesopotamia or the Moslems will fail to succeed for their French ally.

100. "The last one honored amongst the Gauls. Over the enemy man will be victorious: Strength and land in a moment explored. When the envious one will die from an arrow shot." The last one to capture Italy being the Habsburgs honored amongst the Gauls or French in defeat, Over the Moslem enemy man will the Habsburgs be victorious: Moslem strength and land in Italy in a moment of counter attack explored, when the envious one or greedy French will die from an arrow shot or sending supplies.

Nostradamus
Century IV

Nostradamus
Century IV

1.   "Those of the remainder of blood unshed: Venice demands that relief be given: After having waited a very long time. City delivered up at the first sound of the horn." Those from the remainder of Italians whose blood is unshed. Venice, indicating Italy, demands that relief be given from the Moslem captors. After having waited a very long time for the Habsburgs to get organized, the city or Italy delivered up by counter attack of Habsburgs at the first sound of the horn which calls to battle.

2.   "Because of death France will take to making a journey. Fleet by sea, marching over the Pyrenees Mountains, Spain in trouble, military people marching: By the greatest Ladies of France they are taken." Because of death or defeat from Habsburgs, France will take to making a journey to ally with the Moslems, whose fleet by sea attacks Italy while French spies are marching over the Pyrenees Mountains, Spain who governs Italy is in trouble, military people marching: By the greatest ladies, French and Moslem allies at France, they are taken.

3.   "With Arras and Bourges many banners of Dusky Ones; a greater number of Cascone to fight on foot, those along the Rhone will bleed the Spanish: Near the mountain where Saganto sits." With Arras and Bourges, or France, are many banners of the Dusky Ones or Moslems, a greater number of Gascons, or French, to fight on foot as spies, those French and Moslems along the Rhone, which divides France like an alliance, will bleed the Spanish Habsburgs: Near the mountain representing Italy where Sagonto sits indicating Spanish ruling there.

4.   "The impotent Prince angry, complaints and quarrels, Rape and Pillage, by cocks and Libyans: Great it is by land, by sea infinite sails, Italy alone will be chasing Celts." The impotent Prince, Charles V being

undermined, is angry, complaints and quarrels within his borders incited by spies plus Rape and pillage in Italy, all by cocks, France, and Libyans, or Moslems: Great is the espionage by land, and sea infinite sails. Spanish held Italy alone, will be chasing the Celts, or French, secretly allied with Moslems.

5.   **"Cross, peace, under one the divine word accomplished, Spain and Gaul will be united together: Great disaster near, and combat very bitter: No heart will be so hardy as not to tremble."** The cross of Christianity making a peace where, under one religion, the divine Word is accomplished. Spain and Gaul will seemingly be united together because of their one religious belief: However, great disaster from espionage is near, and combat with the Moslems will make things very bitter: No heart will be so hardy as not to tremble.

6.   **"With new clothes after the truce is made, malicious weaving and plotting: First will die he who will prove to be in it, Color of Venetion treachery."** With new clothes, like changing attitude, after the truce or alliance is made with France, the Moslems begin malicious weaving and plotting not in accord with agreement: Such that first to die will be France, who will prove to be in it from the first, Finally, this being the true color of Venetion, or Moslem treachery against France.

7.   **"The minor sons of the great and hated Prince, will have a great touch of leprosy at the age of twenty: Of grief his mother will die very sad and emaciated. And he will die where the loose flesh falls."** The minor sons, or spies, of the great and hated Prince, Francis I, will have a great touch of Leprosy, failing because of Moslem trickery, at the age of twenty, two indicating alliance: Of grief their mother, France, will die very sad and emaciated, defeated and old, and the spies will die, murdered, where the loose flesh falls.

8.   **"The great city by quick and unexpected assault Surprised at night, guards interrupted: The guards and night watchmen by Saint-Quentin Slaughtered, guards and the gates broken."** The great city, or Habsburg held Italy, by quick and unexpected assault from the Moslems, is surprised at night, the time of evil, the Habsburg guards interrupted since not expecting trouble: Habsburg guards and night watchmen by Saint-Quentin, or France, are slaughtered, guards and the gates broken by espionage from French spies helping the Moslems capture Italy.

9.   **"The chief of the army in the middle of the crowd will be wounded by an arrow shot in the thighs, when Geneva in tears and distress will be betrayed by Lausanne and the Swiss."** The chief of the Habsburg army, Charles V, in the middle of the crowd or in his country, will be wounded by an arrow shot in the thighs, indicating French espionage activities inside his country, when Habsburg Geneva in tears and distress from incited disturbances will be betrayed by Habsburg Lausanne and Swiss, showing disputes within Habsburg borders.

10.   **"The young Prince falsely accused will put the army into trouble and quarrels: The leader murdered because of his support, Sceptre to**

pacify: then to cure scrofula." The young Prince Charles V will be falsely accused of wrong doing which will plunge the army into trouble and quarrels among the ranks: The leader of the revolt murdered for his support, in order to pacify the Sceptre, Charles V: then to cure scrofula, indicating the King being in a better disposition, like scrofula cured at a coronation.

11. "He who will have the government of the great cloak will be prevailed upon to perform several deeds: The twelve red ones coming to soil the cloth, with murder, murder will come to be perpetrated." France, having the government of the great cloak or Catholic Church, is prevailed upon to perform several deeds for the Moslems, espionage against the Spanish and Austrians, besides supplying the Moslems: The twelve red ones, Moslems allied like cardinals, coming to soil the Christian cloth, with murder defeating Italy, will come to commit murder of Christians, too.

12. "The greater army put to flight in disorder, will scarcely be pursued further: Army reassembled and the legion reduced, then it will be chased out completely by the Gauls." The greater army of the Habsburgs put to flight out of Italy in disorder, will scarcely be pursued further: The French army reassembled with the Moslems, the Habsburg legion reduced or diminished by the allied attack, then, the Gauls or French spies will also be completely chased out of Italy by the Moslems murdering even French Christians.

13. "News of the greater loss reported, the report will astonish the army: Troops united against the insurgent: The double phalanx the great one will abandon." News of the greater loss suffered from the Moslems murdering Christians will be reported to the French, the report will astonish the French army: French spies were united with the Moslems against the Habsburg insurgent: The double phalanx or alliance of French and Moslems, the great one, Moslems, will abandon as they turn to religious persecution.

14. "The sudden death of the first personage will have changed and put another in the sovereignty: Quickly, late come so high and of small time, such by land and sea one will have to fear him." The sudden death of the first personage, Habsburgs, defeated by the French and Moslem attack, will have caused a change and put another, the Moslems, into the sovereignty of Italy: Quickly, the late arriving Moslems come so high to achieve victory and in small time such that by land and sea one will have to fear him.

15. "From where they will think to make famine come, from there will come the overindulgence: The eye of the sea through canine greed for the one the other will give oil and wheat." From Italy where the Moslems attack, the Habsburgs will think to make famine come by laying siege, but from the Moslem army will come surfeit or over indulgence: The eye of the sea or Moslems capture Italy through canine greed, for the one or Moslems the other, or French, will give oil and wheat because of alliance.

16. "The free city of liberty made servile: The profligates and dreamers taking asylum. The King changed, not so violent to them: From one hundred they become more than a thousand." The free city of Liberty, or

Italy under Christianity, made servile by Moslems: The profligates and dreamers taking their asylum by converting to the Moslem faith. The King changed, not being so violent to those who convert from the Christian faith: From one hundred they become more than a thousand in order to keep from being murdered.

17. **"Changes at Beaune, Nuits, Chalon, and Dijon, the duke wishing to improve the Carmelite (nun) Merchant near the river, fish, diver's beak will see the signal: the gate will be locked."** Changes at Beaune, Nuits, Chalon, and Dijon, or France, where the duke, Francis I, wishes to improve the Carmelite (nun) or France's condition, the French merchant near the river, with fish ready to send to the Moslems, the diver's beak will see the cue or signal of excess fish: the gate will be locked against further Moslem aid.

18. **"Some of those most lettered in the celestial facts will be condemned by illiterate princes: Punished by edict, hunted, like criminals. And put to death wherever they will be found."** Some of those Christian priests and scholars most lettered or educated in the celestial facts or Christian teachings, will be condemned by illiterate Moslem princes, punished by the Moslem king's edict to be hunted like criminals for their negative speech against the Moslem faith, and they will be put to death or murdered wherever they are found.

19. **"Ahead of Rouen the siege laid on the Insurbrians, by land and sea the passages shut up: At Hainaut and Flanders, at Ghent and those of Liege through cloaked gifts they will ravage the shores."** Ahead of Rouen or France, the Moslem siege laid on the Insubrians or Habsburgs ruling Italy. By land and sea, the Habsburg passages to Italy are shut up: at Hainaut and Flanders, at Ghent and those of Liege, all Habsburg territories, cloaked gifts, or bribes from French spies ravage the shores, indirectly helping the assault on Italy.

20. **"Peace and plenty for a long time the place will praise: Throughout his realm the fleur-de-lys deserted: Bodies dead by water, land one will bring there, vainly awaiting the opportunity to be buried there."** Peace and plenty for a long time the place of Italy under Moslem control, praises: Throughout the Moslem realm the fleur-de-lys or family emblem of France, will be deserted: Bodies dead by water and land are murdered French spies and France brought there to Italy and now waiting in vain for the opportunity to be buried there.

21. **"The change will be very difficult: City and province will gain by change: Heart high, prudent established, chased out one cunning, sea, land, people will change their state."** The change to French rule in Italy will be very difficult: City or Italy and province or France will gain by the government change: With heart high or hopes, prudent France will be established, after chasing out the cunning Moslems, sea, lands, people in Italy will then change their state or condition back to Christian government.

22. **"The great army which will be chased out, in one moment it will be needed by the King: The faith promised from afar will be broken, He**

will be seen naked in pitiful disorder." The great Moslem army which will be chased out of Italy, for a moment during the initial invasion will be needed by the king, Francis I, in order to wear down the Habsburg army. The faith by alliance promised from afar by France, will be broken, naked without French supplies, the Moslems will be seen in pitiful disorder.

23. "**The legion in the marine fleet will burn lime, lodestone, sulfur, and pitch: The long pause at the secure place: Port Selyn and Monaco, fire will consume them.**" The Moslem legion in the marine fleet will burn lime, lodestone, sulfur, and pitch, this being Greek fire because of the lime, therefore, indicating the Moslems. With the long pause or siege against the Habsburgs while at their secure place: For Port Selyn or Genoa and Monaco indicating Habsburg strongholds, fire will consume them.

24. "**Hearing beneath the earth the holy Lady voice faint, human flame seen to shine as divine: It will cause the earth to be stained with the blood of the monks, and destroy the holy temples for the impure ones.**" Hearing beneath the earth the holy lady, France, her voice faint with her plans failing human flame of Moslem triumph in Italy seen to shine as divine: Moslems will cause the earth in Italy to be stained with the blood of monks, or Christians, and to destroy the holy Christian temples to substitute the impure Moslem faith.

25. "**Lofty bodies endlessly visible to the eye, coming to obscure for these reasons: Body forehead included, sense and head invisible, diminishing the sacred prayers.**" Lofty bodies of the Moslems coming to rule in Italy are endlessly visible to the eye, coming to obscure or overcloud the Christians in Italy for these reasons: Body, forehead included indicates their outward appearance of the true Moslem faith; sense and head invisible indicates inward perversion of the true Moslem faith with insanity and poor judgment.

26. "**The great swarm of bees will arise, such that one will not know whence they have come: By night the ambush, the sentinel under the vines city delivered by five babblers not naked.**" The great swarm of bees, or Moslems, will arise, such that one will not know whence they have come, having such strength: By night, indicating evil, the ambush of Italy planned, the sentinel, France, under the vines like Napoleon capturing Paris, which was delivered by five babblers bribed or not naked, symbolizing the allied Moslems delivering Italy.

27. "**Salon, Tarascon, Mausol, the arch of SEX, where the pyramid is still standing: They will come to deliver the prince of Denmark, *redemption* reviled in the temple of Artemis.**" Salon, Tarascon, or France and Mausol, the arch of SEX, located where the pyramid or mausoleum is still standing represent the Moslems: Allied they will come to deliver the Prince of Denmark, or Charles V, with defeat in Italy, redemption through Christianity in Italy will be reviled by the temple of Artemis, the Moon Goddess, representing the Moslems.

28.   "When Venus will be covered by the Sun, under the splendor will be an occult form: Mercury will have exposed them to the fire, through war-like noise being placed as an insult." When Venus, or Italy under Habsburg rule, will be covered by the Sun or French, under the splendor of the French will be an occult or mysterious form, indicating the Moslem army: Mercury, the messenger God, like the Moslems, will have exposed Habsburg Italy to the fire, through war-like noise of fighting being placed as an insult.

29.   "The Sun hidden eclipsed by Mercury will be placed only second in the sky: With Vulcan, Hermes will be made into food. The Sun will be seen pure, glowing red and golden." The Sun, France, eclipsed by Mercury, the Moslems, will be placed only second in the sky, indicating France standing by: With Vulcan, god of fire, Hermes identified with Mercury, or the Moslems, will be made into food by defeat from fighting Habsburgs. The Sun, France, will be seen pure, glowing and golden, ready to replace the Moslems.

30.   "Besides eleven times the Moon will not want the Sun. Both raised and lowered by degree: And one put so low that little gold stitched: Such that after famine plague, the secret uncovered." Besides eleven times, like Protestant grace before judgment, the Moon, Moslems, will still not want the Sun, France, though allied together in the end. Both raised and lowered by degree not really together: And France put so low, little gold stitched, prospering little: Such that after famine, plague of war, the secret uncovered concerning the Moslem trickery.

31.   "The Moon in the full of night over the high mountain. The new sage with single mind has seen there: By his disciples invited to be immortal, eyes at 12:00 o'clock. Hands on holy relics, bodies in the fire." The Moon, or Moslems, in full night like judgment time, are over the high mountain capturing Italy. The new Moslem sage with single mind is seen there: with his Moslem disciples invited to be immortal as victors, eyes at 12:00 o'clock or judgment hour, Moslem hands in the holy Christian relics, Christian bodies thrown in the fire.

32.   "In the places and times of flesh giving way to fish. The parish law will be made with opposition: It will hold strongly the old ones, then removed from the midst, the totally social friend." In the places or nations, and church age times, where worldly flesh gives way to Pisces, a double fish, indicating France's alliance, like the end time Catholic parish law brought forth with the Protestant opposition: It will hold strongly these old ones. Then, removed from the midst, the totaly social Catholic friend, like the French, put far behind.

33.   "Jupiter joined more to Venus than to the Moon appearing with white fullness: Venus hidden under the whiteness of Neptune struck by Mars through the stewy white." Jupiter, god of the Romans, or France, seems to lean more towards Venus, the Christian Habsburgs, than towards the Moon, Moslems, appearing with fullness at night: Venus or Habsburgs hidden under the whiteness of Neptune, god of the sea, indicating superior

Moslem forces, struck with Mars of warfare through the stewy white as the Moslems attack.

34.   "The great one led captive from the foreign land. In gold chains offered by King Chyren: Who in Ausonia, Milan will lose the war, and all his army put to fire and sword." The great one, Habsburgs, are led captive from the foreign land of Italy, in gold chains, indicating expensive French aid offered by the French ally, King Henry II: The French who, in Ausonia, Milan, or Italy will lose the war, and all their army of spies there put to fire and sword from religious persecution by the Moslems.

35.   "The fire put out the virgins betrayed by the greater part of the new band: Lightning in sword and lance the lone kings guarding Etruria and Corsica, by night throat cut." The fire of warfare put out or ended, the virgins, or Christian captives and French spies betrayed by The greater Moslem part of the new allied band: Lightning in sword and lance, the lone Kings, French and Moslems guarding Etruria and Corsica, or Italy, then by night France's throat is cut by the Moslem's ignoring their alliance.

36.   "The new sports set up again in Gaul, after victory in the Insurbrian campaign: Mountains of Hesperia, the great ones tied and trussed up: Romania and Spain to tremble with fear." The new sports of celebration set up again in Gaul or France after victory in the Insubrian or Itailan campaign. Mountains of Hesperia, or Habsburg held Italy, the great ones, or allied French and Moslems, have tied and trussed up by capturing: Romania or the Holy Roman Empire and Spain to tremble with fear, losing the fight.

37.   "The Gauls will by leaps come to penetrate the mountains: To occupy the great place of Insurbria: To the greatest depths his army entering, Genoa and Monaco will drive back the red fleet." The Gauls or French will by leaps, with their Moslem allies, come to penetrate the mountains of Italy: To occupy the great place of Insubria or Italy: To the greatest depths France's army entering, Genoa and Monaco or France will in this way drive back the red or Spanish fleet, indicating the Spanish ruling there in Italy.

38.   "While the Duke occupies the King and Queen the Byzantine chief held captive in Samothrace: Before the assault one will eat the other: Reverse swords following the trail of the blood." While the duke, Francis I, occupies the king and queen, Austria and Spain, fighting with them earlier, the Byzantine chief, Suleiman I, is held captive, unable to conquer past Samothrace or Greece: Before the later assault, Turks will ally, eating the French by receiving supplies: Reverse swords will follow the trial of blood, retracing France's path and capturing Italy.

39.   "The Rhodians will demand relief, from the neglect of its heirs abandoned. The Arab empire will discover its help. Through Hesperia, the cause to put right." The Rhodians, representing Italy, will demand relief, from the neglect of its Habsburg heirs, they were abandoned as the Moslems attacked, the Arab empire, or Turks, will discover its help from the French alliance, through Hesperia, or Italy, earlier lost by France, now the cause is to put things right for France by capturing Italy back again.

40. **"The fortresses of the besieged shut up, through gunpowder sunk into the abyss: The traitors will all be locked up alive, never by the Sextons did such a pitiful separating happen."** The fortresses of the besieged Spanish in Italy locked up, through French gunpowder sunk into the abyss, or roadside cliffs, blocking escape: The Spanish traitors will all be locked up alive in the Italian forts, never by the Sextons, or French, in earlier warfare did such a pitiful separation or cutting off from their army ever happen.

41. **"Female sex captive as a hostage will come by night to deceive the guards: The chief of the army deceived by her language will abandon her to the people, it will be pitiful to see."** The female sex, France, captive like a hostage in the alliance, will come by night, like the judgment, to deceive the Moslems guarding Italy: The Moslem chief of the army, deceived by France's language during the alliance to capture Italy, will abandon the French ally in Italy to the Moslem army; it will be pitiful to see.

42. **"Geneva and Langres through those of Chartres and Dole and through Grenoble captive at Montelimar Syssel, Lausanne, through fraudulent deceit, will betray them for sixty marks of gold."** Geneva and Langes being easterly from the Rhone dividing like alliance, represent the Moslems through those of westerly Chartres and Dole, or the French and through Moslem Grenoble captive at Montelimar or the alliance, Seyssel and Lausanne or Moslems through fraudulent deceit will betray the French for sixty marks of gold, six being the number representing work.

43. **"Being heard in the sky, arms clashing: That very same year the divine ones enemies: will want unjustly to discuss the holy laws: Through lightning and war the complacent one put to death."** Being heard in the sky, arms clashing in warfare with the Moslems capturing Italy: That very same year, the Moslem divine ones becoming enemies to France by wanting, according to alliance, unjustly to discuss the holy laws: Through this spiritual lightning and war, the French complacent one put to death as Christians, including the French, are persecuted.

44. **"Two large ones at Mende, at Rodez, and Milhau Cohors, Limoges, Castres bad week by night the entry, by Bordeaux an insult from Perigord at the peal of the bell."** Two large ones, France and Moslems, at Mende, at Rodez and Milhau, Cahors, Limoges, Castres, six French cities indicating work supporting the Moslems, a bad week as by night, like at judgment, the entry into Italy, by Bordeaux, French Christians at the peal of the allied victory bell.

45. **"Through conflict a King will abandon his realm: The greatest chief will fail in time of need: Dead ruined few will escape it, *all* cut up, one will be a witness to it."** Through conflict in Italy with Moslems, a King, Charles V, will abandon his realm of Italy: The greatest chief, Charles V, will fail in time of need, the French spies interfering secretly inside Habsburg lands, dead, ruined in defeat, few will escape the onslaught, Habsburgs all cut up retreating, while the French will be a witness to it.

46. **"The deed through its excellence strongly forbidden, guard yourself Tours from your near ruin: Londres and Nantez will make a defense through Reims not passing further in the time of the drizzle."** The deed by excellence of France sending her army into Italy helping the Moslems, is strongly forbidden by the Moslems, saying Guard yourself Tours, or France, from your ruin near at hand: Londres and Nantes, or France, make a defense through northerly Reims with the French army not passing further in the time of the drizzle of warfare.

47. **"The savage black one when he will have tried His bloody hand at fire, sword and drawn bows: All of the people will be terribly frightened, seeing the greatest ones hung by neck and feet."** The savage black one, Suleiman I, when he will have tried His bloody hand at fire, sword, and drawn bows capturing Italy from the Habsburgs: All the people of France will be so terrified to see the greatest ones, Habsburgs, who earlier conquered the French, now hung by their neck and feet, indicating defeat and loss in Italy.

48. **"The fertile, spacious Ausonian plain will produce so many gadflies with locusts, the solar brightness will become clouded, all devoured, great plague to come from them."** The fertile, spacious Ausonian plain, indicating Italy's Campanian plain, under Habsburg rule, like a born again Christian not yet in God's fullness, will produce so many gadflies, French spies, and locusts, Moslem attackers, that the solar brightness, like the Christian witness, will become clouded, all devoured, great plague, like the great shaking time, to come from invasion.

49. **"Before the people blood will be shed, which will not go far from the high heavens: But for a long time nothing will be heard, the spirit of a lone one will come to bear witness against him."** Before the people, Christian blood will be shed by the Moslems, which will not go far unnoticed from the high heavens or French (sun): But for a long time nothing is heard from the French spies in Italy, the spirit of a lone French Christian will come to bear witness against the Moslems, since he is missing.

50. **"Libra will watch to reign in Hesperias, to take the monarchy of heaven and earth: No one will see the forces of Asia perished, which seven don't take through the heirarchy of succession."** Libra, the seventh sign, indicating France and the Catholic Church, will watch to reign in Hesperias, Italy, to take the monarchy of heaven and earth from their Moslem ally: No one will see the forces of Asia, the Moslems, perished, which seven, or France, doesn't take through the order of the hierarchy by displacing the failing Moslems.

51. **"A Duke eager to follow his enemy will enter within stopping the phalanx: Hurried on foot they will come to pursue so closely that the day's conflict is near Ganges."** A duke, or Francis I, eager to follow or pursue his Habsburg enemy, will enter within Italy, stopping the Habsburg phalanx through spy espionage, helping the Moslems: Hurried on foot behind the

Habsburg defence lines, the French will come; the day's conflict is near Gange, or French spies.

52.   "In the besieged city men and women to the walls, *enemies* outside the chief ready to surrender: The wind will be strongly against the troops, *they* will be driven away through lime, dust, and ashes." In the besieged city, or Italy, the Habsburg men and women run to the walls for safety, the Moslem enemies outside, the Habsburg chief is ready to surrender: The wind will be strongly against them; Habsburgs will be driven away through lime, dust, and ashes as the wind helps the Moslems to smoke out the defenders.

53.   "The fugitives and exiles removed: Fathers and sons greatly garnishing the deep wells: The cruel father and his own people choked: His much worse off sons submerged in the well." The Habsburg fugitives and exiles removed from their rule in Italy as they retreat: Habsburg fathers and sons greatly garnishing the deep wells with their bodies: The once cruel and mighty Habsburg father and his own people choked to death in defeat: His much worse off sons sumberged, drowned in the well because Habsburg captives are murdered.

54.   "Of the name which no Gallic King ever had *never* was there so fearful a thunderbolt, Italy, Spain, and the Anglois trembling, *to* the female, foreigners are very attentive." Of the name, indicating Moslem fame, which no Gallic or French king ever had, never was there so fearful a thunderbolt, symbolizing the Moslem army attacking. Italy, Spain, and the Anglois or French are trembling as even the French are astonished, to the female, or Italy, the foreigners, Habsburgs, French, and Moslems are very attentive to possess.

55.   "When the crow on the tower made of brick *during* seven hours does nothing except cry: Death foretold, the statute stained with blood, *tyrant* murders, people praying to their gods." When the crow on the tower made of brick, like France's role with the Moslems, during seven hours, like seven Catholic ages, does nothing except to cry or warn the Moslems if trouble comes: France's death foretold, the Moslem statute or edict stained with blood, the tyrant murders the Christians, to Moslem gods people are to pray.

56.   "After the victory of the raving tongue, the spirit tempered in tranquillity and repose: Throughout the conflict, the bloody victor makes orations. Roasting the tongue and the flesh and the bones." After the victory of the raving tongue, or Moslems preaching, the spirit of the Moslem faith is gradually tempered in tranquillity and repose: Throughout the conflict, the bloody Moslem victor makes orations to the captives trying to win new converts to the faith, roasting the tongue and the flesh and the bones by murdering the stubborn Christians.

57.   "Ignorant envy upheld by the great King, He will propose forbidding the writings: His wife not his wife tempted by another, more the double dealing couple no longer cries." Ignorant envy of perverted Moslem religion upheld by the great Moslem king. He will propose forbidding the writings of Christianity in Italy: His wife, or French ally, not his wife,

indicating Christian faith. More, the double dealing couple no longer cries, from disagreements as they finally part company.

58. "Sun scorching, from the throat swallowing, with human blood to wash the Etruscan land: The chief, pail of water, to lead his son away, captive lady conducted in Turkish land." The sun scorching, from the throat swallowing, the Moslem army makes the Christians thirst, with human blood to wash the Etruscan land, Italy, of the unwanted religion: The Moslem chief, with French supplied bucket of water for relief, leads his son, or Moslem converts away from drought, the captive or enslaved converts indeed conducted into Turkish lands.

59. "Two beset in burning fervor: Of extended thirst for two full cups, the fort polished, and an old dreamer, to the Genevans of Jura showing the trail." Among the Christian captives taken, two are beset in burning fervor: Of extended thirst for two full cups, indicating Christians pressured by thirst, the fort polished by one who converts to live in slavery while the other is murdered, and an old Moslem dreamer, to the Genevans of Jura, Italy, will show the Moslem trail to salvation.

60. "The seven children left in hostage, the third will come to slaughter his child: Two because of his son will be pierced by the point, Genoa, Florence, he will come to strike against them." The seven children, France symbolizing the Catholic chuch of seven ages, left in hostage, the third or allied Moslems will come to slaughter his child or French spies: Two because half of them will convert, will be pierced by the point or persecuted, Genoa, Florence, or French Christians in Italy, the Moslems will come to strike against.

61. "The old one mocked and deprived of his place, by the foreigner who will suborn him: Hands of his sons eaten before his face, His brother to Chartres, Orleans Rouen will betray." The old one, France, mocked and deprived of his place in Italy, by the Moslem foreigner who will suborn him by taking all the territory for himself: Hands of France's Christian sons eaten before her own face after the Moselms used French spies in capturing Italy. His brother, the Moslems, will betray Chartres, Orleans, Rouen, or France.

62. "A colonel with ambitious intrigue, will seize with the greater part of the army, against his Prince with false invention, and he will be discovered under his arbor." A colonel, Suleiman I, with ambitious intrigue against his prince, or French ally, will seize Italy with the greater part of the allied army, against the prince, or French ally, a false invention pretending to be equal partners, sharing Italy, and the Moslems will be discovered under France's arbor being the victor, like Napoleon when he captured Paris.

63. "The Celtic army close by the mountaineers, who will be against and captured by the piper: Peasants knead working the early presses, All hurled on the sword's edge." The Celtic or French army of spies close by the mountaineers or Habsburgs in Italy, who will be against and captured by the Moslem piper: Peasants who knead working the early presses now owned by their Moslem captors, all these are hurled on the sword's edge as the Moslems persecute Christians to get converts to their faith.

64. "The transgressor in bourgeois garb, will come to try the King with his offense: Fifteen soldiers for the most part bandits, life closing and the greater part with his fortune." The Moslem transgressor in bourgeois garb pretending friendship, will come to try the king, Francis I, with the Moslem offense of trickery. Fifteen soldiers indicates the allies for the most part bandits, or Moslems, like three Protestant ages times five, the number of grace, life closing for France and the chief or Moslems are with his Italian fortune.

65. "To the deserter of the great fortress, after he will have abandoned his place, His adversary will exhibit very great prowess, the Emperor will soon be condemned to death." To the Habsburg deserter of the great fortress, or Italy, after he will have abandoned his place retreating from the fierceness of attack, His adversary, the Moslems and French, will exhibit very great prowess or ability in capturing Italy from them, the Habsburg Emperor, or Charles V, will soon be condemned to death, indicating this defeat in Italy.

66. "Under the feigned color of seven shaven heads *diverse* spies will be scattered: Wells and fountains sprinkled with poisons, at the fort of Genoa men are devoured." Under the feigned color of seven shaven heads, seven indicating the Catholic Church like France, through baldness feigning repentence from fighting Habsburgs before, diverse Fench spies will be scattered: Habsburg wells and fountains sprinkled with poisons indicating espionage caused by them, at the fort of Genoa or Italy, men will be devoured, or murdered, by this espionage.

67. "The year that Saturn and Mars are equal fiery, the air very dry, long trajections: Through secret fires with heat a great place burns, little rain, warm wind, wars, incursions." The year that Saturn, or France, and Mars, or war, are equally fiery in Italy, the air very dry, indicating good timing for igniting the long trajections of spy routes into Italy: Through secret fires with heat indicating espionage, a great place, or Italy, burns, little rain, warm wind, indicating unprepared, vulnerable Habsburgs, wars and incursions there.

68. "In the year very near not far from Venus, the two greatest ones of L'sie and of Africa, from the Rhine and Lower Danube they will be said to have come, cries, tears at Malta and the Ligurian side." In the year (of Saturn and Mars) very near, not far from Venus and Italy, the two greatest ones of Lassay, or France, and of Africa, or Moslems, from the Rhine in the west and Lower Danube east, they will be said to have, come, cries, tears at Malta and the Ligurian side indicate Italy under attack.

69. "The great city taken by the exiles, the citizens dead, murdered, and driven out: Those of Aguileia will promise Parma to show them the entry through the untracked places." The great city, or Italy, will be taken by the French and Moslem exiles, the citizens there dead, murdered and driven out by them: Those of Aguillia, or Venice, will promise Parma, or Italy, to the French and Moslems, to show them entry through the untracked places of (Parma) while the Moslems are heading towards capturing Italy.

70.   "Quite contiguous to the great Pyrenees Mountains, one to direct a great army against the Eagle: Veins opened, forces exterminated, as far as Pau will be come to chase the chief." Quite contiguous, indicating alliance, to the great Pyrenees Mountains, or France, one to direct a great allied army, against the Eagle or Habsburgs, in Italy: Veins opened by French espionage and Moslem attack, the Habsburg forces in Italy are exterminated or defeated, as far as Pau in northern Italy, the Moslems come to chase the chief, Charles V.

71.   "In the place of the bride the daughters slaughtered, *murder* with such wickedness no survivor to be: Within the well vestals drowned, the bride killed by a drink of Aconite." In the place of the bride, or in Habsburg Italy, the daughters, or Christians, are slaughtered, murdered with such wickedness that no Christian survivor will be around: Within the well the vestals, or Christian captives are drowned, the bride, or Habsburgs, killed in the early attack by a drink of Aconite from the French spies doing espionage.

72.   "Those of Nimes through Agen and Lectoure at Saint-Felix will hold their parliament: Those of Bazas will come at the unhappy hour to seize Condom and Marson promptly." Those of Nimes, or the old France, through meeting of two, like Agen, Latinized to indicate Moslems, and Lectoure, the French, at Saint-Felix will hold their parliament: Those of Bazas, or France, will come at the unhappy hour after recent defeat in Italy, to seize Condom or west France and Marson, or East France, indicating the alliance.

73.   "The great nephew by force will test the treaty made by the pusillanimous heart: The Duke will try Ferrara and Asti, when the pantomime will take place in the evening." The great nephew Moslems, will be forced, in capturing Italy, to test the treaty made by the pusillanimous or cowardly heart, indicating France: The Duke, France, like Duke DeBerry and the Catholic Church, will prove Ferrara east and Asti west Italy indicating the alliance when the pantomime will take place in the evening, like the end time church alliance.

74.   "From Lake Geneva and those of Macon: All assembled near those of Aquitaine: Many Germans besides more Swiss, will be routed along with those of Maine." From Lake Geneva, or France, and those of Macon, France, Latinized indicating the Moslems: All assembled by alliance near those of Aquitaine, or France: Many Germans besides more Swiss are both Habsburgs who will be routed by French espionage along with those of Maine, being a river in south Germany indicating Habsburgs defeated by Moslems in Italy.

75.   "Ready to fight one will desert, the chief adversary will obtain the victory: The rear guard will make a resistance, the faltering ones dead in the white territory." The Habsburgs ready to fight in Italy, will desert after unusual losses, the chief Moslem adversary will then obtain the victory: The French rear guard will make a resistance through spy activity; the faltering Habsburgs unable to defend themselves properly are dead or defeated in the white territory, which is French espionage behind the Habsburg front lines.

76. "The people of Agen by those of Perigord will be vexed, holding as far as the Rhone: The union of Gascons and Bigorre to betray the temple, the priest giving his sermon." The people of Agen, France Latinized to symbolize the Moslems, by those of Perigord, or France, will be vexed holding by sharing Italy, as far as the Rhone, symbolizing alliance boundaries like in France: The union of Gascons, France, and Bigorre, variant indicating the Moslems, to betray the Christian temple, the Catholic priest giving his sermon there.

77. "Selin monarch the breadth of Italy, pacified *realms* untied because of the Christian King of the world: Dying he will want to lie in Blois soil, after having chased the pirates from the sea." Selin, or Suleiman I, the Moslem monarch in power through the breadth of Italy, is pacified, Italian realms united under his control, because allied to the Christian king of the world, Francis I will want to lie in Blois, France, Latinized, indicating Italy, after having chased the Habsburg pirates from the sea.

78. "The great army with the civil struggle, because of the night, Parma discovered with the foreign one, seventy-nine murder in the town, the foreigners put all to the sword." The great Habsburg army with the civil struggle in Italy caused by French espionage, because of the night or Habsburg sin, Parma, or Italy, is discovered with the foreign one, or Moslems ruling. Seventy-nine indicates France, seven, and Moslems, multiple of three, murdering in the town, or Italy. The foreigners, French and Moslems, put all to the sword.

79. "Blood Royal flee, Monheurt, Mas, Aiguillon, to be replenished by Bordelais, Les Landes. Navarre, Bigorre points and spurs, deep in hunger to devour acorns of the cork oak." Blood royal, or Habsburgs, flee from Monheurt (Latinized), Mas, Aiguillon or the Moslem invaders, who will be replenished by Bordelais, Les Landes, or France. Navarre, Bigorre, or France, prods and spurs itself to provide supplies for the Moslem army which is deep in hunger to devour (Latinized) acorns of the cork oak, or hungry to conquer Italy.

80. "Near the great river, great ditch, earth drawn out, into fifteen parts the water will be divided: The city taken, fire, blood, cries, and conflict, and the greatest part regards the colosseum." Near the great river Rhone, dividing East, Moslems, and West, French, great ditch, earth drawn out like for irrigation into fifteen parts, the water divided symbolizing the Moslem's share, or three ages times grace or five, the city Italy taken, fire, blood, cries, sad conflict, and the greatest part, or Moslem ally regards the collosseum, indicating Italy.

81. "A bridge one will promptly build of boats. To pass the army of the great Belgian Prince: Poured forth within and not far from Brussels. Passed beyond, seven cut up by pike." France will build a bridge of boats, symbolizing the spy route, to pass the defensive army formed up in Italy by the great Belgian prince, Charles V: French spies also poured forth within and

not far from Brussels, Belgium. Passed beyond deep into Habsburg lands, seven or France will cut them up by pike, symbolizing espionage activity done.

82. **"A throng draws near coming to Slavonia, the old destroyer will ruin the city: He will see his Romania quite desolated. Then he will not know how to put out the great flame."** A throng of Moslem attackers draws near Italy coming to Slavonia. The old Moslem destroyer, like the backslidden Protestants at the end time, will ruin the city, Italy: He will see his Romania, or Italy, quite desolated after the fighting ends. Then he will not know how to put out the great flame, as he begins murdering Christians.

83. **"Combat by night the valiant captain conquered will flee, few people destroyed: His people stirred up, sedition not in vain, His own son will hold him besieged."** Combat with the Moslems by night, like end time Protestant after their time of grace, the valiant captain, Charles V.,conquered, will flee with few of his people destroyed by the Moslems: The Habsburg people stirred up, sedition caused by French spies was not done in vain, His own son will hold Charles V besieged, symbolizing divisions in Habsburg lands.

84. **"A great one by Auxerre will die very miserable, driven out by those who had been under him: Put in chains, afterwards by a strong cable. In the year that Mars, Venus, and Sun are joined in the summer."** A great one, Habsburgs, by Auxerre - French spies, will die very miserable, Driven out of Italy by those French who had been under him: Put in chains of defeat, afterwards, by a strong cable of French and Moslem attackers, in the year that Mars - warfare, Venus -Italy, and Sun - Habsburgs, are joined like new believers in summer.

85. **"The white coal with the black will be pursuing, Made a prisoner, led to the dung cart, His feet are tied together like a rogue, when the next born will let slip the hobby falcon."** The white coal with the black, French and Moslems, will be pursuing the Habsburgs in Italy, Made a prisoner by defeat, the Habsburgs are led to the dung cart, His feet tied together like a rogue, when the next born or Moslem successor to rule Italy will let slip the hobby falcon, symbolizing the French helping them.

86. **"The year that Saturn will be conjoined in Aquarius with the Sun, the very powerful King will be received and anointed by Reins and Aix. Afterwards in conquests he will murder the innocent."** The year that Saturn, or France, will be conjoined in water of defeat along with the Sun, or Habsburgs, the strong and powerful Moslem king will be received and annointed by Reims and Aix, or France, who secretly aided the Moslems capturing Italy. Afterwards through religious conquests, the Moslems will murder the innocent Christians, including French Christians.

87. **"The sons of the King much learned in languages. Different from their senior in the realm: Their handsome father with the greater sons included, will cause their principal adherent to perish."** The sons of the French King are much learned in foreign languages. Different from their senior, Francis I, who deals mostly with the Moslems to capture Italy: Their handsome kingly father, Francis I, with the very great or highly trained sons doing espionage in Habsburg lands, will cause their principal adherent, or Habsburg enemy, to perish by defeat.

88.   **"Anthony, by name great, with a filthy case of lice wasted at his end: One who will want to be affectionate with lead, passing the port, he will be drowned by the elected one."** Anthony, only by name great, since never becoming king of France like his son, indicated France with a filthy case of lice, wasted at his end without possessing Italy: The French, with lead, or amunition, wanting to be affectionate, or friendly, with the Moslems, while passing the Italian port, will be drowned by the Moslem elected one.

89.   **"Thirty of Londres will conspire secretly near their King, the impotent one on the bridge: He and his satellites, the corpse trickling, elected a King blond, native of Frejus."** Thirty of Londres, or France, thirty implying Moslems, like Protestants, allied to France, will conspire secretly near their French king, the impotent one on the bridge, as in command: Francis I and his satellites, or spies, their corpse trickling with blood of earlier defeat, elected a king, Suleiman I, to be blond, native of Frejus, or France, by alliance.

90.   **"The two armies will be unable to unite at the walls, in that instant Milan and Pavia to tremble: Hunger, thirst, doubt will come to plague them very strongly. They will not have a single morsel of meat, bread or victuals."** The two armies, Moslem and French, will be unable to unite at the walls to share the Italian lands. In that instant, Milan and Pavia, or Italy, will tremble from Moslem rulers: Hunger, thirst, doubt will come to plague them very strongly, not having a single morsel of meat, bread or victuals, as the Christians are persecuted.

91.   **"With the Gallic Duke constrained to torment in the duel, the ship of Melilla will not approach Monaco, falsely accused, perpetual prison, His sons will strive to reign before death."** With the Gallic duke, Francis I, constrained to torment by Moslem trickery during the duel to capture Italy, the ship of Melilla, or Spain, will not approach to attack Monaco, or France. Falsely accused Christians murdered, and perpetual prison or slavery for converts, France's sons or spies will strive to reign in Italy before death from Moslem murderers.

92.   **"The life trench of the valiant captain, overthrown before his adversary: Their bodies hung on the sail-yard of the ship, confused he will flee by oars in a contrary wind."** The life trench in Italy, indicating the Habsburg defending army of the valiant captain, Charles V, will be overthrown before his Moslem adversary who is attacking: Their bodies hung on the sail-yard of the ship, indicating Habsburg defeat in Italy. Confused by the French espionage, Charles V will flee Italy quickly as though by oars in a contrary wind.

93.   **"A serpent seen near the royal bed, will be by the lady at night, the dogs not barking: Then to be born in France a Prince so royal, from heaven come all the Princes to see him."** A serpent, the Moslems, like the Duke of Orleans seen near the royal bed in France, will be by the French lady

at night, the Habsburg watch dogs not alerted or barking: Then to be born in France a prince, Francis I, so royal with allied strength like from heaven, that all the princes come to see him.

94.   "Two great brothers will be chased by Spain, the elder conquered upon the Pyrenees Mountains: To redden the sea, the Rhone, bloody Lake Geneva from Germany, Narbonne, Beriera with Agde contaminated." Two great brothers, France and Moslems, are chased by Spain, or Habsburgs, the elder France conquered upon the Pyrenees Mountains, indicating fruitless esplonage: To redden the sea with the Rhone, symbolizing allied attack, and bloody Lake Geneva from Germany by French espionage, Narbonne, France, and Beziers, Latinized indicating allied Moslems, contaminated by Agde, Latinized indicating Moslem trickery.

95.   "The realm left to two they will hold it very briefly, *three* years and seven months passed by they will make war: The two vestals will rebel in opposition, Victor the younger in the land of Armenia." The realm of Italy left to two, French and Moslems, who will hold it very briefly, three years (Moslems,) and seven months (France,) passed, symbolizing the end time churches when grace has run out: Two vestals, France and Moslems, will rebel in opposition even among themselves; Victor the younger, or Moslems, in the land of Armenia, or Italy.

96.   "The elder sister the Ille of Brittany fifteen years after her brother's birth. Because his promised proxy true, will succeed to the kingdom of the balance." The elder sister, from the Ille at Rance of Brittany, or France, fifteen years after her brother, or Moslems, are born, like the Protestants of three ages multiplied by five, the number of grace given them, because the Moslem's promised proxy becoming true (France), will succeed through alliance, to the Italian kingdom in the balance, after defeating the Habsburgs.

97.   "The year that Mercury, Mars, Venus in retreat the line of the great Monarch will not fail: Chosen from the people, the visitor near at Guarda, one who will come to grow very old in peace and reign." The year that Mercury, or Moslems, in Mars, or warfare, Venus in retreat, indicating Habsburgs of Italy, the line of the great Moslem monarch not to fail: Chosen from the people, the visitor, or French spy, near Guarda, Latinized to indicate near inside Italy, France will come there to grow very old in peace and reign.

98.   "Those of Alba passing into Rome. By means of Langres the multitude muffled up. Marquis and Duke pardoning no man. Fire, blood, smallpox no water the crops to fail." Those of Albania, or the Moslems, passing into Rome to capture Italy. By means of Langres, or French spies allied to them, the Habsburg multitude muffled up, Marquis, or French, and Duke, or Moslems, pardoning no man. Fire, blood of warfare from the Moslems, and smallpox, no water, failure of crops from French espionage overwhelming Habsburg Italy.

99.   "The valiant sister of the King's daughter will hurl back the Celts so profoundly. Such that he will cast thunderbolts, so far in such an array

few **and infrequently, then deep into the Hesperias."** The valiant sister, or Moslems, allied to the king's daughter, France, will hurl back the Celts, or France so profoundly by trickery, such that the Moslems will cast thunderbolts so many in such an array, few and infrequently as at first agreed upon by alliance, then deep into the Hesperias, capturing all the Spanish ruled Italian realm.

100. "With the celestial fire from the Royal edifice, when the light of Mars will go out, Seven months great war, people dead through evil Rouen, Evreux the King will not fail." With the celestial fire of fighting from the Royal edifice, or alliance, when the light of Mars, or war, between the Habsburgs and Moslems will dwindle down, seven months, symbolizing France, the great war with people dead through evil of fighting, Rouen, Evreux, or France, the king, Suleiman I, will not fail, capturing all of Italy.

Nostradamus
Century V

Nostradamus

Century V

1.   "Before the coming of ruin from the Celtic, in the temple two will parley dagger to the heart by one mounted on the steed and spurring. They will bury the great one without making any noise." Before the coming of ruin, from the Celtic or French: In the temple two will parley, indicating French allying with the Moslems. Dagger to the heart of the Habsburgs in Italy by the Moslems mounted on a steed and spurring, indicating speedy conquest. They will bury the Habsburg great one without making any noise, indicating secret alliance.

2.   "Seven conspirators at the banquet will cause to shine close by the three, their iron out of the ship: One will have the two fleets brought to the great one. Where through the evil the latter shoots him in the forehead." Seven conspirators, France, at the alliance banquet, will cause to shine close by the three or Moslems, their iron or cannon from on the ship: One will have the two French and Moslem fleets combined into one great fleet, when through the evil of fighting the latter combined force shoots the Habsburgs in the forehead, capturing Italy.

3.   "The successor to the Duchy will come, very far beyond the Tuscan Sea: A Gallic branch will take Florence, with his gyron by agreement with the nautical frog." The successor to the Duchy of Tuscany, or Italy, being the Moslems, will come very far beyond the Tuscan sea fighting: A Gallic branch, indicating Moslems, will take or capture Florence, or Italy, with his gyron or heraldry of French espionage done through agreement of the alliance with the nautical frog, indicating the Moslems attacking by ship.

4.   "The large mastiff expelled from the city will be vexed by the strange alliance. After having chased the stag to the fields the wolf and the bear will defy each other." The large mastiff, or French expelled from the

---

81

city or Italy by Moslem trickery, will be vexed by the strange alliance made, since the Moslems have another religion, after having chased the stag or Habsburgs to the fields or out of Italy, the wolf or France and the bear or Moslems will defy each other with arguments.

5. **"Under the shadowy pretense of removing servitude. He will himself usurp the people and city: He will do worse because of the deceit of the young prostitute, *delivered* in the field reading the false poem."** Under the shadowy or tricky pretense of removing people from servitude under Christianity, the Moslems will themselves usurp the people and city: Moslems will do worse persecuting Christians in Italy because of the deceit of their French ally or young prostitute. Delivered into captivity when the Moslems found them in the field reading the "false" Christian poem.

6. **The Augur putting his hand upon the head of the king will come to pray for the peace of Italy: Be will come to move the sceptre to his left hand. From King he will become peaceful Emperor."** The Augur, indicating Suleiman I, putting his hand upon the head of the allied king, Francis I, will come to pray for the peace of Italy, converting in to the Moslem faith: Suleiman I will come to move the sceptre to his left hand, indicating that from conquering king he will become a peaceful Emperor to Christians becoming Moslem converts.

7. **"From the Triumvir will be found the bones. Looking for a deep enigmatic treasure: Those from thereabouts will not be at rest. This to hollow of marble and metallic lead."** From the Triumvir, indicating France like Napoleon's Directory and like France's Roman image, the bones, or defeated France, will be found looking for a deeply perplexing treasure, the possession of Italy: Those French bones from thereabouts suffering defeat will not be at rest. This land or Italy to hollow of marble and metallic lead like Napoleon's coffin.

8. **"There will be unleashed live fire, hidden death. In the eyes, horrible frightful. By night the city reduced to powder by the fleet. The city afire, the enemy amenable."** There will be unleashed live fire from Moslems attacking and hidden death from French spies, in the eyes of their Habsburg enemy, it is horrible and frightful. By night, the city or Italy is reduced to powder, or ashes, by the Moslem fleet, the city or Italy, afire from the fighting, the retreating Habsburg enemy looking favorable.

9. **"The great arch demolished down to its base. By the chief, the captive mistress forestalled, born of the lady his forehead and face hairy. Then through cunning the Duke tricks by death."** The great arch, France, demolished down to its base. By the Habsburg chief, the captive French mistress forestalled from possessing Italy. Born of the French Lady in Alliance, the Moslem son with forehead and face hairy, like an outcast, then through cunning, the French Duke tricks by feigning death while helping the Moslems capture Italy back.

10. **"A Celtic chief wounded in the conflict near the vault seeing his men struck dead: Pressed by blood and wounds and by enemies, and the**

relief of four unheard ones." The Celtic French chief, wounded in the conflict near the vault or land of Italy, seeing his men struck dead by the Habsburgs and Moslems, is pressed by blood and wounds and the Habsburg enemies. And the allied relief or Moslems who trick France by persecuting Christians, like the four unheard conspirators who tried to kill Napoleon III.

11.   "The sea will not be passed over safely by those of the Sun, those of Venus will hold all Africa; Saturn will no longer occupy their realm, and the Asiatic place will change." The sea will not be crossed safely by those of the Sun or France, though allied with the Moslems, who ruling Venus or Italy will hold all Africa, too, as they expanded to new territories; Saturn, or the old man representing France, will no longer occupy their realm in Italy, and the Asiatic place, Moslem Italy, will change.

12.   "To near the Lake of Geneva will he be conducted, by the foreign maiden wishing to betray the city: Before his murder at Augsburg, the great suite, and those of the Rhine will come to invade it." To near the Habsburg lake of Geneva the Moslems will be conducted by the foreign maiden, or French spies, in alliance, wishing to betray the city of Habsburg Italy: Before the murder or defeat of the Habsburgs at Augsburg, the great suite of Moslems and those French spies of the Rhine will come to invade Habsburg Italy.

13.   "With great fury the Roman Belgian King will want to vex the barbarian with his phalanx: Fury gnashing, he will chase the Libian people from the Pannonias to the Pillars of Hercules." With great fury, the Roman Belgian King, Charles V, will want to vex the Moslem barbarian invader with his Habsburg army: Fury gnashing to do battle, the Habsburgs want to chase the Libyan people or Moslems from their places in the Pannonias or Hungary to the Pillars of Hercules or Gibraltar, wherever they might be found.

14.   "Saturn and Mars in Leo, Spain captive, by the African chief trapped in the conflict Near Malta, Herodde taken alive, and the Roman sceptre will be struck down by the cock." Saturn, or France, with Mars of warfare allied with Moslem Leo, Spanish Habsburgs captive or defeated, by the African chief or Moslems, the Habsburgs are trapped in the conflict, near Malta or Italy. Moslems from Herodde, or Rhodes, take alive and the Roman sceptre, or Habsburgs in Italy, will be struck down by the Cock or France.

15.   "By navigating, the great Pontiff taken captive, the great one thereafter to fail the clergy in tumult: Second one elected, absent his estate declines, His favorite bastard, with death brakes on the wheel." By navigating, or trickery, the great Pontiff or France taken captive, French spies imprisoned, the great one, Moslems, thereafter to fail the Clergy or Christian France, in tumult: The second one, France, elected by alliance, absent from Italy, France's estate declines, His favorite bastard or Moslem ally, with death, brakes France on the wheel, persecuting Christians.

16.   "The Sabaean Frankincense no longer at its high price, from human flesh turned into ashes through death, at the isle of Pharos

disturbed by the Crusaders, when at Rhodes will appear a hard phantom." The Sabaean tear or Arab frankincense, indicating Moslem trade with France, no longer at its high price, from human flesh turned to ashes through death, indicating Christian captives killed, at the isle of Moslem Pharos they are disturbed by the French Crusaders, when at Rhodes, indicating Italy, will appear a difficult phantom of staged French tumults.

17.   "By night the King near an alley passing, Him of Cyprus and the principal guard: The King mistaken, the hand flees the length of the Rhone, the conspirators will set out to put him to death." By night the French king, Francis I, near an alley passing Suleiman I of Cyprus or Italy and the principal guard there: The King, Francis I, mistaken to be causing tumults against the Moslems, whose hand then flees the length of the Rhone or ends their alliance, the Moslem conspirators will set out to put France to death this way.

18.   "The unhappy abandoned one will die of grief, His conqueress will celebrate the hecatomb: Pristine law, free edict drawn up, the wall and the Prince falls on the seventh day." The unhappy abandoned one, or France, will die of grief, his Moslem conqueress will celebrate the hecatomb or great sacrifice of France's death: Pristine or former Moslem law, with free or unrestricted edict, will be drawn up again, the wall of alliance and the French prince fall on the seventh day, like the seventh Catholic Church age.

19.   "The great Royal one of gold, augmented by brass, the agreement broken, quarrel opened by a young man: People lament afflicted because of a chief, the land will be covered with barbarian blood." The great Royal one, of gold or France, augmented by brass or Moslem ally, like the end time allied Catholic and Protestant churches, the alliance agreement broken after a quarrel is opened by a young man, Suleiman I: Christians lament, afflicted by a Moslem chief, Italy will be covered with barbarian or Moslem blood, dominating all of Italy.

20.   "The great army will pass beyond the Alps, shortly before will be born a monster scoundrel: Prodigious and sudden he will turn the great Tuscan to his nearest place." The great army of French spies will pass beyond the Alps to help upset and defeat the Habsburgs in Italy. Shortly before this a monster scoundrel will be born, France allied to the Moslems, combining their strength: Prodigious and sudden the allies will turn the great Tuscan Habsburgs, ruling in Italy, to his nearest place in retreat.

21.   "By the death of the Latin Monarch, those whom he will have assisted through his reign: will light the fire, the booty divided, public death for the bold ones who incurred it." By the death or defeat of the Latin monarch or Habsburgs in Italy, those Moslems who the French will have assisted through their new reign in Italy will light up the fire with tumults, the booty of French controled Italy divided for themselves, public death for the bold French ones who incurred this judgment through Moslem trickery.

22.   "Before the great one has given up the ghost at Rome, Great terror for the foreign army: The ambush by squadrons near Parma, then the

two red ones will celebrate together." Before the great one or Habsburgs have given up the ghost at Rome or Italy, great terror comes for the Habsburg foreign army: The ambush done by squadrons of French spies near Parma or northern Italy. Then the two red ones, red indicating the bloody hands of French and Moslems, will celebrate together the capture of Italy.

23. **"The two contented ones will be united together when for the most part they will be conjoined with Mars: The great one with Africa trembles in terror, Duumvirate disjoined by the fleet."** The two contented ones, France and Moslems, will be united together in agreement, when, for the most part, they will be conjoined with Mars or warfare against the Habsburg Italy: The great one, France, with Africa, or Moslems, trembles in terror when the twin alliance with the Moslem fleet becomes disjoint, the Moslems using trickery against France.

24. **"The realm and low raised under Venus, Saturn will have dominion over Jupiter: The law and realm raised by the Sun, through those near Saturn it will suffer the worst."** The French realm or holdings and law of the Christian faith raised under Venus, or Italy, Saturn or France will this way have dominion over Jupiter, or the defeated Habsburgs: The Law and realm that was raised by the Sun or Christian French will, however, suffer worst through those Moslem allies near Saturn, or France, in Italy.

25. **"The Arab Prince Mars, Sun, Venus, Leo. The rule of the Church will succumb by sea: Towards Persia very nearly a million men, the true serpent will invade Byzantium and Egypt."** The Arab Prince, or Suleiman I, in Mars of warfare when the Sun or Christianity, Venus or Italy, and Leo or Moslems like fifth church age Protestants, are conjoined. The rule of the Christian church will succumb through the sea of Moslem invaders: Towards Persia very nearly a million Moslems, the true serpent, will invade Byzantium and Egypt.

26. **"The slavish people through luck in war will become elevated to a very high degree: They will change their Prince, one born a provincial. To pass over the sea, the army raised in the mountains."** The Slavic or Balkan people indicating the Moslems, through luck in war against the Spanish Habsburgs will become elevated to a very high degree by capturing Italy from them: The Moslems will change Italy's prince to Suleiman I, one born a provincial or uncultured, to pass over the sea his army raised victorious in the mountains of Italy.

27. **"Through fire and arms not far from the Black Sea, He will come from Persia to occupy Trebizond: Pharos, Mytilene to tremble, the Sun joyful, with Arab blood the Adriatic Sea covered."** Through fire and arms of Moslem invaders not far from the Black Sea, Suleiman I will come from Persia to occupy Trebizond in northeastern Balkens: Pharos, or Egypt, Mytilene in Northwestern Balkens to tremble with fear. The Sun or Catholic French are joyful seeing the possibility of success, with Arab blood being their ally, covering the Adriatic sea.

28. "His arm hung and leg bound, face pale, dagger hidden in his bosom, Three, who being sworn with the conflict *against* the great one of Genoa, will unleash the steel." France's arm hung and leg bound, indicating too disabled for waging war by themselves, face pale from earlier defeat, dagger hidden in his bosom for revenge. Three, or the Moslems like the three Protestant church ages, being sworn by alliance in the conflict, against the great one of Genoa, or Habsburgs, will unleash the steel of war.

29. "Liberty will not be recovered, a proud, villainous, wicked black one will occupy it, when the matter of the bridge will be opened, the republic of Venice vexed by the Danube." Liberty to possess Italy will not be recovered by France after Habsburg defeat. A proud, villainous, wicked black one, or Moslems, will occupy it, when the matter of the bridge, or French spy connection, indicating the alliance, will be opened by French request. The republic of Venice, with its Christians, are vexed by the Danube or Moslems.

30. "All around the great city soldiers will be lodged throughout the fields and towns: Paris to give the assault, Rome incited, then upon the bridge great pillage will be carried out." All around the great city or Italy, soldiers or French spies will be lodged, infiltrating the Habsburgs throughout their fields and towns: Paris, or France, to give assault this way, with Rome, or Italy, incited. Then upon the bridge, or French spy network, great pillage against Christians will be carried out by the Moslems tricking their ally.

31. "From the Attic land fountain of wisdom, at present the rose of the world: The bridge ruined and its great pre-eminence will be subjected, a wreck amidst the waves." From the land of Attica, the fountain of all wisdom, indicating southeast Greece, or the clever Moslems, at present being the rose of the world by capturing Italy: The bridge or French spy system ruined and its great pre-eminence or alliance will be subjected, a wreck beneath the waves with Moslem persecution against the Christians in Italy.

32. "Where all is good, the Sun all beneficial and the Moon being abundant, its ruin approaches: From the sky it advances to change their fortune: To the same state as the seventh rock." Where all is good, the Sun or France being all beneficial sending spies and supplies, and the Moon or Moslem soldiers being abundant, Habsburg Italy's ruin approaches: From the sky, smokey from battles, the allied warfare advances to change Habsburg fortune, to the same state or condition of defeat that the seventh rock or France earlier suffered.

33. "The principal ones in the city rebelling who will strive mightily to recover their liberty: The males cut up, unhappy fray, cries, groans from Nantes pitiful to see." The principal ones, or French in the city or Italy, rebelling, who will strive mightily to regain Italy's liberty from Habsburg rule through an allied war effort, the French males are cut up by Moslem persecution, unhappy fray as the Moslems and French are seen quarreling among themselves; cries, groans from Nantes, or France, pitiful to see.

34. "From the deepest part of the Anglois West where the head of the Isle Brittany is a fleet will enter the Gironde for Blois, with wine and salt, fires hidden in the casks." From the deepest part of western Anglois, or France, where the head of L'Isle of Brittany is, a fleet will enter through the Gironde River heading for Blois implying secret activity with indirect destination routes, with the wine and salt, firearms hidden in the cargo casks as France sends aid to the Moslems in Italy.

35. "For the free city with the great Crescent sea, which still carries the stone in its stomach, the Anglois fleet will come with the drizzle to seize a branch, war opened by the great one." For the free, liberated city, or Italy, with the great Crescent sea or Moslem government that still carries the stone of tolerance for France in its stomach, the Anglois or Allied French fleet will come with the drizzle of spy infiltration, to seize a branch of Italy, the Moslem great one will open the war by invading.

36. "The sister's brother through the quarrel and deceit will come to mix dew in the mineral: On the cake presented to the slow old woman, she dies tasting it being simple and rustic." The French sister's Moslem brother, through feigned quarrel and deceit will come to mix poisonous dew of death into the mineral: On the cake of their alliance, presented to the slow old French woman, she dies tasting it, being simple and rustic or unable to think clearly, after the Moslems begin ignoring their alliance agreements with France.

37. "Three hundred will be in accord with one will, to come to the execution of their blow, twenty months after all memory their king betrayed simulating feigned hate." Three hundred, indicating Moslems, like the three Protestant ages, will be in accord by alliance with one will or desire, to come to the execution of their blow by capturing Italy: Twenty months, indicating alliance, after which all memory of it is forgotten, their French king is betrayed by the Moslems pretending a hatred against the Christians.

38. "He who will succeed the great monarch on his death will lead an illicit and wanton life: Through unconcern be will give way to all, so that in the end the Salic law will fail." Suleiman I, who will succeed the great Habsburg monarch upon his death or defeat in Italy, will lead an illicit and wanton life, not in accord with sound Moslem doctrines: Through unconcern for their ally, Suleiman I will give way to the will of all the Moslems, so that, in the end, Salic or Moslem law will fail France.

39. "Issued from the true branch of the fleur-de-lys, placed and lodged as heir of Etruria: His ancient blood woven by many hands, He will cause the escutcheon of Florence to bloom." Issued or sent from the true branch of the fleur-de-lys, or France, to aid the Moslems, French spies are placed and lodged as heirs of Etruria or Italy: France's ancient family line woven by many hands as the spies enter with documents, they make their coat of arms to bloom and appear true in Florence, or Italy.

40. "The blood royal will be so very mixed, Gauls will be embarrassed at Hesperia: One will wait until his term has expired, and until the memory of his voice has perished." The blood royal or Habsburg leadership will be so very mixed in their ancestory, Gauls or French spies infiltrating will be constraining the Habsburgs at Hesperia or Italy: The Moslems will wait or delay their attack, until the term of the French spies has expired, and until the memory of the Habsburg voice in government has perished.

41. **"Born in the shadows and during a dark day, He will be sovereign in realm and goodness: Causing his blood to rise again in the ancient urn, *renewing* the age of gold with that of brass."** France, born in the shadows and during a dark day, like the end time Catholic Church resurrecting for final judgment, France will be sovereign in realm and goodness outwardly: Causing his blood to rise again in the ancient urn with a last attempt to possess Italy; renewing the age of gold with that of brass, indicating the alliance.

42. **"Mars raised to his highest belfry will cause the Savoyards to withdraw from France: The Lombard people will cause very great terror to those of the Eagle included in the balance."** Mars of warfare raised to its highest belfry after France's alliance with Moslems, will cause the Savoyards, or Habsburgs, being defeated in Italy, to withdraw from France: Lombard or French spies in Italy, will cause great terror to those of the Eagle, or Habsburgs, in the balance of suspence (Seventh sign) like seventh church age saints chastised.

43. **"The great ruin on the holy ones is not far off, Provence, Naples, Sicily, Sees and Pons: In Germany, at the Rhine and Cologne, vexed to death by all those of Maine."** The great ruin of the holy ones, like the Habsburgs, is not far off, Provence, or France in Naples and Sicily, or Italy, Sees and Pons, two religion-oriented cities in France, similar to the end time church alliance: In Germany, at the Rhine and Cologne, Habsburgs are vexed to death by all those spies from Maine, France.

44. **"On sea the red one will be taken by pirates, because of him peace will be disturbed: Anger and greed will he expose through a false act, the army doubled by the great Pontiff."** On sea the red one, or Habsburgs, bloodied and taken by Moslem pirates attacking, because of Suleiman I, peace will be disturbed for Habsburg Italy: Anger and greed will the Moslems expose through a false or tricky act of alliance, the army doubled by the great pontiff, or France, like the end time Catholic Church confederating with the Protestants.

45. **"The great Empire will soon be desolated and transferred to near the Ardennes: The two bastards beheaded by the oldest one, and Bronzebeard the hawk-nose will reign."** The great Habsburg Empire will soon be desolated or defeated and Italy will be transferred to the Moslems who are near the Ardennes Forrest, or France, by alliance: The two bastards or enemies, Spanish and Austrian Habsburgs, beheaded in Italy by the oldest one, France, and the Bronzebeard, or French-like Hawk-nose, Suleiman I, will then reign in Italy.

46. **"For the red hats quarrels and new schisms when the Sabine will have been elected: They will produce great sophisms against him, and**

Rome will be injured by those of Alba." For the red hats, or Spanish in Italy, quarrels and new schisms caused by French spies, when the Sabine or Spanish Habsburgs will have been elected into their positions in government: The French spies will produce great sophisms against Charles V, and Rome or Habsburg Italy will also be injured by those of Alba, indicating Moslem invasion beginning.

47.   "The great Arab will march far forward, He will be revealed by the Byzantinians: Ancient Rhodes will come to meet him, and greater harm for the Austrian Hungarians." The great Arab, Suleiman I, will march far forward expanding his empire, He will be revealed or discovered first by the Byzantinians: Ancient Rhodes or Greece will then come to meet Suleiman I in the forefront as the Moslems advance farther. And greater harm will then begin for the Austrian Hungarians (Latinized), indicating Italy, where Moslems begin attacking.

48.   "After the great affliction of the sceptre, two enemies, by them there will be defeat: A fleet from Africa will appear before the Hungarians, by land and sea horrible deeds will take place." After the great affliction from French espionage against the sceptre or Habsburgs, two enemies, the Moslems and French, by them there will be defeat for Italy: A fleet from Africa, indicating the Moslems, will appear in battle before the Hungarians (Latinized) to indicate Habsburg Italy. By land and sea, horrible deads of allied warfare will take place.

49.   "Not from Spain but from ancient France will one be elected for the trembling bark, to the enemy will promise be made, He who will cause a cruel plague in his realm." Not from the Habsburgs of Spain, but from ancient France will one be elected for the sake of the trembling bark or Christianity to rule in Italy, to the Moslem enemies will a promise of alliance be made, which will cause a cruel plague of murder in France's realm in Italy, when Moslems persecute the French Christians.

50.   "The year that the brothers of the lily come of age one of them will hold the great Romania: The mountain to tremble, Latin passage opened, Agreement to march against the fort of Armenia." The year that the brother of the lily, fleur-de-lys, French and Moslems, come of age by alliance, one of them, the Moslems, will hold the great Romania or Italy: The mountains of Italy to tremble with this Latin passage opened, agreement by French and Moslem for Suleiman I to march against the Spanish fort of Armenia in Italy.

51.   "The people of Hungary, Angleterre, Poland, and of Bohemia will make a new league: To pass beyond the Pillars of Hercules. For the Barcelonans and Tuscans they will prepare a cruel plot." The people of Moslem Hungary (Dacia) of Angleterre or France, Moslem Poland and of Moslem Bohemia, will make a new league of alliance: To pass beyond the Pillars of Hercules or Spanish defenders in Italy, for the Barcelonans or Spanish and Tuscans or Italians the French and Moslems will prepare a cruel plot of attack and turmoil.

52. **"There will be a King who will give opposition, the exiles raised over the realm: The pure poor people to swim in blood, and for a long time will he flourish under such a device."** There will be a king, Suleiman I, who will give opposition invading Italy, the French exiles or spies raised up over the realm to incite rebellions: The pure, poor Spanish rulers there to swim in blood from this allied warfare, and for a long time the Moslems will flourish in conquest under such a device or alliance with France.

53. **"The law of the Sun and Venus contending, *appropriating* the spirit of prophecy: Neither the one nor the other will be understood, the law of the great Messiah will be held by the Sun."** The law of the Sun or Christianity and Venus or Moslem Italy contending, appropriating the spirit of prophecy from their own religions: Neither the one, Moslem faith, nor the other, Christian faith, will be understood when they try witnessing to each other. The law of the great Messiah Jesus will be held by the Sun or Christianity.

54. **"From beyond the Black Sea and great Tartary, there will be a King who will come to see Gaul. He will pierce through Alania and Armenia, and within Byzantium will he leave his bloody rod."** From beyond the Black Sea and Great Tartary, or Turkish lands, there will be a king, Suleiman I, who will come to see Gaul, making an alliance with France. He will pierce through Alania and Armenia, and within Byzantium will he leave his bloody rod as he conquers these lands on his path west through the European countries.

55. **"From the country of Arabia Felix there will be born one powerful in the law of Mahomet: To vex Spain to conquer Grenada, and more by sea at the Ligurian people."** From the country of Arabia, Felix, now divided indicating secret alliance, there will be born one powerful in the law of Mahomet, Suleiman I, wanting to expand his Moslem realm: To vex Spain in with French spies, to conquer (Old French) Grenada or Spanish Italy, and more from Moslems by sea against the Ligurian people or Habsburgs in Italy.

56. **"Through the death of the very old Pontiff a Roman of good age will be elected, of him it will be said that he weakens his see, but long will he sit and in biting activity."** Through the death of the very old pontiff, France, being a type of dead Catholicism, a Roman through alliance, Suleiman I, of good age, will be elected by France to capture Italy. Of him it will be said that he weakens the Holy Seat by persecuting the Christians, but long will Suleiman I sit and in this biting activity.

57. **"There will go from Mont Gaussier and Aventin, one who through the gate will warn the army: Between two rocks will the booty be taken, of Sectus mausoleum the renown to fail."** There will go from Mont Gaussier (Moslems) and Aventin (France), indicating alliance, France who, through the gate of spy activity, will warn the Moslems concerning Habsburg defenses: Between two rocks, French and Moslem, will the booty or Italy be taken. Of Sextus Mausoleum, again indicating alliance, the renown to fail as the Moslems later persecute the Christians.

58. "By the aqueduct of Uzes over the Gard, *through* the forest and inaccessible mountain, in the middle of the bridge there will be cut in the hand the chief of Nimes who will be very terrible." By the aqueduct of Uzes, over the Gard River, or spy route, through the forest and inaccessible mountain, French spies are sent into Italy. In the middle of the bridge, or spy route, there will be cut in the hand by Moslem trickery, the chief of Nimes, Francis I, who will be very terrible using spies against Habsburgs.

59. "The Anglois chief of Nimes stays too long, near to Spain Redbeard to the rescue: Many will die by war opened that day, when a bearded star will fall in Artois." The Anglois or French chief of Nimes, France, stays in Italy too long, near Habsburg Spain, Redbeard or Charles V to the rescue in counter attack against the allies there: Many will die by war opened that day, when a bearded star, Charles V, will come near Artois, or France, in Italy, by defeating the Moslems there.

60. "For the shaven head a very bad choice will come to be made, overburdened he will not pass the gate: He will speak with such great fury and rage. That to fire and blood he will consign the entire sex." For the shaven head, or defeated France, a very bad choice of alliance will come to be made. Overburdened by Moslem trickery, France will not pass the port to dwell inside Italy: Suleiman I will speak with such great fury and rage against the French that he will consign all of sex, or France, to fire and blood.

61. "Child of the great one not by his birth, will subjugate the high Apennine Mountains: Causing to tremble all those of the balance, and from the Pyrenees in Mont Cenis." The Moslem child, by alliance with the great one, France, not according to his birth since of another nationality and another religious faith, will subjugate the high Apennine Mountains by capturing Italy: Causing to tremble all those sitting in the balance, or Austrian Habsburgs, and those from the Pyrenees in Mont Cenis, indicating Spanish Habsburgs in Italy.

62. "One will see blood to rain near the high rocks, Sun in the East, Saturn in the West: Near Orgon fighting, for Rome great evil to be seen, ships sunk to the bottom, and the Tridental taken." One will see blood from fighting to rain near the high rocks, the Moslem Sun France-like; in the East, and Saturn or France in the West: From Moslems near Orgon or France comes war, for Rome or Italy great evil or instigated revolts to be seen, ships sunk to the bottom and Habsburg Tridental taken.

63. "From the vain enterprise honor and undue complaint, boats tossed about among the Latins, cold, hunger, waves not far from the Tiber the land stained with blood, and diverse plagues will be upon mankind." From the vain enterprise to capture Italy, honor of victory for Moslems and undue complaint from France because of trickery, boats tossed about among the Latins or Habsburgs in Italy as cold, hunger waves not far from the Tiber, the land stained with blood from Moslems attacking and diverse plagues from French spies will be upon mankind.

64. **"Those assembled with the tranquility of the great number, by land and sea counsel countermanded: Near Antonne Genoa, Nice in the shadow from fields and towns revolting against the chief."** Those French and Turks, assembled with the tranquility of their great number after capturing Italy, by land and sea their allied counsel countermanded as the Turks trick the French: Near Autun, France, Genoa, Italy, Nice, France, indicating the French in Italy in the shadow, from French fields and towns in Italy revolting against the Moslem chief.

65. **"Suddenly coming, the terror will be great, the principal ones of the affair hidden: And the lady will no longer be in sight by the brewery, Thus little by little the great ones will be angered."** Suddenly coming, the terror of French revolts will reportedly be great, the principal ones or Moslem instigators in the affair of staged revolt, keeping hidden: And the Lady, France, will no longer be in sight by the brewery, celebrating Habsburg defeat; thus, little by little, the great ones, French and Moslems, will be angered with each other.

66. **"By the ancient vestal edifices, not far from the ruined aqueduct: From the Sun and Moon are the shining metals, the Trojan lamp engraved with gold burning.** By the ancient vestal edifices or property of aging France, not far in time from the ruined aqueduct or French spy route that helped Moslems capture Italy: From the Sun or France and Moon or Moslems are shining metals or sword of quarreling, the Trojan or Moslem lamp engraved with gold or France, through alliance, is burning.

67. **"When the chief of Perugia will not venture his tunic Sons in the shade without any cover and quite naked Seven will be taken Aristocratic deed, Father and son dead through a point in the collar."** When the Moslem chief of Perugia or Italy will not venture his tunic to help, sons or France, in the shade without any cover and quite naked: Seven, or France, will be taken by the instigated Aristocratic deed or revolts, Father and son, indicating the alliance relationship, dead through a point in the collar from Moslem soldiers.

68. **"From the Danube and the Rhine will come to drink the great camel, not being sorry for it: To shake from the Rhone, and much more so those of the Loire, and near the Alps the Cock will ruin him."** From the Moslem Danube, and French Rhine will come to drink the great camel or Moslem invaders, not being sorry for it: To shake from the Rhone or alliance and much more so from those of the Loire or French spies, and near the Alps or in Italy, the Cock or French spies will ruin the Habsburgs.

69. **"No longer will the great one be in his false sleep, *uneasiness* will come to replace tranquility: A Phalanx of gold, azure and vermilion arrayed Africa to subjugate and gnaw them to the bone."** No longer will the great one, or Habsburg Charles V, be in his false sleep, resting with fortified Italy; uneasiness of war will come to replace this tranquility: To array the battle Phalanx with gold, azure, and vermilion, Africa or the Moslems to subjugate the Habsburgs and gnaw them to the bone by driving them out of Italy.

70.   "From the regions subject to the Balance, they will trouble the mountains with great war, Captives the entire sex enthralled and all Byzantium, so that at dawn they will spread the news from land to land." From the Italian regions subject to the Balance or Habsburgs, the French and Moslems will trouble the mountains there with great war, Captives, or Habsburgs defeated, the entire sex, or France, enthralled and all Byzantium, of the Moslems, too, so that at dawn they will spread the news from land to land, telling their great victory.

71.   "In the fury of one who will wait for the water, in his great rage the entire army agitated: Seventeen boats loaded by the noble, the carrier comes late along the Rhone." The Moslems in fury will wait for the water to arrive. In his great rage, the entire Moslem army agitated: Seventeen boats, seven indicating France, loaded by the noble French ally, the French carrier, or ship, comes late along the Rhone, symbolizing alliance, with his fresh water to supply the Moslem army, since French spies poisoned the wells.

72.   "For the pleasure of the voluptuous edict, one will mix poison in the faith: Venus will be in a course so virtuous As to becloud the whole quality of the Sun." For the pleasure of the voluptuous Moslem edict, Suleiman I, like end time Protestants, will mix poison in the law, allowing Christians to be persecuted: Venus, indicating Moslems in Italy, will be in a course or walk so virtuous, in their opinion, as to becloud or outshine the whole quality of the Sun, symbolizing Christianity and their French allies.

73.   "The church of God will be persecuted, and the holy Temples will be plundered, the child will put his mother out in a shift, being Arabs with (Pollons) Peillon rallying." The church of God or French Christians, like the end time Catholic Church, will be persecuted, and the holy Christian temples will be plundered by the Moslems, like end time Protestants. The Moslem child will put his French mother, related by alliance, out in a shift of policy. Being Moslem Arabs with Peillon or allied French rallying against themselves.

74.   "Of Trojan blood will be born a Germanic heart who will rise to very high power: He will drive out the foreign Arabic people, returning the Church to its pristine pre-eminence." Of Trojan blood, similar to France by Christian faith, will be born a Germanic heart, Charles V, who will rise to very high power, similar to the Christian receiving the greater anointing through God's full end time revelations: He will drive out the foreign Arabic people from Italy, returning the Church to its pristine pre-eminence, or the Christian faith.

75.   "He will rise high over the estate more to the right, He will remain seated upon the square stone, towards the south facing to his left, the crooked staff in his hand his mouth sealed." The Habsburgs will rise over the estate more to the right against the eastern Moslems, Charles V will remain seated like repentant saints, upon the square (Pyramidal) stone of God's fullness. Towards the south facing to his left, is France, like the end time

Catholic Church, the crooked staff of perversion in his hand, his mouth sealed in shame.

76. **"In a free place will he pitch his tent, and he will not want to lodge in the cities: Aix, Carpentras, L'Isle, Vancluse Mont. Cavaillon, *throughout* all these places will he abolish his trace."** In a free place, Italy recaptured, the Habsburgs pitch their tent, and they will not want to lodge in the cities of Aix, Carpentras, L'Isle, Vancluse, Montfayet, and Cavaillon, French cities indicating Christianity under man's corrupt doctrines,.Throughout all these places will the Habsburgs abolish the French and Moslem trace, symbolizing the end time Catholic and Protestant perversions.

77. **"All the degrees of Ecclesiastical honor will be changed in Jupiter to Quirinus: In Mars the priest of Quirinus, then a King of France will make him Vulcanal."** All the degrees of Christian Ecclesiastical honor will be changed in Jupiter, or Habsburg Italy, to Quirinus, the new Italic divinity, indicating the Moslem faith: In Mars of warfare, the priest of Quirinus, or Suleiman I, is seen expanding his empire. Then a king of France, Francis I, will make Suleiman I Vulcanal or more fiery through an alliance.

78. **"The two will not remain united for very long, and during thirteen years with the Barbarian Satrap: On both sides they will cause such loss that one will bless the Bark and its cope."** The two, France and Turks, will not remain united very long, and during thirteen years, symbolizing end time United States Christians, with the Barbarian Satrap, or Moslems, like three Protestant ages: On both sides, they will cause such loss by perverting the faith that end time Protestants will bless the Bark and its cope, allying with the Catholic Church.

79. **"The sacred pomp will come to lower its wings, by the coming of the great legislator: He will raise the humble, he will vex the rebels, and His like will not appear on this earth."** The sacred pomp, or France, will come to lower its wings like Napoleon making aristocrats out of the lowly, by the coming for alliance of the great legislator, Suleiman I: France will raise the humble Moslems and vex the Habsburg rebels, His like, similar to end time uniting of Catholics and Protestants, will not appear on this earth again.

80. **"Ogmios will approach great Byzantium. The Barbaric League will be driven out: Of the two laws the heathen one released, Barbarian and Frank in perpetual strife."** Ogmios, the Celtic Hercules, indicates France, who will approach great Byzantium or the Moslems for alliance. The Barbaric League or Habsburgs will then be driven out of Italy: Of the two laws, Christian and Moslem, the heathen or Moslem one is released to rule Italy, Barbarian Moslem and Frank, or French Christian, then fall into perpetual strife.

81. **"The royal bird over the city of the Sun, Seven months in advance will deliver a nocturnal omen: The Eastern wall will fall, lightning thunder, Seven days the enemies directly to the gates."** The royal bird, France, over the city of the Sun, or Habsburg Italy, Seven months in advance, like seven church ages completed, will deliver a nocturnal omen of perversion:

The Eastern wall of Italy will fall with lightning and thunder of fighting Seven days, indicating French spies as the enemies directly to the gates in Italy.

82. "At the conclusion of the treaty beyond the fortress He who is placed in despair will not go: When those of Arbois, of Langres against Bresse will have the mountains of Dole an enemy ambush." At the conclusion of the treaty or ceasefire, with Habsburg defeat, beyond the fortress in Italy. France, placed in despair from trickery, will not go: When those of Arbois, symbolizing the alliance, becoming as Langres or Moslems against Bresse of France, will have the mountains of Dole as an enemy ambush, indicating Moslem trickery.

83. "Those who will have undertaken to overthrow, an unparalleled realm, powerful and invincible: will act through deception three nights to warn when the greatest one will read his Bible at the table." Those Moslems who will have undertaken to overthrow an unparalleled realm, Habsburg Italy, powerful and seemingly invincible, will act through deception of perverted Moslem faith three nights to warn, like Protestants of three church ages perverting their faith, when the greatest one, Habsburg Italy, symbolizing the believer, will read his Bible at the table, seeking the truth.

84. "He will be born of the unmeasured gulf and city. Born of obscure and dark family: Who revered the power of the great King, will want to destroy through Rouen and Evreux." The Moslems who will be born of the unmeasured gulf and city, Born of obscure and dark family similar to the various origins of the Protestant churches Who revered the power of the great Habsburg King, representing the true Christian believer, will want to destroy Charles V through Rouen and Evreux, two French cities indicating alliance with France.

85. "From the Suevi and neighboring places, they will be at war on account of the clouds: Swarm of marine locusts and gnats, the faults of Geneva will be laid quite bare." From the Suevi or Swiss and neighboring places, the Habsburgs will be at war on account of the clouds of Moslems attacking Italy: Like a swarm of marine locusts and gnats coming to land from the sea, the faults of Geneva, indicating Habsburg weaknesses, will be laid quite bare as they are defeated, like end time saints chastised.

86. "Divided by the two heads and three arms, the great city will be vexed by waters: Some great ones among them led astray in exile, Byzantium hard pressed by the head of Persia." Divided by two heads, Habsburgs against Moslems, and three arms indicating the secret French ally, too, the great Habsburg city, Italy, will be vexed by waters, indicating French and Moslems: Some great ones among them, Habsburg and French Christians, led astray in exile, Byzantium, or western Moslems, hard pressed by the head of Persia for more slaves.

87. "The year that Saturn is out of bondage, from the Frank land he will be inundated by water: With Trojan blood will his marriage be and it will be confined safely from the Spaniards." The year that Saturn, or France, is out of bondage of despair from defeat in Italy, from the French land the Habsburg countries will be flooded by water when French spies instigate revolts: With Trojan or French blood, will the Moslem marriage by alliance be made, and it will be safely confined in secrecy from the Habsburgs.

88.   "Through a frightful flood upon the sand, a marine monster from other seas found: Near the place will be made a refuge, Savona taking the slave of Turin." Through a frightful flood of invaders upon the sand of shores of Italy, a marine monster, the Moslems from other seas are found, invading Italy with their army: Near the place farther inside Italy a refuge will be made for French spies to operate, Savona or France taking the slave of Turin or Habsburg Italy, in secrecy.

89.   "In Hungary from Bohemia, Navarre, and through the banner feigned insurrections: Through the fleur-de-lys region carrying the bar, against Orleans they will cause disturbances." In Moslem Hungary, from Bohemia, Navarre, or France, and through the banner of alliance with the French, feigned insurrections are started by the Moslems: Through the fleur-de-lys or French controled region carrying the bar or Bourbon emblem, symbolizing the cross of Christianity, against Orleans or France, the Moslems will this way cause disturbances, which ruins the alliance.

90.   "In the Cyclades, in Perinthus and Larissa, in Sparta and the entire Peloponnesus: Very great famine, plague through false striving, *nine* months will it last and throughout the entire peninsula." In the Cyclades, in Perinthus and Larissa, in Sparta and the entire Peloponnesus, indicating Moslem lands: Very great famine and plague of persecution started against the French, through false or invented striving of Christians against Moslems, nine months will it last. Nine being a multiple of three indicating Moslem instigators, similar to end time Protestants from three ages.

91.   "From the great marche which they call that of liars. The entire Tourain and field of Athens: will be surprising them with light horses, from those of Alba when Mars is in Leo and Saturn in Aquarius." From the great French Marche, what they call those secretive liars, the entire Tourain, or France, and field of Athens or Moslems: will be surprising Habsburg ruled Italy with light horses, from those of Moslem Albania, when Mars of war is in Moslem Leo, fifth or beginning Protestant age, and French Saturn in eleventh hour Aquarius.

92.   "After the siege has been held seventeen years, Five will change within the same period of time: Then one will be elected at the same time, who will not be too conformable to the Romans." After the siege has been held seventeen years, symbolizing France like ending of seven Catholic ages, five indicating the Moslems like the fifth church age Protestants, change within the same end time period: Then the Moslem one by alliance will be elected to rule the same time, who will not be too conformable to the Romans or French.

93.   "Under the land of the round lunar globe, when Mercury will be dominating: The isle de Crozon will produce a light, that will put, the Anglois in confusion." Under Italy, the land of the round lunar globe, or Moslems, when Moslem Mercury, closest to the French Sun, like alliance, will

be dominating Italy: The isle de Crozon, or France, will produce a light of Christianity, which will put the Anglois or French into confusion from Moslem trickery when they deceive the French and take over all Italy.

94.   "He will transfer to great Germany Brabant and Flanders, Ghent, Bruges, and Boulogne: The truce feigned, the great Duke of Armenia will assail Vienna and Cologne." French spies will transfer (Old French) to great Germany to trouble the Habsburgs at Brabant and Flanders, Ghent, Bruges, and Boulogne: The alliance truce with the French feigned by the Moslems who wanted to capture Italy, the great Duke of Armenia, French-like Suleiman I, leading the Moslems, will assail Vienna and Cologne, attacking the Spanish Habsburgs in Italy.

95.   "The nautical frog will invite those of Ambrois, then it will come to stir up the great Empire: In the Aegean Sea those of Kemba with wood will obstruct the diverted Tyrrhenian Sea." The nautical frog, or seafaring Moslems, will invite those of the shadows, or defeated France, into an alliance, then Moslems will come to provoke the great Habsburg Empire by attacking Habsburg Italy: In the Aegean Sea those of Kembs or France with wood or ships bringing supplies helping the Moslems, will obstruct the Tyrrhenian Sea or Habsburgs.

96.   "The rose upon the middle of the great world, from new deeds public shedding of blood: To speak the truth, one will have a closed mouth, then at the time of need, the invited one will come late." The rose or Moslems upon the middle of the great world with Italy captured, from new deeds of Moslem edicts, begins public shedding of blood against Christians: To speak truth according to the Moslem faith, the Christian will have a closed mouth, then at the time of need, the awaited defense comes late from France raising objections.

97.   "The one born deformed suffocated in horror, in the habitable city of the great King: The severe edict the captives revoke, hail and thunder, Condom inestimable." France, born into alliance deformed, suffering from earlier defeat, suffocated in horror from Moslem trickery, in the habitable city of the great King, or Italy under the triumphant Moslem king: The severe Moslem edict enslaving and murdering Christian captives in Italy, is finally revoked, but the hail and thunder, to Condom or France, inestimable in damage.

98.   "At the forth-eighth climacteric degree, at the end of Cancer very great dryness: Fish in sea, river, lake boiled hectic, Bearn, Bigorre in distress through fire from the sky." At the 49th climacteric degree, indicating France, at the end of Cancer, fourth sign of the Zodiac symbolizing four Catholic Church ages past, very great dryness or famine for God's Word: Fish in sea, river, lake boiled hectic from heat, Bearn, Bigoree or France, symbolizing the dead Catholic Church, in distress through judgment fire from the sky.

99.   "Milan, Ferrara, Turin and Aquileia, Capua, Brindise vexed by the Celtic nation: With the Lion and his eagle phalanx, when the old

Britannique chief will have Rome." Milan, Ferrara, Turin and Aquileia, Capua, Brindisi Italy vexed by the Celtic or French people when they earlier captured Italy alone: With the Lion or France and his imperial phalanx or French army, when the old Britannique, French chief, Francis I, will have Rome or Italy by defeating the Habsburgs and driving them out.

100. "The incendiary in his fire tricked, by fire from the sky at Carcassonne and the Comminges: Foix, Auch Mazeres, the high old man escaped, through those of Hesse and Thuringia, and some Saxons." The incendiary or French army in his fire or attack trapped By fire or Habsburg counter attack from the sky at Carcassonne and the Comminges: Foix, Auch, and Mazeres, indicating France, the high old man, or Francis I, escaped through those of Hesse and Thuringia, and some Saxons, all German states, indicating Habsburgs, allowing Francis I release after his capture.

Nostradamus
Century VI

Nostradamus

Century VI

1. **"Around the Pyrenees Mountains a great throng of foreign people to aid the new King: Near the Garonne the great temple of Le Mas. A Roman Chief will fear it in the water."** Around the Pyrenees Mountains, indicating French, a great throng of foreign people, French allies, to aid the new Moslem king ruling in Italy: Near the Garonne the great temple of LeMas, indicating French cities and the Christian faith, a Roman chief, Suleiman I, will fear the French Christians in the water rebelling against the Moslem cities in Italy.

2. **"In the year five hundred eighty more or less, one will await a very strange century: In the year seven hundred and three the heavens witness thereof, that several kingdoms one to five making a change."** In the year 580 more or less, indicating six, the number of work, France will await a very strange century sharing Italy: In the year 703, seven indicating Catholic and three Protestants, the heavens or believers witness thereof, that several Protestant realms, like Moslems, and one to five, or Catholics like France, making a change by trickery.

3. **"The river that the new Celtic heir tries will be in great discord from the Empire: The young Prince through the ecclesiastical people will remove the sceptre of the crown of concord."** The (Rhone) river indicating alliance, that the new Celtic or French heir of Italy attempts using, will be in great discord from the Italian Empire: The young prince Suleiman I through the ecclesiastical French spies who rebel against Moslem cities, will remove the Moslem sceptre (variant indicating Moslems) of concord and put the French rebels to death.

4. **"The Celtic river will change its course, no longer will it include the city of Agrippina: All changed except the old language, Saturn, Leo,**

Mars, Cancer in plunder." The Celtic river (Rhone being French and Moslem alliance) will change its course. No longer will it include the city, western Agrippina, symbolizing France: All changed in Italy to the Moslem faith but not to the Moslem language, Saturn, Leo or French and Moslems in Mars of quarreling, Cancer or four Catholic ages, like France, in plunder.

5.   **"Very great famine through pestiferous wave, *through* long rain the length of the northern Po: Samarobryn one hundred leagues from the hemisphere, they will live without law except from politics."** Very great famine of loss for the French through pestiferous wave of quarreling through long rain of Moslem instigated rebellions the length of the northern Po, indicating Italy: Amiens (Samarobryn) or France being one hundred leagues (alone) from the hemisphere or shared Italy, will live without law causing rebellions against the Moslems wherever exempt from French politics.

6.   **"There will appear towards the North not far from Cancer L'Etoil full of filaments: Suna, Siena, Boeotia, Eretria. The great one of Rome will die, the fight over."** There will appear towards the North, Strasburg (easterly) indicating Moslems, not far from Cancer, fourth sign or France like four Catholic Church ages. Place de L'Etoil, or Moslems, full of filaments or tricks Susa, Siena, French in Italy, revolt against Moslem Boeotia and Eretria, the great one of Rome, Suleiman I, will die, indicating losses, the night rebellions over.

7.   **"Norneigre and Dacia and the isle Britannique through the united Monks will be vexed: The Roman chief issued with Gallic blood and his forces hurled back into the forests."** Norneigre (variant for Normandy) and Dacia both indicating Moslem regions in Italy, and L'Ile Britannique or French regions, through the united French monks rebelling, will be vexed: The Roman chief, Suleiman I, issued with Gallic blood or French allies sharing in ownership of Italian lands, and his Moslem forces hurled back into the forests by the French rebellions started.

8.   **"Those who were in the realm for knowledge will become impoverished at the change of King: Some exiled without support, having no gold, the lettered and letters will not be at a high premium."** Those French who were in the Italian realm because of their knowledge as spies, will become impoverished at the change of the king, Suleiman I: Some French exiled without support having no gold after the Moslems plundered them, the lettered or educated Christians and letters of Christian teachings will not be at a high premium to the Moslems.

9.   **"In the sacred temples scandals being perpetrated. Reckoned being as honors and commendations: Of one of whom they engrave medals of silver and of gold, the end will be in very strange torments."** In the sacred Moslem temples being perpetrated by French rebels as scandals those things reckoned being for honors and commendations for the Moslem rulers: Of one Moslem leader they will engrave award medals of silver and of gold, the end of his success will be in very strange torments as the French rebels capture and torture him.

10.   "In a short time the temples with colors of white and black of the two intermixed: Red and yellow ones carrying them and their possessions, blood, land, plague, famine, fire extinguished by water." In a short time, the temples with colors of white Christian and black Moslem, with the two intermixed in Italy under allied rule: Red and yellow ones, indicating bloodied Moslems, with changed color or attitude carrying off the French rebels and their possessions, blood, land, plague, famine, or persecutions, the fire of rebellions extinguished by Moslem water.

11.   "The seven branches to three being reduced, the elder ones being surprised by death, the two being seduced to fratricide, the conspirators being dead while sleeping." The seven branches, indicating France like the end time Catholic Church from seven church ages, being reduced to three, or Moslem rule only, in Italy, like end time Protestants, the elder ones, France, being surprised by death after rebellions, the two being seduced to fratricide, the French conspirators being dead while sleeping, being off guard, killed by Moslem trickery.

12.   "To raise forces to ascend the empire in the Vatican, the Royal blood will be anxious: Flamans Anglois, Spain with Aspire against Italy the French will contend." To raise rebel forces to ascend to the original size of the French empire, in the Vatican or Christian churches, the Royal blood, or French, will be anxious against the Moslem ally ruling Italy with them: Flamanville and Anglois or French, Spain (Habsburgs) with Speyer (Germany Habsburgs) indicating French spies, against Italy the French contend by rebellion.

13.   "A doubtful one will not come far from the realm, the greater part will want to uphold him: A capital will not want him to reign at all, He will be unable to bear his great burden." The doubtful one, or French, will not come far with success in the Italian realm, because of instigated rebellions. The greater part or France itself will want to uphold the French in Italy: A capital (Rome), symbolizing the French rebels, will not want the Moslems to reign at all, unable to bear his great burden of government.

14.   "Far from his land a King will lose the battle, at once escaped, pursued, then captured, ignorant one taken under the golden mail, under false garb, and the enemy surprised." Far from his land, a king, Francis I, will lose the battle initially in Italy and be captured by Habsburgs. At once, escaped through his release, Francis I pursued, then captured Italy back again. Ignorant one, or Moslems, taken under French golden mail, under false garb by secret alliance helping the Moslems, and the Habsburg enemy surprised in Italy.

15.   "Under the tomb will be found a Prince who will be valued above Nuremberg: The Spanish King in Capricorn thin, deceived and betrayed by the great Wittenberg." Under the tomb of defeat will be found a prince, Francis I, who will be valued by the Moslems above Nuremberg or Habsburgs who rule in Italy: The Spanish King of Italy in Capricorn, tenth sign of Zodiac,

indicating alone and thin without Austrian help, deceived and betrayed by the great Wittenberg or Austrian Habsburgs because of quarreling.

16. **"That which will be carried off by the young Hawk, by the Normans of France and Picardy: The black ones of the temple of the Black Forest place will make an inn and fire of Lombardy."** The Italian realm carried off by the young Hawk, Suleiman I, by allied help from Normans of France and Picardy: The Moslem black ones will of the Italian temple under the Black forest place, or Habsburgs, like the partially anointed end time believer, make an inn of drunk confusion and fire of military defeat of Lombardy or Habsburg Italy.

17. **"After they burned penances, the ass-drivers, will be obliged to change different clothes: Those of Saturn burned by the hooded crows, except the greater part which will not be protected."** After French Christians burned penances again in Moslem-held Italy, the ass-drivers or Moslems will be obliged to change into different clothes or change their attitude against France because of rebellions: Those of Saturn or France burned or murdered by the hooded crows or Moslems, except the greater French part, which is not protected inside Italian lands.

18. **"The great King abandoned by the Physicians, by fate not the Labrede art he remains alive, He and his kindred pushed high in the realm, Pardon given to the race which denies Christ."** The great king, Suleiman I, abandoned by the physicians, or French ally, through the French rebellions. By fate not the medical art of Labrede, or France, Suleiman I remains alive possessing Italy alone, He and his Moslem kindred pushed high in the Italian realm. Pardon given to the Christian race which denies Christ and converts to the Moslem faith.

19. **"The true flame will devour the lady who will want to put the Innocent Ones to the fire: Before the assault the army is inflamed, when from Seville a monster will be seen in the black cattle."** The true flame or Moslems will devour the French lady who will want to put the Moslem Innocent Ones to the fire through rebellions: Before the assault the Moslem army is inflamed when in Spanish Seville, or French spies who had Spanish credentials, a monster, indicating the rebellions, will be seen in the black cattle or Moslems.

20. **"The feigned union will be of short duration, from some changed, the greater part reformed: In the vessels people will be in suffering, then Rome will have a new Leopard."** The feigned union or alliance between France and Moslems will be of short duration, from Moslems, changed in attitude, tricking the French, most of the Christians reformed becoming Moslems to avoid the persecution: In the vessels fleeing people will be in suffering because of the Moslems, then Rome will have a new (yellow) Leopard, Suleiman I, acting differently.

21. **"When those by the northern pole are united together, great terror and fear in the East: Newly elected, the great trembling supported, Rhodes, Byzantium stained with Barbarian blood."** When those French and Moslems by the Northern pole are united, indicating their alliance together, great terror and fear from warfare is started in the East by Moslems: Newly elected, the great trembling of war from the Moslems attacking Italy is supported by alliance, Rhodes, Byzantium or Moslems stained with Barbarian or Habsburg blood during Italy's capture.

22. **"Within the land of the great heavenly temple, Nephew murdered at Londres through feigned peace: The bark will then become schismatic, Sham liberty will be proclaimed everywhere."** Within the land of the great heavenly temple, indicating Italy after it is captured, Nephew from Londres or France, indicating French spies, murdered through feigned peace in Italy: The bark or French Christians will then become schismatic with people converting to the Moslem faith for safety. Sham liberty for Moslems, and not Christians, will be proclaimed everywhere.

23. **"Defenses undermined by the spirit of the realm, and people will be stirred up against their King: New peace made, holy laws become worse. Paris was never in so very severe an array."** The allied Moslem and French defenses are undermined by the Moslem spirit of the Italian realm, and French people will be stirred up against their Moslem kingking, Suleiman I, through Moslem trickery: New stricter peace made, Moslem holy laws become worse, allowing persecution against Christians. Paris, indicating France, was never in so very severe an array or loss.

24. **"Mars and sceptre will be found conjoined under Cancer calamitous war: Shortly afterwards a new King will be anointed, one who for a long time will pacify the earth."** Mars and the sceptre of Moslem forces will be found conjoined underneath Cancer, fourth sign like France and the first four Catholic ages, calamitous war for the Habsburgs: Shortly afterwards, a new king, Suleiman I, will be anointed by the French ally to govern Italy, one who for a long time will pacify the earth with Moslem rule.

25. **"Through adverse Mars will the monarchy of the great fisherman be in ruinous trouble: The young red black one will seize the hierarchy, the traitors will act on a day of drizzle."** Through adverse Mars of war the monarchy of the great fisherman, Charles V, will be in ruinous trouble: The young red black one, indicating red or Spanish-like French spies and allied black Moslems, will seize the Habsburg hierarchy in Italy. The French traitors will act on a day of drizzle (Old French), indicating French spies working under cover.

26. **"For four years, the see will be held with some little good, one libidinous in life will succeed to it: Ravenna, Pisa, and Verona will give support, longing to elevate the Papal cross."** For four years, like first four Catholic Church ages of grace, the see, or Italy, will be held with some little good. One libidinous or lewd in life, Suleiman I, will succeed to it: Ravenna, Pisa, and Verona, owned by the French, will give support to Moslem government, longing to elevate the Papal cross with French sharing Italy.

27. **"Within the Isles by five rivers to one, from the expansion of the great Chyren Selin: From the drizzles in the air the fury of one, Six**

escaped, hidden in bundles of flax." Within the Isles, by five (grace) rivers or routes to one of them, from the expansion of war into Italy by the great Chyren Selin of French and Moslem allies: Through the drizzles in the air, indicating French spy activity, and the fury of one, the Moslem army, Six (work) Habsburgs escaped hidden in bundles of flax.

28. **"The great Celt will enter within Rome, leading a throng of the exiles and banished: The great Pastor will put to death all the men who were united at the Alps for the cock."** The great Celt, Francis I, will enter within Rome, leading a throng of exiled French spies and banished Moslems, under Suleiman I against Italy: The great Pastor, like the end time Catholic Church and Francis I, will put to death all Habsburg men who were on account of the cock or French allied effort united at the Alps against the Moslems.

29. **"The saintly widow hearing the news, of her offspring placed in perplexity and trouble: He who will be instructed to appease the quarrels, through his pursuit the shaven heads pile up."** The saintly widow, Austrian Habsburgs like the end time chastised saint, hearing the news, of her offspring like Habsburg city subdivisions, placed in perplexity and trouble from rebellions: He who will be instructed (Old French, indicating French spy influence) to appease the quarrels, through his pursuit the shaven heads of quarreling Habsburgs pile up with even more complications.

30. **"Through the appearance of feigned sanctity the see will be betrayed to the enemies: In the night when they trusted to sleep in safety, near Brabant will march those of Liege."** Through the appearance of France's feigned holiness or non-involvement, the seat, or Habsburg Italy, will be betrayed to the Moslem enemies through French spies causing trouble: In the night when the Habsburgs trusted to sleep in safety away from the front line fighting, near Brabant will march those of Liege as rebellions are instigated among Habsburg cities.

31. **"The King will find that which he desired so much when the Prelate will be unjustly taken: Reply to the Duke will leave him dissatisfied, who in Milan will put several to death."** The King, Charles V, will find that which he desired so much because of optimistic French spies, when the prelate or bishop will be taken unjustly: Reply to the Duke will leave him dissatisfied who in Milan will put several to death in reprisal as he too is encouraged by French spies instigating seditions among the Habsburg leadership.

32. **"Beaten to death by rods for treason, captured he will be overcome through his disorder: Frivolous counsel held out to the great captive, when Berich will come to bite his nose in fury."** Beaten to death by rods for treason, indicating the French spies causing seditions among Habsburgs, Italy captured, Charles V will be overcome through his disorder of confusion from rebellions: Frivolous counsel held out to the great captive Italy, when Berich (variant) or Duke de Berry, symbolizing the Moslems, will come to bite the Habsburg nose in fury of attack.

33. **"His last hand through Alus bloody, He will be unable to protect himself by sea: Between two rivers he will fear the military hand, the black and irate one will make him be sorry."** The last hand of Charles V, bloody from war with Alice St. Reine, or France, Charles V will be unable to protect himself by sea when the Moslems attack: Between two rivers, France and Moslems, he will fear the military hand of the Moslems. The black one, or Moslems, and irate one, France, will make Charles V to be sorry in defeat.

34. **"The device of flying fire will come to trouble the great besieged chief: Within there will be such sedition that the profligate ones will be in despair."** The device of flying fire done by catapults will come to trouble the great besieged chief, Charles V, when the Moslems attack Italy: Within the Habsburg Empire, there will be such sedition caused by French spies infiltrating the government, that the profligate ones, or extravagant Habsburgs, influenced by spies, will be in despair, unable to properly defend themselves.

35. **"Near the Rhone (Rion) and close to the white wool, Aries, Taurus, Cancer, Leo, Virgo, Mars, Jupiter, the Sun will burn a great plain, woods and cities letters hidden in the candle."** Near the Rhone (Rion) or alliance and close to the Blanc (wool) mountains or eastern Moslems, Aries, Taurus, Cancer, Leo, Virgo representing Catholic and Protestant church ages being allied: Mars or Moslem warfare in Jupiter or Habsburg Italy, the Sun or French spies will burn a great plain, including woods and cities, secret letters hidden in the candle.

36. **"Neither good nor evil through terrestrial battle will reach the confines of Paris, Plea to rebel, Florence to see an evil existence, King by night wounded near a mule with black housing."** Neither good nor evil through the terrestrial battle will reach the confines of Paris, representing France—supposedly uninvolved. Pisa or Habsburgs in Italy to rebel through French spy influence, Florence or Italy to see and evil existence during warfare, Habsburg king wounded secretly by night, from French spies near a mule with black covering, or Moslem attackers.

37. **"The ancient deed will be finished, from the roof evil ruin will fall upon the great one: Dead they will accuse an innocent one of the deed, the guilty one hidden in the misty woods."** The ancient deed of spies will be finished, from the roof of his own Habsburg house, evil ruin instigated by spies will fall upon the Habsburg great one: Dead through rebellions, they will accuse an innocent one among their own Habsburgs of the deed, the guilty one or French spy hidden in the misty woods of secrecy.

38. **"For the profligates at peace, the enemies, afterwards to have Italy conquered: The bloodthirsty black one, red, will be exposed, Fire, blood shed, water colored by blood."** For the profligates or vanquished French who seem at peace, the enemies or Moslem army afterwards to have Italy conquered: Black blood-thirsty, the Moslems, red from battle, will be exposed or visible compared to French spy activity, Fire, blood shed of the Moslems fighting, water colored by blood of Habsburg victims as French spies poison the wells.

39. **"The child of the realm, through his father, captured will be plundered to deliver it: Near the Lake of Perugia the azure surprised, the troop hostage through too much drunkenness."** The Habsburg child in the Italian realm captured, through the father, Charles V, neglecting him, will be plundered (variant) by the Moslems, who deliver Italy free again: Near the Lake of Perugia or Italy, the azure or blue blood Habsburg child is surprised from the Moslem assault, the Habsburg troop hostage through too much drunkenness encouraged by spies.

40. **"The great one of Maine to quench the great thirst will be deprived of his great dignity: Those of Cologne will come to complain so loudly when the great rump will be thrown into the Rine."** The great one of Main (Latinized) indicating French in Italy, to quench his great thirst by greed, will be deprived of his great dignity losing Italian possessions: Those of Cologne or France will come to complain to the Moslems so very loudly, when the great rump (Low Latin) or France, is thrown into the Rhine, losing Italy.

41. **"The second chief of the realm of Annemark, *through* those of Prisia and of L'Ile Britannique, will spend more than one hundred thousand marks, to the vain traveling to Italy."** The second chief, Francis I, by alliance, or the realm of Annemark, captured by Moslems and included in allied lands, through those French spies of Frisia or Holland and L'Ile Britannique or France, will spend (Old French) more than one hundred thousand French marks, indicating their allied support, to exploit the vain Moslems traveling to Italy for the attack.

42. **"To Ogmios will be left the realm with the great Selin, who will in fact do more: Throughout Italy will he extend his banner, it will be ruled by a prudent counterfeit."** To Ogmios, the Celtic Hercules indicating France, will be left the Italian realm with the great Selin, or Suleiman I, who will in fact do more in taking control than the French: Throughout Italy will the French extend their banner ruling together with the Moslems. Italy will be ruled by a prudent counterfeit as Suleiman I will trick France.

43. **"For a long time will she remain uninhabited, where the Seine and the Marne comes around to water: Tried by La Tamise and warriors, the guards deceived in trusting in the repulse."** For a long time, Italy will remain uninhabited by the Habsburgs, where the Seine and Marne or France allied to Moslems, come to gush forth against them: Tried by La Tamise, or French, and warriors of the Moslem army, the Habsburg guards are deceived in trusting (Old French) in the repulse with the recent victory over the French.

44. **"By night in Nantes the Loire will appear, with marine arts stirring up rain: In the Gulf of Arabia a great fleet will fuse, in Saxony a monster will be born of a bear and a sow."** By night in Nantes, France, the Loire River will appear with Moslem marine arts, stirring up rain or war for Italy: In the Arabian Gulf, a great Moslem fleet will fuse by alliance. In Saxony or

Habsburg territory, a French spy monster, born of a Moslem bear (Pic de L'Ours by Frejus) and French sow (Troo on the Loire).

45. **"The very learned governor of the realm, not wishing to consent to the royal deed: The fleet at Melilla through contrary wind will deliver him to his most disloyal one."** The very learned Habsburg governor of the Italian realm, not wishing to consent to the royal deed of his leader, Charles V, being done in poor judgment, supposedly: The fleet of Melilla, indicating Spanish Habsburgs in Italy, through contrary wind of rebellion will deliver Charles V to his most disloyal one, another rebellious Habsburg, who causes him some problems.

46. **"A just one will be sent back into exile, *through* pestilence to the confines of Senigallia, His reply to the red one will cause him to be misled, the King withdrawing to the Lorraine and L'Aigle."** A just Habsburg is sent back into exile, through pestilence of rebellions to the confines of Senigallia (Nonseggle) in Italy, Charles V's reply to the red one or Spanish governor there, will cause the governor to be misled against Habsburg best interest, Charles V withdrawing unknowingly to Lorraine and L'Aigle, or French spies who advise towards French advantage.

47. **"Between two mountains the two great ones assembled abandoning their secret quarrels Brussels and Dole through Langres overthrow, in order to execute plague at Malines."** Between two mountains or down on the plain, the two great Habsburg leaders assembled for conflict among themselves, abandoning their formerly secret quarrel (Old French) indicating French spy instigation: Brussels and Dole, Habsburg cities, through French Langres or Spies encouraging them, overthrow in rebellion, in order to execute plague of revenge at Malines, another Habsburg city.

48. **"The sanctity too false and seductive, accompanied by an eloquent tongue: The old city, and Parma too hasty, rendering Florence and Siena more deserted."** The sanctity or goodness of Habsburgs too false and seductive, accompanied by an eloquent tongue of French spies prodding them to the point of quarrel: The old city, Rome, and Parma too hasty, rendering Florence and Siena in Italy more deserted from rebellions as these Habsburg cities fight with each other over arguments incited by French spies.

49. **"With the party of Mars the great Pontiff will subjugate the confines of the Danube: To pursue the cross through sword hook or crook, captives, gold, jewels more than one hundred thousands rubies."** With the party of Mars or Moslem attack in Italy, the great pontiff, or France, will subjugate the confines of the northern Habsburg Danube: To pursue the cross or Habsburgs through Moslem sword and hook or crook of French spy activity, Habsburg captives, gold, jewels, more than one hundred thousand rubes, one indicating alone without Habsburg reinforcements.

50. **"Within the wells the bones being found, being from incest committed by the stepmother: The condition changed, they will demand fame and praise, and will have Mars meanwhile as their star."** Within the wells the bones of Christians being found, being from incest of persecution to gain converts, committed by the stepmother or Moslems wanting their religion to be the mother instead of Christianity: The condition of the Moslems changed, they will demand fame and praise and will have Mars of warfare meanwhile as their star of glory.

51. **"People assembled to see a new spectacle, Princes and Kings amongst many bystanders, Pillars walls to fall: but as by a miracle King saved and thirty of the ones present."** People assembled by the Moslem victors to see a new spectacle of ruin upon the cities in Italy, Habsburg princes and kings disguised amongst many bystanders; pillars, walls to fall as the cities are ruined: but as by a miracle the king saved and thirty of the Habsburg leaders present, indicating thirty-one years tribulation escaped by saints.

52. **"In place of the great one who will be condemned, outside the prison, his friend in his place: The Trojan hope in six months herewith, born dead, the Sun in the urn rivers with ice."** In place of the Habsburg great one, who will be condemned by defeat, outside the prison in Italy his French friend in his place for tribulation: The Trojan or French hope in six months, six the number of work, herewith born dead by Moslem trickery, the Sun or France in the urn, rivers with ice, indicating disagreements.

53. **"The great Celtic Prelate suspected by the King, by night in flight will leave the realm: Through a duke fruitful for his great Bretaine King, Byzantium to Cyprus and Tunis unsuspected."** The great Celtic or French Prelate suspected by the king, Charles V, by night in flight will leave beyond the realm avoiding discovery: Through a French duke found fruitful to his Bretaine or French King (variant indicating secretly allied to the Moslems, too) Byzantium to Cyprus and Tunis or the Moslems unsuspected (Old French) of French ties.

54. **"At daybreak of the second crowing of the cock, those of Tunis, of Fez and of Bougie, with the Arabs captured the Moorish King, the year sixteen hundred and seven, of the Liturgy."** At daybreak of the second crowing of the French cock, like the end time revived Catholic Church, those of Tunis, Fei, and Bougie with the Arabs capture the Moorish or Spanish king in Italy like end time Protestant churches gaining. The year sixteen hundred, multiple of initial four Catholic ages and seven ages including end time Catholic liturgy revival.

55. **"By the appeared Duke in drawing up the contract, Arabesque sail seen, sudden discovery: Tripolis, Chios, and those of Trebizond, Prize the Duke, the Black Sea and the city deserted."** From the appeased Duke, Francis I, drawing up a contract of alliance with the Moslems, the Arab sail seen, a sudden discovery near Italy as the Moslems attack: Tripolis, Chios from the Aegean and those Moslems of Trebizond prize the French Duke for the alliance, the Black Sea and the city deserted as Moslems leave to capture Italy.

56. **"The dreaded army with the Narbonne enemy will frighten very greatly the Hesperians: Perpignan destitute through the blind one of Argon, then Barcelona by sea will present the offence."** The dreaded Moslem army with the Narbonne enemy or French spies, will frighten very greatly the Habsburg Hesperians in Italy: Perpignan or Spanish Habsburgs in Italy destitute through the blind spy of Narbonne, or France, supposedly helping the Habsburg defenders. Then Barcelona by sea or Spanish Habsburgs in Italy will present the offence against the Moslem army.

57.   **"He who was well forward in the realm, *having* a red chief close to the hierarchy, harsh and cruel, and will make himself much feared. He will succeed to the sacred monarchy."** Suleiman I, who was well forward during the assault in the realm of Italy, having a red or Spanish chief, actually a French spy, close to the Moslem hierarchy, harsh and cruel with his army capturing Italy, will make himself much feared by his success. He will succeed to the sacred monarchy of Italy after the Habsburg defeat.

58.   **"Between the two monarchs alienated, when the Sun through Selin clearly lost: Great enmity between two indignant ones, who restored the Isles and Siena to liberty."** Between the two French and Moslem monarchs, alienated by Moslem instigated rebellions, when the French Sun clearly lost Italian lands through Selin or the Moslems murdering French landholders: Great enmity is between too indignant French and Moslem ones, not being happy now, who earlier restored the Isles and Siena of Italian lands to liberty from Habsburgs.

59.   **"The Lady in fury through rage of adultery, will come to her Prince to entreat him not to tell: But soon will the blame be known, so that seventeen will be put to martyrdom."** The lady, France, in fury through rage of adultery against the alliance after French rebellions discovered, will come to her Moslem prince to entreat him not to tell: But soon will the blame be known by more rebellions occurring, so that being put to martyrdom are seventeen, representing France losing Italian possessions as in the end time of seven Catholic ages.

60.   **"The Prince outside his Celtic land will be betrayed, deceived by the interpreter: Rouen, La Rochelle through those of Brittany at the port of Blaye deceived by monk and priest."** The prince or France outside his Celtic land trying to govern lands in Italy will be betrayed, deceived by the bribed interpreter through Moslem trickery: Rouen, La Rochelle through those French men of Brittany also ruling in Italy; at the port of Blaye, indicating another French city in Italy, deceived by monk and priest, indicating religious problems instigated.

61.   **"The great carpet folded will not show but by halves the greatest part of its history: Driven far out of the realm he will appear harsh, so that everyone will come to believe in his warlike deed."** The great alliance carpet folded will not show but by halves the greatest part of its history, indicating the Moslem role in capturing Italy: The Habsburgs driven far out of the Italian realm, the Moslems will appear harsh, or a great threat, so that everyone will come to believe in his warlike deed seemingly done without assistance.

62.   **"Too late both the flowers will be lost, the serpent will not want to act against the law: The forces of the Ligurians confounded by the**

French, Savona, Albenga through Monaco great martyrdom." Too late, the two flowers, the allied French and Moslems, will be ruined by quarrels, the Moslem serpent will not want to act against the law and tolerate rebellions: The Moslem forces of the Ligurians of Italy confounded, supposedly, by the French rebellions, French Savona and Albenga cause great martyrdom for Moslem Monaco (Latinized, indicating Moslems).

63. "**The lady left alone in the realm extinguished by one first on the bed of honor: Seven years will she be weeping in grief, then long life with great good fortune for the realm.**" The lady, France, at first left alone in the realm of Italy, extinguished by the unrivaled Moslems on the bed of legal honor: Seven years, indicating France like the Catholic Church of seven ages, will be weeping in grief from these losses; then, seemingly long life to the Italian realm through great good fortune of the Moslems.

64. "**No peace agreed upon will be kept, all the subscribers will act with deceit: In peace and truce, land and sea in protest, over the Barcelona fleet seized with ingenuity.**" No peace agreed upon by the French and Moslems will be kept, as the Moslems by trickery instigate rebellions, all the French subscribers living in Italy will supposedly act with deceit: In peace and truce after capturing Italy, land and sea in protest of rebellions, over the captured spoils of the Spanish Barcelona fleet, siezed with ingenuity.

65. "**Gray and brown in half opened war, by night being assaulted and pillaged: The brown captured will pass through the lock, His temple opened, two cover up the slip.**" Gray or Moslem and brown or French in half-opened war, indicating French secrecy, against the Habsburgs, by night being assaulted and pillaged by the Moslems: The brown or French spies captured by mistake, will pass through the prison to freedom, His Christian temple opened in Italy, the two, French and Moslems, cover up the slip or mistake.

66. "**At the foundation of the new sect, being the bones found of the great Roman, A sepulchre covered by marble will appear, Earth to quake in April, poorly buried.**" At the foundation of the new Moslem sect, being the bones found of the great Roman, or French Christians, a French sepulchre covered by marble, like the end time Catholic Church, will appear, Earth to quake in April from the Moslems attacking Italy, the French bones poorly buried, since the graves opened, indicating French zones appearing in Italy.

67. "**To the great Empire, quite another one will attain,** *kindness* **distant more so happiness: Ruled by one sprung not far from the bed. To rush the realms to great misfortune.**" Quite another one, France, to attain Italian holdings from the great Habsburg empire, kindness through alliance with Moslems; happiness because of later Moslem trickery: Ruled by the Moslems who sprung not too far from the bed of French alliance sharing Italy, to rush the French and Moslem realms to great misfortune from instigated rebellions.

68. "**When the soldiers in a seditions fury against their chief will cause steel to flash by night: The enemy from Alba acts with furious hand, then**

to vex **Rome and seduce the principal ones.**" When the French soldiers, in a seditious fury against their allied Moslem chief in Italy, will cause steel to flash by night with rebellion, the French enemy from Alba, or France, will supposedly act with furious hand against the innocent Moslems, then to vex Rome, or Italy, and seduce or beguile the principal Moslem leaders feeling safe.

69. "**The great pity will occur before long, those who gave will be obliged to take: Naked, starving, from cold and thirst banding together, to pass over the mountains committing a great scandal.**" The great pity of France losing Italian possessions will occur before long. Those French who gave to supply their Moslem ally in capturing Italy will be obliged to take as beggers: Naked and starving from cold and thirst banding together, to pass over the mountains heading back to France after supposedly committing a great scandal through rebellions.

70. "**To the chief of the world will the great Chyren be, plus further hereafter, loved, feared, dreaded: His fame and praise will go beyond the heavens, and with only the title of Victor will he be quite satisfied.**" To the Moslem chief of the world will the great Henry or France be, further hereafter more loved, feared, and dreaded: France's fame and praise will go beyond the heavens because of skill against the Habsburgs using spies and with only the title of victor will France be quite satisfied since French rebels lost the Italian possessions.

71. "**When they will come to give the last rites to the great King before he has entirely given up the ghost: (To) him who will come to grieve over him the least, by Lions, Aigles, cross crown sold.**" When the Moslems come to give the last rites to the great French king, before he has entirely given up the ghost, or before the Moslems begin murdering the French Christians, to the Moslems who will come to grieve over France the least, by Lyons and Aigles, or French rebellions, the cross and Italian crown is sold.

72. "**Through feigned fury of divine emotion the wife of the great one will be violated: The judges wishing to condemn such a doctrine, the victim from the ignorant people allied.**" Through feigned fury of Moslem divine or religious emotion retaliating against the French rebellions, the wife, or Christianity, of the great one, or France, will be violated by persecution when the Moslems force French Christians to convert: The Moslem judges, wishing to condemn such a Christian doctrine, the Christian victim from the ignorant people killed for not converting.

73. "**In a great city a monk and artisan, lodged near by the gate and walls, Speaking secretly and emptily against Modena, betrayed for acting under the guise of nuptials.**" In a great city, Italy, a French monk and artisan rebel, lodged near by the gate and walls where most of the busy activity usually takes place in a city, speaking secretly and emptily against Modena (variant indicating the Moslems), betrayed for acting under the guise of nuptials or French allies while also conspiring against the Moslems.

74. "She chased out of the realm will return, her enemies found to be conspirators: More than ever her time will triumph, Three and seventy to death very sure." Moslems, chased out of the realm by French rebels will return, her enemies found to be French conspirators hiding behind alliance: More than ever, the Moslem time will triumph in Italy, Three, or Moslems, like the three Protestant church ages, and seventy, or France, like the seven Catholic ages, to death very sure for the alliance agreement.

75. "The great Pilot will be commissioned by the King, to leave the fleet to fill a higher post: Seven years afterwards will be rebellion, Venice will come to fear the Barbarian army." The great pilot, Suleiman I, will be commissioned by the king, Francis I, to leave the fleet to fill a higher post of allied invasion to capture Italy: Seven years afterwards, indicating France, like the end time Catholic alliance, having captured Italy, will be in supposed rebellion, Venice or Italy will come to fear the Barbarian or Moslem army retaliating.

76. "The ancient city the creation of Antenor, no longer able to bear the tyrant: The false one-armed one in the temple to cut a throat, the people will come to put his followers to death." The ancient French city (Padua) in Italy, the creation (Old French) of Antenor, a Trojan, indicating a French city through alliance, no longer able to bear the Moslem tyrant: The false one-armed one (variant for Moslem instigation) in the Moslem temple to cut a throat rebelling; the Moslems will come to put his Christian followers to death.

77. "From the victory through fraudulent deceit, Two fleets one, the revolt of the cousin: The chief murdered and his sons in the tent, Florence and Imola pursued into Romania." From the French victory by fraudulent deceit of rebellion against Moslems, two fleets, Moslem and French, become one, indicating fighting among themselves, the revolt against the cousin (variant, indicating Moslems): The Moslem chief and his sons murdered in the tent by French rebels, Florence and Imola, both French-controled cities pursued Romania (variant indicating Moslems) in Italy.

78. "To proclaim the victory over the great expanding Selin: By the Romans the Aigle will be proclaimed, Pavia, Milan, and Genoa will not consent thereto, then the great Basileus demanded by themselves." To proclaim victory over the great Selin or Moslems expanding their realm over the world: by the Romans or French in Italy, L'Aigle or France, will be proclaimed the victor; Pavia, Milan, and Genoa or French-controled Italy will not consent to Moslem partnership. Then, the great Basileus, Greek indicating Moslems, countering them demanded Italy by themselves.

79. "Near the Ticino the inhabitants of the Loire, Garonne and Saone, the Seine, the Tain and Gironde: Erecting a promontory beyond the mountains. Conflict given, Po seized submerged in the wave." Near the Ticino, or Italy, the inhabitants of the Loire, Garonne, and Saone, the Seine, the Tain and Gironde, indicating French rebels fighting the Moslems, and six the number of work: Erecting a promontory, the realm of Italy beyond the

mountains, conflict given, Po, or Italy, seized (Erratum - Moslem instigated) submerged in the wave of French rebellions.

80. **"From Fez the realm will reach those of Europe, their city ablaze and the blade will cut: The great one of Asia by land and sea with a great troop, so that blues, Paris, and cross he will pursue to death."** From Fez, indicating the east, the Moslem realm will reach those of Europe, their city, Italy, ablaze from attack and the Moslem blade will cut: The great one of Asia, Suleiman I, by land and sea with a great troop. So that Habsburg blues, Paris or French rebels, and Christian cross he will pursue (Old French) to death.

81. **"Tears, cries and laments, howls, terror, heart inhuman, cruel, black, and chilly: Lake of Geneva, the Isles the notables of Genoa, blood to pour out, hunger for wheat, to none mercy,"** Tears, cries from Habsburgs, laments, howls, from French rebels terror (Old French) to French Christians, the Moslem heart inhuman, cruel, black, and chilly: Lake of Geneva or Habsburgs, the Isles or French rebels, and the Christian notables of Genoa, blood to pour out for Habsburgs, hunger for wheat (variant) to French rebels to remaining Christians no mercy.

82. **"Through the deserts of the free and wild place, the descendents of the great Pontiff will come to wander: Stunned by seven with a heavy club, *through* those only afterwards filling the chalice."** Through the deserts of the free and wild place or Italy, the French descendents of the great pontiff, France, like the end time Catholic Church, will come to wander into Moslem cities: Stunned by seven, or France, with a heavy club of French rebellions, through those same French only afterwards with Italy's capture, filling the chalice and celebrating.

83. **"He who will have so much honor and flattery at his entry into Gaul Bellecour: A while after he will act very rudely, and he will act very warlike against the flower."** The Moslems who will have so much honor and flattery towards France at his entry into Gaul or French Bellecour, indicating the initial alliance: A while after when Italy has been captured by them, the Moslems will act very rudely instigating French revolts, and will act very warlike against the flower or France by murdering the rebels.

84. **"He who in Sparta, and being lame could not reign He will do much through seductive means: So that by the short and long, he will be accused of making his perspective against the King."** Suleiman I, who in Sparta and lame or insufficient by himself could not reign in Italy, will do much in gaining lands through seductive means including French alliance: So that by the short and long of it, he will be accused (Old French) by French rebels of aiming his objectives to enlarge possessions against the French King's share.

85. **"The great city by Tarsus through the Gauls will be destroyed, captives, all of Turin: Help by sea from the great one of Porto Gaulois, first day of summer Urban's consecration."** The great Habsburg city or Italy, by Tarsus the Moslem army through the Gauls or French allied help, will be destroyed, captives, all of Turin, or Italy: Help by sea from the great one of

Porto, or French spies, first day of summer when most wars are begun and at Urban's (Langres-France) consecration, like end time Catholic revival.

86. **"The great Prelate, one day later, his thinking interpreted contrary to its meaning: From Gascony a monk will come unexpectantly, one who will cause the great prelate of Sens to be elected."** The great Habsburg prelate, after making a governing decision, one day later, his thinking interpreted contrary to its meaning through French spy influence: From Gascony, or France, a monk (Provencal) or French spy will come unexpectedly, who will cause the great prelate of Sens or French leanings to be elected in Habsburg Italy, taking the other's place.

87. **"The election made in Frankfort will be voided, Milan will be opposed: That follower closer will seem so very strong that he will drive him out into the marshes beyond the Rhine."** The election of a Habsburg city, will be voided as Milan, another Habsburg city this time in Italy, will be opposed to it: The follower closer to French leanings will seem so very strong, politically, that he will drive the governor out into the marshes beyond the Rhine, losing his job.

88. **"A great realm will be left desolated, near the Ebro they will be gathered in assemblies: The Pyrenees mountains rendering consolation, when in May the earth is being shaken."** The great realm of Habsburg Italy will remain desolated of solid Habsburg unity, near the Ebro in Spain the Spanish Habsburgs will be gathered in assemblies for rebellions: The Pyrenees Mountians, rendering consolation to France as spy routes as they cause confusion, when in May the earth is being shaken in Italy by attack from the Moslems.

89. **"Between two boats feet and hands cling, face anointed with honey, and sustained with milk: Wasps and flies, paternal love angered, cup-bearer to falsify, chalice tried."** Between two boats (Old French) indicating French, Moslem feet and hands cling by alliance, French face anointed with honey, and Moslems sustained (Latin) with milk as both cooperated: French wasps and Moslem flies, paternal love of the Moslem government in Italy angered, the French cupbearer to falsify (Old French) by rebellions, chalice tried, indicating influenced while drinking.

90. **"The disgrace offensive and abominable, after the deed is congratulated: The great excuse to not be favorable, that Neptune will not be persuaded to peace."** The disgrace of French rebellion in Italy offensive and abominable to the Moslems, after the deed is congratulated by other French cities rebelling too: The great excuse of rebellions will serve for the Moslems to not be favorable to their French ally, so that Neptune or the Moslems will not be persuaded to peace with the rebels.

91. **"By the leader of the naval war, Red one unbridled, severe, horrible quarrel, Captive escaped from the elder one in the bale, when there will be born a son to the great Agrippa."** By the Moslem leader of the naval war capturing Italy, the red one, French spies disguised as Spanish Habsburgs, unbridled or released from prison, severe, horrible quarrel of

French rebellions begun, captive Moslems escaped in the bale from the elder French rebels when there will be born a French son to the great Moslem Agrippa sharing Italy.

92.   "Prince of beauty so comely, in his head a plot, the second deed disclosed: The city to the sword with powder the face burned, through too great murder the head of the King hated." Prince (variant, indicating Suleman I) with beauty so comely (Latin) capturing Italy, in France's head a plot against their ally, the second deed to ruin the Moslems disclosed: The city, Italy, to the sword, then with powder the face burned by French rebels fighting. Through too great murder by more rebellions, the head of the king, Francis I, hated.

93.   "The greedy prelate deceived by ambition, nothing too much for him, he will come to reckon: His messengers and he completely trapped, will see all in reverse, he who cut the wood." The greedy French prelate in Italy deceived by ambition to displace the Moslems, nothing too much for himself, he will come to reckon: His messengers, or French rebels, and he completely trapped by the tricky Moslem (the prelate), will see all in reverse concerning French position, the French who cut the wood, indicating supplies given the Moslems.

94.   "A King will be angry with the sea breakers, when bewildered being outfitted for war: The poison tainted in the sugar for the strawberries, by themselves murdered, dead, saying land, land." The Moslem king will be angry (Old French) with the seat breakers or French rebels, when bewildered by French cities outfitted for war against the Moslems: The poison by Moslem trickery, tainted in the sugar for the strawberries (Latinized). With the French themselves murdered, the dead from French losses saying land, land, dying because of their greed.

95.   "By the detractors, calumny against the younger born, when enormous and warlike deeds will take place: The least part doubtful to the elder one, Yet soon in the realm there will be partisan deeds." By the French detractor, calumny or slander against the younger born Moslem cities in Italy, when enormous and war-like deeds of French rebellions are taking place: The least part or one city rebelling counted as doubtful to the elder one or France, yet soon in the Italian realm there will be partisan deeds by other French cities.

96.   "Great city abandoned by the soldiers, never was mortal tumult so close: Oh, what a hideous calamity draws near, except one offense it will not be spared." Great city or Italy abandoned to the Moslem soldiers to get revenge. Never was there mortal tumult so close, being against their own ally sharing the Italian lands together: Oh, what a hideous calamity for the French and Moslem alliance draws near, except one rebellious offense, which the Moslems could tolerate, the alliance will not be spared.

97.   "At forty-five degrees the sky will burn, fire to approach the great new city: In an instant, a great scattered flame will leap up, when one will want to have proof of the Normans." At forty-five degrees, indicating

French responsibility, the sky will burn, symbolizing French rebellion to approach the great new city, Naples, in Italy: In an instant, a great scattered flame will leap up, indicating other diverse cities also rebelling against the Moslem government, when the Moslems will want to have proof from French Normans of their innocense.

98.   **"Ruin for the Volcae with fear so very terrible, their great city stained, pestilential deed: To plunder the Sun, the Moon yet to violate their temples: And to redden the two rivers flowing with blood."** Ruin for the Volcae, or France, with their fear very terrible, their great city in Italy stained by the pestilential deed of rebellions supposedly begun by the French: To plunder the Sun, or French, the Moon or Moslems yet to violate French temples, persecuting the Christians: And the two rivers of alliance to redden with blood flowing.

99.   **"The learned enemy will find himself confused, His great army sick, and defeated by ambushes, the Pyrenees and Pennine Alps will be denied him, near the river discovering ancient funeral urns."** The learned Moslem enemy will find himself confused, His great Moslem army sick and defeated by French ambushes (actually instigated by the tricky Moslems), the Pyrenees and Pennine Alps, indicating French protection, will be seemingly denied to the Moslems. Near the river discovering ancient funeral urns, symbolizing the French rebels hiding in position ready to ambush them.

Incantation of the Law Against Inept Critics

100.   **"Let those who read this verse consider it profoundly, let the profane and ignorant herd keep away: And far away all Astrologers, Idiots, and Barbarians, may he who does otherwise, be priest to the rite."**
100.   **"Daughter of the L'Aure, habitation of the unhealthy, where the amphitheater is seen on the horizon: Prodigy seen, your evil is very near, you will be captive, and more than four times."** Daughter of the Loire (Latinized), indicating the French daughter in Italy, habitation of the unhealthy rebels, where the amphitheater of persecution is seen on the horizon: Prodigy or unusual occurrence of rebellion seen, your evil by Moslem revenge is very near; you will be captive like the Catholic Church, yet times more than after four first church ages.

Nostradamus
Century VII

Nostradamus
Century VII

1.   "The Ark with treasure through Achilles deceived, by the procreated ones the quadrangular known: The invention will be known by the royal deed, body seen hung in the sight of the people." L'Arc or France with treasure of Italian lands, through Achilles or French rebels, deceived, by the procreated ones (variant) indicating Moslems, the quadrangular (Museum in Louvre) representing French plundering, will be known: The invention (Latinized) in Italy will be known by the royal deed of French rebellions. Body, or Moslems, seen hung in the sight of the people.

2.   "Opened by Mars Arles will give him battle, by night will the soldiers be astonished: Black and white deceived indigo on land, under the feigned shadow traitors swept and sounded." Opened by Mars of rebellions, Arles or France will give him (variant), Moslems, battle; by night will the Moslem soldiers be astonished: Black, Moslems, and white, French, deceived indigo (blue), Habsburgs, on land warring through secret alliance, under the feigned shadow of night the French traitors swept away the Habsburgs and later sounded rebellion against the Moslems.

3.   "After the naval victory of France, those of Barcelona, the Saillimons, those of Marselles: Robber of gold, the anvil enclosed in the ball, those of Ptolon will be a party to the fraud." After the naval Victory of allied France, those Habsburgs of Barcelona (Latinized), the Moslems of Saillimons (Latinized), those French spies of Marseilles (Latinized) all in battle, French robber (Old French) of gold, allied secretly like an anvil enclosed in the ball, those of Ptolon, indicating Moslems, will be a party to the fraud as they capture Italy.

4.   "The Duke of Langres besieged at Dole, *accompanied* by Autun and those of Lyons: Geneva, Augsburg, joined those of Mirandola, to

pass over the mountains against those of Ancona." The French duke of Langres besieged in Dole (East of Rhone), indicating the Moslems accompanied by French rebels sent from Autun and those of Lyons: Geneva and Augsburg, or Habsburgs, join those Moslems of Mirandola being against France, the Moslems to pass over the mountains against those French of Ancona (a papal city) defeating the French rebels.

5.   **"Of the wine on the table some will be spilled, the third one will not have that which he claimed: Twice descended from the black one of Parma, Perugia will do to Pisa that which he believed."** Of the victory, wine on the table with Habsburg defeat, some will be spilled, the third one, France, will not have that which he claimed: Two times descended in losses, this time from the Moslem black one of Parma, Perugia or French rebels will do to Pisa, or Moslems, that which Moslems believed (Old French), starting rebellions.

6.   **"Naples, Palermo, and all Sicily, through Barbarian hand it will be uninhabited: Corsica, Salerno, and the Isle of Sardinia, Famine, plague, war, end of evils extended."** Naples, Palermo, and all Sicily, indicating Moslem possessions, through Barbarian or French hand, will be uninhabited, as French rebels drive out the Moslems: Corsica Salerno, and the Isle of Sardinia or Moslem-held cities, famine, plague war by the French rebelling against them, end of evil extended (Latinized) as the Moslems are chased out of Italy.

7.   **"Upon the struggle of the great light horses, they will proclaim the great crescent destroyed: By night to kill in the mountains, shepherds' garb, red gulfs in the deep ditch."** Upon the struggle, by rebellions, of the great light horses (White indicating the French), the rebels will proclaim the great crescent or Moslems destroyed (Old French) by them: By night of Moslem trickery, the Moslems to kill in the mountains wearing shepherds garb, disguised as French, red gulfs of blood shed in the deep ditch of rebellions.

8.   **"Florence, flee, flee the approaching Roman, at Fiasole will battle be given: Blood shed, the greatest ones taken by hand, neither temple nor sex will be spared."** Florence (variant), indicating Moslems, flee, flee the approaching Roman or French rebels, at Moslem Fiesole (Latinized) in Italy battle will be given through French rebellion: Blood shed, the greatest ones or French taken by hand as the Moslems return fighting, neither Christian temple nor sex (French) will be spared as the Moslems even banish Christianity from Italy.

9.   **"The Lady in the absence of her great captain will be wooed by the Viceroy: Feigned promise and unfortunate luck, into the hands of the great Prince of Bar."** The lady, French in Italy, in the absence of her great captain, Francis I, will be wooed by the Viceroy or Moslem instigators in Italy: Feigned promise of ousting the Moslems and unfortunate luck for the French rebels, into the hands of the great prince of bar or Moslems who tricked them, returning back to Italy and retaliating.

10.	"By the great Prince bordering on Le Mans, Brave and valiant chief of the great army: By land and sea with Bretons and Normans, to pass Gilbraltar and Barcelona the isle sacked." By the great Moslem prince bordering on Le Mans or French allied support, Brave and valiant Moslem chief of the great allied army (Latinized) attacking the Habsburgs: By land and sea with Bretons (Old French) and Normans or French spies aiding them, to pass Gibraltar and Barcelona or the Spanish, the Isle or Italy sacked with Habsburg defeat.

11.	"The royal child will scorn his mother, eye, feet wounded, rude, disobedient: Strange and very bitter news to the lady, more than five hundred of her followers will be killed." The royal child, or French rebels, will scorn his mother, France, eye being greedy, feet wounded as Moslems stop the French rebels who are rude and disobedient (Old French) to France's policy of coexistance: Strange and very bitter news to the lady, France. More than five hundred of her French citizens will be killed, grace (Five) ending.

12.	"The great cadet will put an end to the war, before the Gods he assembles the pardoned: Cahors and Moissac will go far from the confinement, at Lectoure refusal, those of Agen shaved." The great cadet or seemingly inferior Moslems will put an end to the war of French rebellion, before the Gods or Moslem doctrines he assembles the pardoned or French who convert: Cahors and Moissac or French converts will go far from the confinement (Old French), at Lectoure refusal to convert, those French of Agen shaved or humiliated.

13.	"From the marine and tributary city the shaven head will take the satrapy: To chase the sordid one who will then be against him, for fourteen years he will withstand the tyranny." From the marine and tributary Moslem city, the shaven head or degraded French will take the satrapy or Moslem government by rebellion: To chase the sordid or selfish Moslems who will then be against them, for fourteen years (indicating French rebels, alone, like the end time Catholic Church from four ages) French rebels will fight the Moslem tyranny.

14.	"They will come to expose the false topography, the jugs of the tombs will be opened: Sect and holy philosophy to multiply, for the whites the blacks, and for the ancient the new." The Moslems will come to expose the false topography of secret alliance, the funeral urns from tombs opened of French regions in Italy: Christian sect and holy Moslem philosophy to multiply together, for the whites or French the blacks or Moslems supporting each other, and for the ancient or old Christian faith the new Moslem faith befriends.

15.	"Before the city of the Insubrian region, the siege will be laid for seven years: The very great King will enter therein, city then free its enemies out." Before the Moslem city of the Insubrian region or Italy, seven years French, like end time Catholic Church of seven ages, will lay siege through rebellions: The very great King, Suleiman I, will enter therein, city or

Italy then free, its French enemies out as the rebels are killed and French Christians forced to convert to the Moslem faith.

16.   "**The deep entry made by the great Queen will render the place powerful and inaccessible: The army of the three Lions will be defeated, causing within a hideous and terrible event.**" The deep entry made by the great Queen, France, through French rebellions against the Moslems will render Italy powerful under French leadership and inaccessible for the Moslems: The arm of the three Lions, three indicating the Moslems like Protestants from three ages, will be defeated by French, causing within Italy a hideous and terrible event of rebellions.

17.   "**The Prince rare in pity and mercy will come to change through death great cognizance: Through great tranquility the realm cultivated, when the great one soon will be fleeced.**" The Moslem prince, rare in pity and mercy towards other nations, will come to change its cognizance towards France who had before been friends: Through great tranquility, the Italian realm cultivated under Moslem government sharing Italy with France, when the great one, Suleiman I, soon will be fleeced by French rebels trying to take over all of Italy.

18.   "**The besieged coloring their pacts, Seven days after making a cruel sortie: Hurled back within, fire, blood, Seven put to the ax the Lady who had woven the peace captive.**" The besieged French rebels, coloring or disavowing their agreements (Old French), Seven days, or France, like end time Catholic Church of seven ages, after making a cruel sortie or rebellions, hurled back within, fire, blood, seven or French rebels, put Moslems to the ax, the French Lady who had woven the peace or Moslem alliance, captures Italy for herself.

19.   "**The fort of Nice will not be engaged: It will be conquered by shining metal which deed will be discussed a long time, to the citizens strange and frightful.**" The French fort of Nice will not be engaged in battle with the Moslems: It will be conquered by shining metal or Moslem threat, after French flee Italy, whose deed of Italian domination will be discussed a long time, to the French citizens strange and frightful after the change of Moslem policy, even to persecuting the Christians.

20.   "**Ambassadors of the Tuscan tongue, in April and May to pass the Alps and sea: He of the calf will deliver the oration, the Gallic life not coming to wipe out.**" French ambassadors of the Tuscan tongue or Italy, in April and May to pass the Alps and sea returning to France to escape the Moslems who persecute and chase them out: The French in calf skin, after being plundered, will deliver the oration that the Gaulic life or French were not coming to wipe out the Moslems.

21.   "**By the pestilential enmity of Languedoc, dissimulated the tyrant will be driven out: On the bridge of Sorgues will be made the deal to put to death him and his adherent.**" By the pestilential enmity of Languedoc, or French rebels in Italy, dissimulated or made different into an enemy, the Moslem tyrant will be driven out of the regions during French rebellions: On

the bridge of Sorgues, indicating the French already in Italy, will be made the deal to put to death the Moslems and their adherent religion.

22. **"The citizens of Mesopotamia angry with their friends of Catalonia: Games, rites, banquets, a whole people lulled to sleep, Vicar at the Rhone, city taken those of Ausonia."** The citizens of Mesopotamia, indicating the Moslems, angry with their French friends of Catalonia, indicating Spanish credentials obtained earlier by French spies against Habsburgs: Games, rites, banquets celebrating victory against Habsburgs, a whole people, Moslems, lulled to sleep, vicar or France, like the end time Catholic Church, at the Rhone of alliance, city taken, those Moslems of Ausonia.

23. **"The royal sceptre will be obliged to take that which his predecessors had invested *since* they will pretend not to understand about the ring, *when* they will come to sack the palace."** The royal sceptre, or France, will be obliged to take that which his predecessors, or Moslems, had invested in Italy since the French rebels will pretend not to understand about the ring, indicating alliance agreement sharing Italy like a marriage, when the French rebels will come to sack the Moslem palace during rebellions against the Moslem inhabitants.

24. **"The buried one will come out from his tomb, He will cause the fort of the bridge to be bound with chains: Poisoned with Barbel eggs, the Great One of Lorraine by the Marquis du Pont."** The buried one, France, will come out of his tomb, like the end time Catholic Church. He will cause the strong one of the bridge, allied Moslems, to be bound with chains: Poisoned by Barbel (fish) eggs, indicating Barbezieux or French rebels, the Great One of Lorraine, Francis I, through the Marquis du Pont or French rebels as second in command.

25. **"Through long war the entire army exhausted, so that they will not find money for the soldiers, instead of gold and silver, they will come to coin leather, Gallic boldness, see, cresent Moon."** Through long war of rebellions in Italy the entire army of French rebels exhausted so that they will not find money for the French soldiers indicating an unsuccessful rebellion, instead of gold and silver of victory, they will come to coin leather indicating poverty, Gallic boldness after rebellion resulting with siege by the Moslem crescent Moon retaliating.

26. **"Foists and galleys around seven ships, a mortal war will be fought: The Chief of Madrid will receive a wound from arrows, Two escaped, and five brought to land."** Foists and galleys of Moslems around seven ships, indicating France like seven Catholic ages, a mortal war to the death will be fought with Moslem retaliation: The chief of Madrid indicating French rebels, formerly spies with Spanish credentials, will receive a wound from arrows, two ships escaped back to France, and five (grace ended) brought to land.

27. **"At the waist of Vasto the great calvalry, near Ferrara impeded by the baggage: Suddenly at Turin carrying on such robbery, when in the**

fort ravaging their hostage." At the waist (Old French) of Vasto near Chieti Italy, a French city, the great French cavalry, near Ferrara (variant, indicating Moslems), the French rebels impeded by the baggage of spoils: Suddenly (variant, indicating Moslems), at Turin carrying on such robbery against the Moslems, when in the fort ravaging the Moslem hostages during the French rebellions.

28. "The captain will lead a great flock, on the mountain closer to the enemy: Surrounded by fire he will cut such a path, all escaped except thirty put on the spit." The French captain will lead a great flock of French rebels, on the mountain closer to the Moslem enemy: Surrounded by fire of French rebellions, the French will cut such a path against the Moslems, all of the Moslems escaped except thirty, indicating Moslems like the three Protestant ages, put on a spit by the French rebellions.

29. "The great Duke of Albe will come to rebel, He will betray his great ancestors: The great one of Guise will come to vanquish him, led captive and a monument erected." The great Duke of Albe, an old Latian city long destroyed near Rome, indicating French, will come to rebel. He will betray his great ancestors, indicating France, who desired friendship with the Moslems: The great one of Guise, French rebels, will come to vanquish the Moslems, led captive, and a monument of French success erected possessing Italy.

30. "The sack approaches, fire, great shedding of blood, Po, great rivers, enterprise by the cow-keepers: From Genoa, Nice, after a long wait, Fossano, Turin, at Savigliano the capture." The sack by French rebellions approaches, fire, great shedding of blood against the Moslems, in Italy, Po becomes great rivers by flooding of rebellions, enterprise by the cow-keepers or former French helpers: From Genoa, Nice, after a long wait of Moslem friendship, Fassano, Turin, two more French rebellious cities, at Savigliano (Suillan indicating Moslems) for the capture.

31. "From Languedoc and Guienne more than ten thousand will want to pass over the Alps again: The great Savoyards to march against Brindisi, Aquino, and Bresse coming to drive them back." From Languedoc and Guienne or France, more than ten thousand not wanting to share Italy, indicated by ten instead of the allied twenty, will want to pass over the Alps again capturing Italy: The great Savoyards (Latinized), or French rebels, to march against Moslem Brindisi, Aquino, and Bresse, indicating France seemingly coming to drive the Moslems back.

32. "From the royal mount will be born from a bank One who boring and calculating will come to tyrannize, to prepare a force in the confines of Milan, to drain Faenza and Florence of gold and men." From the Royal mountains or Alps will be born from a bank on the Italian side one who, boring and calculating, will come to tyrannize, indicating the French rebels: to prepare a force (Latinized) in Italy from the marche of Milan, a French holding, to drain Faenza and Florence, or Moslem cities, of gold and Moslem men.

33. "Through guile the realm stripped of its forces, the fleet blockaded, passages for the spy: Two feigned friends will come to rally, hatred long dormant to awaken." Through guile of French rebellions, the Italian realm stripped of its Moslem forces, the Moslem fleet blockaded, being former passages for the French spy when friendly with Moslems: Two feigned friends, the French and Moslems will come to rally because of French rebellions started, Hatred long dormant against the Moslem faith to awaken as French Christians rebel.

34. "From great grief will the Gallic people, Vain and light of heart, think rashness: No bread, salt, wine, water, venom or ale, Greater captivity, famine, cold, need." From great grief, after tolerating the Moslems, will the Gallic or French people in Italy, vain and light of heart after success against the Habsburgs, think rashness through starting rebellions: No bread, salt, wine, water, hard liquor or ale will be given to the Moslems as before, greater captivity for them instead through famine, cold, and need.

35. "The great fishery will come to complain and weep over the choice it has made, deceived about his age: He will want to remain with them scarcely at all, He will be deceived by those of his own tongue." The great fishery, or Moslems will come to complain and weep over the choice of alliance made, deceived about France's age, thinking it old and in weakened condition: The Moslems will want to remain with the French scarcely at all as they flee the rebels, the Moslems deceived by those of his own tongue, indicating allied partner.

36. "God, heaven all the divine word in the waves, carried by seven red shaven heads to Byzantium: Against the anointed three hundred from Trebizond will set two laws, and horror, the credence." God, heaven, all the divine word of Moslem religion in the waves, carried by seven red shaven heads, or France, like the end time Catholic Church from seven ages, to Moslem Byzantium: Against the anointed three hundred, from Trebizond, Moslems like Protestants of three ages, two religious laws sitting, and horror of rebellion, then credence by retreating Moslems.

37. "Ten sent, captain of the ship put to death, by one warned in the fleet: Confusion, the chief and another, prick and bit on another at the Lerins and Hyeres islands ships, prow in the bottom." Ten sent, indicating disallied Moslems, French captain of the ship (Latinized) at Italy put to death, by Moslems, warned in their fleet about French rebellion: Confusion of fighting, the Moslem chief and French stab and bite one another, at the Lerins and Hyeres (Latinized) islands, indicating French ships at Italy, bow in the bottom (Old French), sinking.

38. "The elder royal one upon a prancing steed, to spur so rudely it will come to pursue: Mouth, pout, foot complaining in the embrace, dragged, pulled, to die horribly." The elder royal one, or French rebels, upon a prancing steed, to spur so rudely with the French rebelling, it will come to pursue against the Moslems: Mouth of the Moslems will pout, foot complaining in the embrace of alliance, the Moslems dragged as from the styrrup, pulled, to die horribly at the hand of French rebels.

39. **"The leader of the French army, thinking to ruin the principal phalanx: Upon the pavement of oats and slate, will undermine themselves through the foreign people of Genoa."** The rebel leader of the French army, thinking to ruin the principal Moslem phalanx and control all Italy: Upon the pavement of oats and slate, or Moslem trickery, like a horse coaxed along the path with oats on the ground ahead of him, will actually undermine themselves through the foreign people, or Moslems, of Genoa taking revenge.

40. **"Within casks anointed outside with oil and grease being twenty-one shut up before the port: At the second watch through death performing a feat to win the gates, and be felled by the watch."** Within burial casks, anointed outside with oil and grease of alliance, the French arise, Being twenty-one, seven or France shut up or allied to three or Moslems before the Italian port: At the second watch or France's resurrection from earlier death or defeat, performing a feat to win the Italian gates and by the Moslem watch felled.

41. **"The bones of the feet and of the hands locked up, because of noise the house long uninhabited, being dug up through dreams unearthed, house healthy and without noise inhabited."** The bones of the feet and of the hands of France locked up in the tomb, because of noise of earlier warfare with Habsburgs, the Italian house long uninhabited by French residents, being dug up, through dreams of recapturing Italy unearthed, House of Italy healthy and without noise of more war, now inhabited by French and Moslems.

42. **"Two in possession of poison newly arrive *through* the kitchen of the great Prince to pour out *through* the scullion both caught by the deed seized he who thought to vex the elder one with death.** Two, French and Moslems, newly arrived in Italy, in possession of poison, to pour out through the kitchen of the great Habsburg prince: Through the scullion, both French and Moslems caught the Habsburgs by deed of secret alliance like a poison; siezed, the Habsburgs who thought to vex the elder French earlier through death of defeat.

43. **"When one will see two unicorns, the one lifting, other lowering, World in the middle, to bend to the limit the nephew will run away laughing."** When one, the Habsburgs of Italy, will see two unicorns, French and Moslems, finally recognized as allied enemies, the one lifting and the other lowering indicating French rebellions occurring, World or Italy in the middle, to bend the limit in tribulation, the Habsburg nephew will run away laughing as the Habsburg leadership escaped any difficulty.

44. **"Then when a Bourbon will be very clever, bearing in himself the impression of justice, with his blood then bearing the long name through unjust flight he will receive his punishment."** Then when a Bourbon or French rebel will be (variant) very clever, bearing in himself the impression of justice against the Moslems, with his blood then bearing the long name of his true French origin instead of his alias, through unjust flight because of Moslem trickery, France will receive his punishment by losing his possession in Italy.

73. **"Reinforced by sieges, maniples yet plunder the changed holy one and die upon the advice, taken and captives do not stop the almost triple, put in the uttermost depths, raised, put on the throne."** Reinforced by sieges, maniples (A Roman military unit) or French rebels yet plunder the changed Moslem holy religion and die in Moslem retaliation upon the tricky advice to rebell, taken and the Moslem captives do not stop the threefold, like Protestants of three ages, put in the uttermost depths, raised, put back on the Italian throne.

80. **"The West free the Isles Britanniques the recognized one to pass low, then high Discontented sad Rebel cross of Escotiques then to rebel much more and by warm night."** The West or France free, including the Isles Britanniques or French rebels, the recognized French to pass low at first helping the Moslems capture Italy, then high after rebelling the discontented sad Rebel cross of Asco (Escotiques) France then to rebel much more after other French cities in Italy rebel and by warm night indicating Christian unity.

82. **"The stratagem in the quarrel will be uncommon the death en route from the country rebellion: On the return from the Barbarian voyage they will exalt the Protestant entry."** The stratagem in the quarrel (Old French) against the French will be uncommon as trickery is used, the death by feigned defeat enroute from the French country rebellion: On the return from the Barbarian or Moslem voyage after initial retreat, Moslems will exalt the (Protestant) or Moslem entry by retaliating against the French, like end time Catholics.

83. **"Wind warm, counsels, tears, timidity, by night in bed assailed without arms: Great calamity from oppression, the wedding song converted, weeping and tears."** Wind warm to the French united rebellion, counsels by Moslem trickery indicate tears and timidity from the retreating Moslems, by night in bed, assailed without his arms or weapons by French rebels in Italy: Great calamity from the rebel oppression, supposedly, the wedding song of their contented alliance converted to weeping and tears by Moslems feigning defeat.

Epistle
Nostradamus to Henry II,
King of France II

12.   —It is much like seeing in a burning mirror, with clouded vision, the great events, sad, prodigious, and calamitous events that in due time will fall upon the principal worshippers. First, upon the temples of God, being the type; secondly, upon those wicked, represented by the condemned churches, which, sustained by the earth, approach such decadence; also, a thousand other calamitous events that will be known to happen in due time, France II indicating resurrection at the judgment.

13.   For God will take notice of the long barrenness of the great dame, representing the Catholic Church, which, thereupon, will conceive two principal children, representing end time Catholic and Protestant churches in alliance. But she will be in danger, and the female to whom she will have given birth will also, both being the Catholic Church at different periods, because of the temerity or foolishness of the age, be in danger of death in her eighteenth year, at the prime of life for the World Council of Churches, and will be unable to live beyond her thirty-sixth year when it will be cut off like the wicked who blaspheme God at the judgment, if not even beforehand. She will leave three males (Protestants out of three church ages) and one female (Catholic Church at this time of being cut off from God) but in an altered condition, and of these two will not have had the same father, indicating the different denominations of the Protestant churches.

14.   There will be great differences between the three brothers, indicating, again, the different denominations and then there will be such great cooperation and agreement between them with the World Council of Churches, that the three (Protestants) and four parts (Catholic Church added) of Europe will tremble, similar to the French and Moslem alliance to capture

Italy. The youngest of them, Moslems, will sustain and augment the Christian monarchy, or France, sharing Italy with them, and under him sects, or Moslems like end time Protestant denominations, will be elevated with friendship and then suddenly cast down by instigated French rebellions. Arabs will be driven back, kingdoms of French holdings united in Italy and new laws promulgated to oust the Moslems from Italy.

15.   The oldest one, France, will rule Italy, whose escutcheon, or shield, is that of the furious crowned lions, or Moslems like Protestants of three ages, with their paws resting on intrepid or fearless arms, which, at first, helped in Italy's capture.

16.   The Moslems, second in age accompanied by the Latins, or French spies stationed in Italy, will penetrate far into Italy, when a second path has been beaten through the Great St. Bernard Pass bordering between France and Italy. From there, the French will descend to mount the Pyreness, which will not, however, be transferred to the French crown, because of Moslem trickery. And this third one, Moslems like three end time Protestant church ages, will cause a great inundation of human blood against the French and then against all Christianity, and for a long time Lent, a Christian tradition, will not include March.

17.   The daughter, Italy, will be given for the preservation of the French Christian church during initial Moslem friendship. Italy's Lord or governor will fall into the pagan sect of the new infidels, or Moslems. Of Italy's two children, French and Moslems, one will be faithful to the Catholic Church and the other an infidel, indicating the Moslem faith.

18.   The other, the Habsburgs, who, to their great confusion by defeat and later repentance, will want to ruin Moslem-held Italy, claiming three widely scattered regions, namely Roman (Italy), Germany, and Spain, setting up diverse governments by armed force, leaving the fiftieth to fifty-second-degree latitude, or Germany, to attack Italy.

19.   And all (Italy, Germany, and Spain) will render homage of ancient religions, indicating the Christian and Moslems, to the region of Europe north of the forty-eighth degree latitude, or Germany, with the Habsburg Empire, which will have trembled first in vain timidity from the Moslem takeover of Italy; but afterwards, the regions, west, south, and east will tremble. Such is Habsburg power, when recapture of Italy is brought about by invincible concord and union in the Habsburg Empire with warlike conquests.

20.   In nature of belonging to the Habsburg Empire, Italy, Germany, and Spain will be equal, but very different in faith as the Reformation spreads in Germany and Italians had converted to Islam to survive the Moslem persecution.

21.   After this the barren dame, defeated France, with greater power as second in the new alliance, will be recognized as two nations through allied strength, with the Moslems first, who are obstinate to France with Moslem power above all and France second.

22.   And with the third, or Habsburgs, who extended their forces towards the circuit of the east of Europe to the Pannonias (Hungary), will be overwelmed (variant) and slaughtered by the Moslem marine sail. The Moslems will make their extensions to Adriatic Sicely through Macedonia and Germany, with all the Habsburgs succumbed, and the barbarian (Habsburgs) sect will be greatly afflicted and driven out by all the Latins, or French spies in Italy.

23.   Then the great Empire of the Antichrist, begun through Attila and Xerxes, indicating the Moslems allied to France, will descend with great and countless numbers, attacking Habsburg lands, such that the coming of the Holy Ghost proceeding from the forty-eighth degree, like the Habsburgs from Germany, makes a transmigration, like the end time rapture into God's full Word, chasing out the abomination of the Antichrist by the power of God's Word, making war against the royal one who is the great vicar of Jesus Christ, being the pope, and against his church, and his reign, for times and the occasion of times, indicating three and half years or last half of its life in judgment.

24.   And this will be preceded by a solar eclipse more dark and gloomy than, be it so, existence since the creation of the world, except at the death and passion of Jesus Christ, as His second coming in the light of His Word revealed, will outshine the sun as though it darkened, and from that till now will be in the month of October, tenth month like ten centuries of poetry by Nostradamus interpreted, that, however, the great translation, or spiritual rapture to higher clouds of glory, will be made and such that one will think the gravity of the earth has lost its natural action and being plunged into perpetual night,

25.   being formerly in the times of spring, France resurrecting with the alliance, and thereafter the extreme changes, reversals of realms, as when French and Moslems lose Italy, with mighty trembling of the land, accompanied by the earlier procreation by alliance with the new Babylon. Moslems, the miserable daughter, France, risen after the abomination of the first holocaust, where Habsburgs defeated France in Italy before, and it will not last but seventy, indicating one lifetime, as the resurrected wicked at judgment time, three years and seven months, indicating three Protestant and seven Catholic ages in initial end time alliance, their judgment coming the last three and one half years or last half of their resurrected existence.

26.   Then there will issue from the stock (of France which had remained after the last war losses, barren for so long like Catholic Church after the Reformation proceeding from the fiftieth degree and south with Habsburgs Italy captured, France, which will renew the whole Christian church. A great peace will be established with union and concord between some of the children, French and Moslems, of opposite ideas, who have been separated by diverse realms, like Catholics and Protestants originally were; and such will be the peace that the instigator and promoter, France, will remain chained to the deepest pit, after French rebellions caused from the diversity of the religions,

and the whole kingdom united by the furious Moslems retaliating, who counterfeit, or trick the French sage out of Italian possessions.

27.   The French countries, towns, cities, realms, and provinces which, having abandoned their old customes or Christianity to gain liberty in Moslem ruled Italian lands, captivating themselves still more by doing so, having secretly wearied of their liberty gained by converting to Islam, and lost in the perfect Moslem religion, the French converts beginning to strike to the left only to return to the right, and Moslem holiness for a long time overcome through alliance concessions, now restoring to the earlier and stricter Moslem writings.

28.   That after the great dog, the biggest of curs, or Moslems, will go forth and destroy all the Christians, who made such great destruction by rebellions, even that which before was being perpetrated against Moslems, Christian temples being set up again as in ancient times, and the Christian clergyman will be restored to his original position, judging through rebellions against the heathen Moslems, and Christians will begin their whoring and luxury, and will supposedly commit a thousand crimes, indicating alliance partnership (two thousand) with the Moslems being discarded.

29.   And extending close to another desolation for France, when she is atop her most high and sublime dignity, raising up some potentates and warlords through French rebellions in Italy, and taking away the Moslem's two swords or allied share in Italian holdings, and France will leave them only the insignia or sign of continued friendship, from which the means of curvature attracts them for mutual benefit, the Christian people making the Moslem convert to Christianity to go to the right (indicating freedom) and not wanting to submit themselves to the opposite extreme of those Moslems with the hands in acute position touching the ground in their worship, wanting to excite.

30.   until to those Moslems born of a branch long sterile of successes, who will deliver the people of the world from this benevelant servitude of Christianity, be submitting to allied French support in Mars, or war, stripping Jupiter, or Habsburgs, of all the honors and dignities in the free city, or Italy, afterwards appointed and established as another scant Mesopotamia, or Moslem territory. And the French chief and governor will be cast out from the middle and hung up in the air, ignoring the plot of the conspirators with the second Thrasibulus, or Moslem instigators, who, for a long time, will have directed all this French rebellion.

31.   Then the Christian impurities and abominations in Italy, being in a great shame, caught in rebellions, will be brought out and manifested in the shadows of the veiled Moslem light that passes judgment on them, and (Christianity) will cease towards the end of the change in the Moslem reign, and the Moslem chiefs (variant) of the church, being backward in the love of God, and several of them apostatizing from the true Moslem faith, and of the three sects, indicating their end time Protestant counterparts, whose (chiefs) who are in the middle, because of their own partisans, or Moslem followers, will be thrown a bit into decadence. The first one, subborn Christians,

exterminated throughout all Europe (Italy) and most of Africa by the third one, Moslems, making use of the poor in spirit Christians who convert, Moslem through madmen elevate themselves to libidinous luxury adultering.

32. The Moslem common people will rise up, contending with and chasing out the rebellious French adherents from the allied legislators, and it will appear from the way the realm becomes weakened by the Moslem Easterners retaliating against the French rebels, that God the Creator has loosed Satan from the prisons of hell to give birth to the great Dog and Donon (in east France, indicating Moslems in the alliance partnerships, who will make such a great abominable breach in the Christian churches that neither the reds (Spanish) nor the whites (French) without eyes to see the true instigators and without hands to make a correction, will know what to make of it, and from these Christians will be taken their power, or rights in Italy.

33. Then will commence more of persecution to the Christian churches, the like of which was never seen. And to these meanwhile a plague of Moslem retaliation will arise so great that more than two thirds of the (world) or Italian property of French Christians and French converts to Islam (among the Moslem one third), will be removed so that one will be unable to ascertain the true owners of fields and houses that remain, and weeds growing in the streets of the cities will rise higher than the knees from neglect. For the Christian clergy, there will be but utter desolation and usurping from the Moslem warlords of what is returned to the Moslems from the city of the Sun, Rome, from Malta and the Isles of Hyeres, and the great Moslem chain will be opened, of the port which takes the name from the marine ox, Marseilles, indicating friendly relations can then resume with France, again.

34. And a new incursion will be made by the Habsburg maritime shores, wishing to deliver the Sierra Morena or Spanish Habsburgs from the first Mahometan recapture of Italy. Their assaults will not all (variant) be in vain against the Moslems, and the country which once was the abode of Abraham (Moslems) will be assaulted in Italy by Habsburgs, who hold in respect the Jovialists (followers of Jupiter) or secretly allied Moslems who earlier defeated them. And this city of Sechem (near Armageddon) indicating the Moslems in Italy, will be surrounded and assailed on all sides by a most powerful force of Habsburg warriors, their Moslem maritime forces being weakened by the Habsburg westerners, and great desolation will fall upon this Moslem realm of Italy and its greatest Moslem-held cities, being depopulated of Christians, and those Moslem enemies who, entering within, are captured under the vengeance of the wrath of God, symbolized by the Habsburg assault, a type of the end time spiritual battle of Armageddon.

35. The sepulchre, France's regained holdings in Italy, like the end time Catholic Church, for long an object of such great veneration, will remain in the open, exposed to the sight of the heavens, the Sun and the Moon, the end time son of perdition revealed in churches. The French holy place, Italy, like the end time Catholic Church, will be converted into a stable for a herd, both large and small (churches) and used for profane purposes like end time perverted

teachings. Oh, what a calamitous affliction will pregnant women bear at this time, similar to the Catholic witness not being powerful enough to bring a prospective convert to the delivery, or salvation.

36.   For hereupon, the principal Moslem Eastern chief will be vanquished by the Habsburg Northerners and Westerners, and most of his Moslem people, stirred up in battle, will be put to death, overwelmed, or scattered; and his Moslem children, offspring of many women, will be imprisoned like Protestant children in the end time who are not yet hardened in the perverted faith. Then will be accomplished the prophecy of the Royal Prophet David—Let the believers, like the Habsburgs, hear the groaning of the captives, that by witnessing, he might deliver the innocent children (young or adult) from those wicked sinners who are doomed to die.

37.   What great oppression, like the great tribulation, will then fall upon the princes and governors of kingdoms, especially those which will be maritime and Eastern, or Moslems, whose tongues will be intermingled with a great French partnership: the tongue of the Latins, or French spies in Italy, and of the Arabs, via the Phoenician communication or alliance, and all these Eastern Moslem kingkings being chased, overthrown, and exterminated, but not altogether, by means of the forces of the Habsburg kings of the North, and by means of the drawing near of our end time age, the Moslems, similar to the end time Protestants of three church ages, united by alliance with France, searching for death to Habsburgs by conquests in Italy, treacherously laying traps for one another like end time Christians. This renewed triumvirate or three Protestant church ages, indicating Protestants, will last for seven years, indicating time allied to the Catholic Church of seven ages, when the renown of this allied sect of the World Council of Churches will make its extension around the world. The sacrifice of the holy and immaculate Catholic communion wafer will be sustained or tolerated by Protestants,

38.   and then the Lords of Aquilon (the North) indicating Habsburgs, two in number, indicating Austria and Spanish Habsburgs, will be victorious over the Easterners or Moslems, and so great a noise and bellicose tumult will the Habsburgs make amongst them that all the East will tremble in terror of these brothers, yet not brothers, of Aquilon (the North) or Habsburg Empire, like the end time believer with the double annointing of God's fullness.

41.   After a while, I (Nostradamus), found the time when Saturn or France turns to enter Jupiter or alliance with the Moslems with Mars of warfare in Venus or Italy, where Mercury or French spies are helping. After that, Saturn or France in Capricorn, tenth sign indicating French rebellion (twenty indicating the alliance friendly), Jupiter or alliance in Aquarius, eleventh sign indicating the midnight hour of judgment is near, Mars of fighting in Scorpio, eighth sign indicating the age following the seven church ages, Venus or Italy in Pisces the twelfth sign indicating judgment, Mercury, the messenger god indicating French spies for a month in Capricorn (rebellion), Aquarius (prior to Moslem retaliation with judgment), and Pisces (during that judgment), the Moon or Moslems in Aquarius (the approach of its own judgment time), the

Dragon's head or Satan in Libra or seventh sign indicating the Millennium: its fall in opposition (being bound for a thousand years) following a conjunction of Jupiter or French alliance with Moslems, like Catholic Church allied with Protestant churches, with a quadrature or squaring off of Mars (quarrels) and Mercury or French spies rebelling,

41.   and the Dragon's head, indicating Satan revealed, coinciding with a conjunction of the Sun or Habsburgs and Jupiter or allied Moslems and French like the end time where the saints witness against the allied Catholic and Protestant perversions with the fullness of God's Word revealed to the believers.

42.   and not at all will they be comprehending, the commencement of the Millennium that will long endure, and beginning with this year, the Christian church will be persecuted more fiercely by exposed sin in their midst than Christianity ever was persecuted by Africa or Moslems who ruled in Italy for a time, and this sporadic fighting will last up to the year 1792, which they will believe to mark a renewal of time, France becoming a republic, similar to the altered condition of end time churches after their judgment:

43.   after this, the Roman people, France like the end time Catholic Church, will begin to re-establish themselves, chasing away some obscure shadows of corrupt government and recovering a bit of their ancient glory, likening themselves to the Republic of Rome, but not without great division and continual changes during the fires of great tribulation, forming their new government. Thereafter, Venice, indicating Roman-like France and the Millennial Catholic Church after its judgment, will raise its wings very high in great force and power of God's Word preached, not far short of the might of ancient Rome.

44.   At that time, to the great sails of Moslem Byzantium allied with the Ligurians or French spies in Italy earlier for their support and power, Habsburg Aquilon will give impedement so greatly that the two Cretans, France and Moslems, will be unable to maintain their faith. The arks built by the Habsburg warriors of ancient times will accompany them to the waves of Neptune, or now weakly allied French and Moslems. In the Adriatic, great discord will arise and the allied partnership that will have been united will be separated by Moslem greediness. To a house will be reduced by the Habsburg army that Moslem stronghold that was and is a great city, including Pampotamia (variant) or Italy, and Mesopotamia, or Moslem-held Greece in Europe at 45 and others at 41, 42, and 37:37 degrees.

45.   It will be at this time and in these countries that the infernal Moslem power will set against the Church of Jesus Christ or French partner, the power of Moslem adversaries to her law, like the end time Protestants tricking their Catholic partner, which will constitute the second Antichrist of the endtimes, who will persecute that Catholic Church and its true Vicor or Pope, by means of the power of temporal kings indicating Protestants out of the last three church ages, who in their ignorance will be seduced by tongues, the strong

delusion sent down from heaven, which in the hands of madmen- Protestant ministers, will cut up more souls than any sword.

46.   The sad reign of the (first) Antichrist will last only to the death of the Catholic Church, which was born close to the Millennial age and of the other Protestant Antichrist like Moslems, with the city of Lyon or France associated in alliance with the elected one of Modon tribe (in Greece, indicating Moslems) with Ferrara, France who maintained the Adriatic Ligurians, or Moslems, and with the proximity of the great Sicily filled with French spies: then they will symbolically cross the Great St. Bernard pass leading into Italy as the Moslems and French capture Italy.

47.   The Gallic Ogmios or France will be accompanied by so great a number of Moslems that the Empire of his great law will extend very far. For some time thereafter, the blood of the innocent Habsburgs will be shed profusely by the recently elevated guilty ones, French and Moslems. Then, because of great floods of Habsburg counter attack, the memory of things contained (doctrines) in these instruments (Catholic and Protestant) will suffer incalculable loss, even literature, which is similar to the Aquiloners or Habsburgs who represent the end time saints.

48.   And even in the times of scum Satan, when he will be bound for one thousand years. And the universal peace will be established among men, and the Church of Jesus Christ (like Habsburgs) will be delivered from all tribulations although (Old French) the Philistines (variant), indicating allied French and Moslems like Catholic and Protestant churches, would like to mix in the honey of malice and their pestilent seduction. This will be near the seventh millenary in the end time when also the sanctuary of Jesus Christ (like the Habsburgs representing the saints) will no longer be trodden down by the infidels, the sanctuary coming from Aquilon like end time saints, the world will be approaching a great conflagration like the Great Tribulation, although according to my calculations in my (Nostradamus) prophecies, the course of time runs much further (indicating the end time parallel).

50.   During this astrological calculation, harmonized with the Holy Scriptures, the persecution of the Ecclesiastical folk or Christians will have its origin with the force or army of the kings of Aguilon or Habsburgs, united in battle with the Easterners or Moslems who captured Italy from them. This persecution of Christians will last for eleven years or somewhat less, for then the chief king of Aquilon, or Habsburgs will fall by losing Italy, short of judgment at twelve.

51.   Thereupon, the same thing will occur in the South or Italy, where for the space of three years, three, indicating Moslems typing the Protestants of three church ages, the Church people or French Catholics will be persecuted even more fiercely through the Apostatic seduction or trickery of the Moslems, who will hold all the absolute power of government of the militant or rebellious Christian church. The holy Moslem man of God, the observer of his law in Moslem religion, will be persecuted fiercely by French (like end time Catholic rebellions, and such will be their affliction that in Moslem

(Protestant) retaliation the blood of the true Christian Ecclesiastics (like end time Catholics) will flow everywhere.

52.   And one of the horrible temporal Moslem kingkings will be told by his adherents, as the ultimate in praise, that he has shed more of human blood of innocent Christian Ecclesiastics than anyone else could have spilled of wine: and this Moslem king will commit incredible crime against the Christian church. Human blood will flow in the public streets and temples like water after an impetuous rain, coloring the nearby rivers red with blood. The ocean itself will be reddened by another naval battle, Moslems against French rebels, such that one Moslem king will say to another, Naval battles have caused the sea to blush, indicating embarrassment to the Christians.

53.   Then, in this same year and in those following, there will ensue the most horrible pestilence upon Christianity, made more stupendous by the preceding famine of Christians in Italy after Moslem retaliating against French rebellions. Such great tribulations similar to end time judgment upon the Catholic Church will never have occurred since the first foundation of the Christian church. It will cover all Latin regions or Italian lands, and will leave traces in some countries of the Spanish Habsburgs, indicating Christian captives from earlier Habsburg defeat who are also persecuted in Italy.

54.   Thereupon, attacking the third king (like end time protestants out of three ages), Aquilon, or Habsburgs hearing the lament of the captives of his principal Habsburg title, will raise a very mighty army and defying the tradition or Moslem faith of his Moslem predecessors in Italy, will put almost everything back in its proper place, in the Christian faith, and the great vicar of the hood like end time Catholicism with the pope will be put back in his former state as a more legitimate church again: but desolated by war and then abandoned by all to the Moslems in Italy, he will turn to find the Holy of Holies destroyed by Moslem paganism, and the old and new Testaments thrown out and burned, as the end time perverted Catholic dogmas also destroyed during endtime judgments.

55.   after the second Antichrist (represented by Moslems taking all of Italy), will be the infernal prince. Then all the kingdoms of Christendom will tremble and even (later on) those of the Moslem infidels for the space of twenty-five years, symbolizing the great Tribulation and wars and battles with French rebellions and Moslem retaliation will be more grievous and towns, cities, counties, and all other edifices will be burned, desolated, and destroyed, with great effusion of vestal, of Christian blood, married women and widows violated sucking children dashed and broken against the walls of towns. By reason of Satan, Prince Infernal (now the second Antichrist) working through the Moslems to attack the French, so many kinds of evils will be committed, through end time Protestants against Catholics, that nearly all of the world will find itself undone and desolated: before these events, some rare birds will cry in the air: Today, today, as end time ministers predicting the rapture, and some time later they will vanish because of their folly.

56.   After this has endured for a long time, there will be almost renewed another reign of Saturn, (France) representing the Millennial Catholic Church, and golden age as God's fullness is in the earth. Hearing the affliction of His people, God the Creator will command that Satan be taken and bound in the depths (variant, indicating the Protestant as well as Catholic perverted dogmas) of hell in the deep pit. Then, a universal peace will commence between God and man, and Satan will remain bound for around a thousand years, and finally Satan will fashion in his very great strength, the Ecclesiastical force again on earth and then all will be unbound for the Great White Throne judgment at the end of the Millennium.

Nostradamus
Century VIII

Nostradamus

Century VIII

1.   "PAU, Nay, Oloron will be more of fire than blood, to swim in praise, the great one to flee to the confluence: The magpies he will refuse entry, Pompon, the Ourance, will keep them confined." PAU, NAY, OLORON (west) indicates France more with fire through espionage then in blood (from combat) is, to swim in praise (Old French), the great Habsburg army to flee the allied confluence: The magpies (Provencal) or Moslems will refuse French entry later. Those of Pompou (Great French spy bridge) the Ourance East indicating Moslems) will keep confined.

2.   "Condom and Auch and around Miranda, I see fire from the sky encompassing them: Sun and Mars conjoined in Leo, them at Marmande lightning, great hail, wall falls into the Geronne." Condom and Auch and around Miranda indicating France, I see fire of French rebellions encompassing the Moslems: Sun or French Christians and Mars of rebellions conjoined in Leo, fifth sign, like the fifth church age reformation fighting, reoccurring, then at Marmande or France, lightning, great hail, from the Moslems retaliating, the alliance wall falls into the Garonne.

3.   "In the strong castle of Vigilanne and Reavieres the cedar of Nancy will be confined: Within Turin the first ones being burned when Lyons will be numbed by grief." In the strong castle of Vigilanne (watchful) and Reavieres (successful) Moslems in Italy, the cedar of Nancy (France) will be confined, indicating French rebels caught and imprisoned: Within Turin (Italy), the first rebellions, French being burned through Moslem retaliation when Lyons or France will be numbed by grief, not realizing the Moslem trickery, to control all Italy.

4.   "The Cock will be received into Monaco, the Cardinal of France will appear: By the Roman Legation will he be deceived, weakness for the

Eagle and strength for the Cock will develop." The Cock, or French spies, will be received into Monaco or Habsburg-ruled Italy, the Cardinal of France will appear as in new friendship: By the Roman Legation (variant) indicating the allied French and Moslems, will Habsburgs be deceived when the Moslems attack Italy. Weakness for the Eagle (Habsburgs) and strength for the Cock (France) will develop.

5.　　"**A glittering ornate temple will appear, the lamp and candle at Borne and Breteuil: For Lucerne the Canton turned aside, when one will see the great Cock in his tomb.**" A glittering ornate Christian temple will appear in Italy, the Lamp and candle from Borne and Breteuil (France): For Lucerne the center in Switzerland, indicating Habsburgs, turned aside retreating out of Italy, when one will see the great Cock, France, in his tomb (Italy) where the bones become visible as France shares captured lands with the Moslems.

6.　　"**Lightning brightness at Lyons visible shining, Malta is taken, suddenly it will be extinguished: Sardon, Maurice will treat deceitfully. Geneva or Londres to the Cock feigned treason.**" Lightning brightness at Lyons indicates French visible shining with Italy captured from the Habsburgs, Habsburgs Malta taken suddenly through allied efforts, will be extinguished or defeated: Habsburg Maurice (of Saxony) influenced by French spies, will treat Habsburg Sardinia deceitfully and Geneva (Habsburgs) at Londres (French spies) for advice, to the Cock (French spy) who feigned Habsburg treason.

7.　　"**Vercelli, Milan will give intelligence, within Pavia the wound will be made: To run from the Seine water, blood, fire through Florence, unique one to fall from high to low while calling for help.**" Vercelli, Milan (French spies) will give intelligence information to Moslems, within Pavia the wound will be made by Moslems invading Italy: To run from the Seine (France) water, blood, fire from French espionage through Florence (Italy) against the Habsburgs, unique one (Habsburgs) to fall from high to low while calling for help (Old French) from deceitful French.

8.　　"**Near Focia enclosed in some casks, Chivasso will plot for the Eagle, the elected one driven out he and his people shut up, within Turin rape bride led away.**" Near Focia (Italy), French bones enclosed in some casks as French spies infiltrate, Chivasso (Italy) influenced by spies will plot for the Eagle (Habsburg offices), the Habsburg elected one then driven out by French inspired quarrels. The competitor and his people shut up from ruling, within Turin (Italy) rape, bride (Habsburg governor) led away after the quarrels.

9.　　"**While the Eagle and the Cock at Savona will be united, Sea, Levant and Hungary: Their army at Naples, Palermo, March of Ancona, Rome, Venice by the Beard great outcry.**" While the Habsburg Eagle and French Cock at Savona (Italy) will be united by the deceitful French spies infiltrating within the Habsburg defenses and government, Sea, Lavant, and Hungary (all Moslem-controled), their army attacking at Naples, Palermo, March of Ancona, Rome, and Venice from the Habsburg barbarians a great outcry from the sudden surprise attack.

10.   "A great stench will come out of Lausonne, such that one will not know the source of the fact, they will put out all the remote people, fire seen in the sky, foreign people defeated." A great stench of problems will come out of Habsburg Lausonne to the north, such that one will not know the source of the fact that French spies kept hidden. The French spies will put out the remote Habsburg people through deceitful activities, fire of the Moslem attack seen in the sky, the Habsburg foreign people defeated.

11.   "Countless people will appear at Vicenza without force, fire to burn the basilica: Near Lunage the great one of Valenza defeated, when Venice through death will take up the quarrel." Countless French spies will appear at Vicenza (Venice) as they enter secretely without force of armed conflict, fire set by the French spies to burn the basilica there: Near Lunage (in Genoa) the great governor of Valenza (Milan) defeated, and ousted when Venice through death from the basilica fire will take up the quarrel blaming Valenza's governor.

12.   "He will appear near Buffalosa. The high and tall one entered into Milan, the Abbot of <**> with these of Saint-Maur will do mischief dressed like serfs." The Venician Habsburgs will appear near Buffalosa (Milan). These high and tall Habsburgs influenced by French spies, entered into Milan to possess their city, because of the basilica fire, the abbot of Foix (Augustinians who synthesized pagan culture) indicates the Venice Habsburgs who, against Saint-Maur Milan Habsburgs (Benedictines - keeping the faith pure), will do mischief dressed like villains.

13.   "The crusader brother through unbridled love will cause Ballerophon to die for Proetus. Fleet to Milano the woman gone mad, the potion drunk, both thereupon to perish." The crusader Venician brother through unbridled love for pure Christianity, will cause Bellerophon (Milan governor) to die for Proetus (Venician revenge), fleet (Venecians) to Milan as the woman Anteia like Augustinians in Venice) gone mad from the basilica fire, the potion of French trickery drunk, both (Venician and Milanians) thereupon to perish as the Moslem army invades.

14.   "The great credit, the abundance of gold and silver will cause honor to be blinded by lust, known will be the offense of the adulteress, which will occur to his great dishonor." The great credit, the abundance of gold and silver taken from Milan by the Venecian Habsburgs, will cause Christian honor to be blinded by lust, known will be the offense of the adulteress (<**> like Augustinian Venecians) rebelling to unite the Habsburgs in one faith, which will occur to her great dishonor as the Moslems suddenly invade.

15.   "Great exertions toward Aquilon by the mannish woman, to vex Europe and almost all the world, the two eclipses put into utter route, and reinforce life and death for the Pannonians." Great exertions toward Aquilon (Latinized) Habsburgs in Milan Italy by the mannish woman (Anteia like Venecian Habsburgs) to vex Europe and almost all the world, the two eclipses or quarrels caused by French spies put the Habsburgs in utter route,

and to the Pannonians (Moslems coming from Hungary), life and death reinforced to favor the allied victory.

16.   **"From the place where Jason had his ship built. There will be a flood so great and so sudden That one will have no place or land to fall upon, the waves to mount Olympian Fesulan."** From the place in Greece where Jason (variant indicating the Moslems) had his ship built, there will be a flood of Moslems so great and so sudden attacking Italy that the Habsburgs will have no place or land to fall upon in their retreat. The waves of Moslems to mount in Fiesole (central Italy) in Olympic numbers.

17.   **"Those well off will suddenly be removed, through the three brothers the world put in trouble, the enemies will seize the marine city, famine, fire, flood, plague and all evils doubled."** Those Venician Habsburgs well off after looting treasure from Milan, will suddenly be removed, through the three brothers or Moslems (like end time Protestants from three ages) the world (Habsburg Empire) put in trouble, the Moslem enemies will seize the marine city (in Venice). Famine, fire, flood, plague and all evils doubled by the French and Moslem allies.

18.   **"From Flore issued the cause of his death, once before by young and old to drink, as the three lilies will force him to quite stop. Through his offspring safe as raw meat is watered."** From Flore (France) issued spies, the cause of Habsburg death, at times before with young and old to drink of French espionage, as the three lilies (Moslems allied to French) will force the Habsburgs to quite a stop from Moslem victory, through his offspring (Moslem army) safe as raw meat of Habsburgs is watered with French poison.

19.   **"Riches to defend the great cope troubled. In order to enlighten them the reds will march: By death a family will be almost ruined. The red red ones knocking down the red one."** Riches for Benedictine Habsburgs in Milan to defend, the great Augustinian Venician cope (Old French) troubled by spies, in order to enlighten them the reds (Augustinians) will march after their basilica burned: A family (Habsburgs) will be almost ruined by death from quarreling, the red red ones (Benedictines - double anointed) knocking down the red ones, or Augustinians.

20.   **"The false message about the sham election. To run through the city, peace prevented: Advice acquired, chapel stained with blood, and to another one the empire contracted."** The false message about the sham Augustinian election in Venice perverting Christianity, to run through (Latinized) the Benedictine city in Milan, peace (Old French) prevented: Advice from French spies acquired, the Venecian chapel stained with blood in the fire, and to another one (Augustinians in Venice) the empire contracted as they attack Milan Benedictines for revenge.

21.   **"Three foists will enter the port of Agde, carrying the infection, not faith and pestilence: Passing the bridge they will carry off millions, and the bridge interrupted for the third resistance."** Three (Moslem, like end time Protestants from three ages) foists will enter the port of Agde (France), carrying the infection (French spies), not faith (true Habsburg

friends) (but) pestilence of espionage: Passing the bridge or spy route, the French spies will carry off millions of Habsburgs, and the bridge (spies) interrupted Habsburg defenses for the third (Moslem) resistance.

22.   Coursan, Narbonne, through the salt to warn, Tuchan, the grace Perpignan betrayed, the red town will not want to consent thereto, in high flight a gray cloth life failed." < * * >, Narbonne (French spies) through the salt (ocean) to warn the Moslems about defenses, Tuchan (France) betrayed the grace of Perpignan (Spanish Habsburgs) who earlier had defeated France in fighting. The red (Habsburg Spanish) town will not want to consent with other double anointed Habsburgs. In high flight (like end time rapture), gray cloth of worldliness having failed.

23.   "In the Queen's coffers letters found, place of signiture without any name of author: The proposals being concealed for the strategy, so that they will not know who the lover is." In the Queen's (France's) coffers letters found from the Moslems, place of signature in the letters without any name of author: For the strategy (Old French) of secret alliance to capture Italy the proposals will be concealed, so that the Habsburgs will not know who the allied French lover is, in case the letters were somehow intercepted.

24.   "The lieutenant in the doorway of the house will knock down the great one of Perpignan: In thinking to save himself at Montpertius. The bastard by Lusignan will be deceived." The Moslem lieutenant in the doorway of the house (invading Italy) will knock down the great one of Perpignan (Spanish Habsburgs who ruled in Italy): In thinking to save himself (Old French) at Montpertius, (Purtus Pass) spy route indicating supposed French friends, the Habsburg bastard by Lusignan (France) deceived as no help is provided by French spies.

25.   "The heart of the lover unlocked by stealthy love in the stream will cause the lady to be ravished: The half hurt one will feign lustful. The father to two will deprive the body of soul." The heart of the Habsburg lover unlocked by stealthy French love, in the stream while helping Italy will cause the Lady (Habsburgs), through French deceit, to be ravished by the Moslems attacking: The half hurt French will feign lustful, the father (Alliance) to the two allies will finally deprive the body of its soul, Habsburg lands captured.

26.   "The bones of Cato found in Barcelona, placed, exposed place refound and ruined: The great one who holds and does not hold will want Pamplona, for the abbey of Montserrat drizzle." The bones of Roman Cato (French spies) found in Barcelona Spain placed, exposed the Italian place to Moslem attack, Italy found again and ruined by Moslems: The great Habsburg one who holds and later does not hold Italy will want contested Spanish Pamplona for the (Benedictine) abbey (variant) of Montserrat (near Barcelona), during spy influenced drizzle confusing the Habsburgs.

27.   "The auxiliary way one arch upon the other with le Muy deserted except for the brave one and his jennet. The writing of the Phoenix

Emperor seen by him that which with none other is." The auxiliary way, sharing Italy like one arch upon the other with Le Muy, Roman-built canal in France, deserted except for the brave one (Moslems) and his jennet (small captured Spanish horse), the writing of the Phoenix emperor (Suleiman I like Hannibal returned) in governing Italy Seen by Habsburgs as that which with none other (French partner) is.

28. "The semblance of gold and silver inflated. Which after the theft was thrown into the raging fire. At the discovery all dulled and troubled, on the marble inscriptions, prescripts inserted." The semblance of gold and silver inflated, which after the theft through French rebellions upon the Moslem temples, were thrown into the raging fire, indicating disappearance of the booty, at the discovery of these French rebellions, all the Moslems dulled and troubled, on the marble inscriptions, indicating Roman laws, prescripts inserted against the French by the Moslems.

29. "At the fourth pillar where they dedicate to Saturn. By earthquake and flood split: Under the Saturnin edifice an urn found. Of gold carried off by Caspio and then restored." At the fourth pillar (Catholic Church before the Reformation) where France dedicated rebellions to old Saturn (France). By earthquake and flood Moslems and French split: Under the Saturnin edifice or Catholic Church built over earlier French defeat. An urn found of gold carried off by Caspio (symbolically by French rebels) and then restored back to the Moslems.

30. "Within Toulouse not far from Beluser. Making one deep pits, palace of spectacle: The treasure one found will come to vex everyone. And from two places all and near the delvasacle." Within Toulouse (France) not far from Bellac Bussiere (representing shared Italy). Making one deep pits by French rebellions, palace of spectacle for Christianity in Italy: The treasure (Italy) found during Moslem retaliation, will come to vex everyone and from two places. (Old French) Moslem and French, all (Italy) found and near the Delphic oracle (delvasacle) or Moslems.

31. "First great fruit of the Prince of Peschiera. But then will come one very cruel and evil: Within Venice he will lose his proud glory. And put to evil by the more youthful Selin." First great fruit, or treasures, captured by the French rebel prince of Peschiera or Italy. But then will come the Moslems back very cruel and evil retaliating: Within Venice (or Italy) the Moslems will lose their proud glory after French rebellions, and put to evil by retaliation from the more youthful Selin (variant) or former Moslem doctrines.

32. "Gallic King, beware of your nephew. He who will do so much that your only son will be murdered making a vow to Venus. Accompanied at night by three and six." Gallic King, beware of your nephew or Moslem ally. He who will do so much by trickery that your only son, French occupying Italy, will be murdered after making a vow for taking over Venus (Italy) by rebellions. Accompanied at night by three Moslem instigators, three like end time Protestants, and later by six (reinforced Moslems during retaliation).

33. "The great one will be born of Verona and Vicenza. Who will bear a very unworthy surname. He who at Venice will want to take vengeance. He himself taken by a man of the watch and sign." The Moslem great one will be born of Verona and Vicenza (Italy shared with the French), who will bear a very unworthy surname, the unwanted Moslem faith. Moslems at Venice (Italy) will want to take vengeance on French Christians. After Moslems themselves taken by a rebel Frenchman at the watch, and a man of the Christian sign.

34. "After the victory of the Lion with the Lion. Moreover the Jura Mountain slaughter. Floods and dusky ones seventh million. Lyons. Ulm at the Mausoleum death and tomb." After the victory of the Moslem Lion with the other allied French Lion. Moreover, the Jura Mountain of Habsburg slaughter, floods (Latinized) of Moslem invaders in Italy and dusky ones (Old French) or Moslems with the seventh million Lyon (or French partner), Ulm (German city indicating Habsburgs) at the Mausoleum through death by defeat and tomb.

35. "Within the entry of the Garonne and Baisa and the forest not far from Damazan. Discoveries of the sea frozen, then hail and cold. In the Dordonnais frost through error of month." Within (Italy) the entry of the Garonne and Baisa (allied French and Moslems) and the forest (Italian lands) not far from Damazan (French spies). Discoveries of the sea (Old French) frozen (indicating French espionage), then hail and cold of Moslem invasion. In the Dordonnais (north of the Garonne) frost (Old French) through error of month (French deceit).

36. "It will be committed against the anointed brought on Lons-le-Saunier. Saint-Aubin and beautiful work to pave with marble picked from distant towers Bletterans not to resist and masterpiece." Espionage will be committed against the anointed (Habsburgs like end time believers), brought (Provencal) by French spies on Lons-le-Saunier and Saint-Aubin bordering on France, and beautiful work of deceit to pave the way for Moslem attack upon Italy, with marble picked from distant Habsburg towers, Bletterans (Habsburg border town) not to resist and this being a French masterpiece.

37. "The fortress close to La Tamise will fall when the King is locked up within: Near the bridge in his shirt will be seen One confronting death, then barred from the fort." The fortress (Italy) close to La Tamise (Habsburg border town) being under the same Habsburg government, will fall when the Habsburg king within the empire is locked up from French espionage: Near the spy bridge (network) in his shirt (unprepared) will be seen One (Habsburgs) confronting death by Moslem attackers, then barred from the Habsburg fort of defense.

38. "The King of Blois to reign in Avignon once again the people not-in-the-city In the Rhone he will cause to bathe by the banks up to five the last one near Nolle." The king, Francis I, of Blois, to reign in Avignon (on the Rhone symbolizing alliance). Once again, the Habsburgs are not in the city (Greek). In the Rhone (allied attack) by the walls, French spies will cause to bathe (in blood). Up to five (grace allowed the allies like end time Catholics and Protestants), the last one (Moslems) near (variant) Nole attacking Italy.

39. "He who will have existed by the Byzantine Prince will be taken away through the Prince of Toulouse: The faith of Foix through the chief of Tolentino will fail him, not refusing the bride." The Habsburgs who will have existed in Italy. By the Byzantine prince (Suleiman I) attacking them will also be taken away (Old French) through the Prince of Toulouse (Francis I): The faith or friendship of Foix (France), through the Habsburg chief of Tolentino (Italy) will fail Charles V, not refusing the bride indicating French spy infiltration hindering the Habsburg government.

40. "The blood of the just through Taur and La Daurade. In order to avenge itself, close by the Saturnines. In the new lake, the band immersing will march against those of Alba." The blood of the just Habsburgs through Taur and La Daurade (French spies). In order to avenge itself against the Moslem attackers, stay close by the Saturnines (French advisers). In the new lake (under Taur where the gold by legend was cast) of French alliance the Moslem band (Provencal) immersing in blood will march against Habsburgs of Alba.

41. "A Fox will be elected without saying a word. Playing the saint in public living on barley bread. To tyrannise afterwards very suddenly. Putting his foot on the throats of the greatest ones." A Fox (Moslems) will be elected to govern without saying a word about their secret French partner in Italy. The Moslems playing the saint in public by tolerating Christianity and living on barley bread showing humbleness. To tyrannise afterwards very suddenly (Old French) against the French. Putting his foot on the throats of the greatest ones (French).

42. "Through greed, through force and violence the chief of Orleans will come to vex his supporters. Near Saint-Memire assault and resistance. Dead in his tent they will say that he sleeps within." Through greed, through force and violence of rebellions the chief of Orleans (Francis I) will reportedly come to vex his Moslem partners in Italy. Near San Marino (Italy) assault by rebellions and then resistance by Moslem retaliation. Francis I dead in his tent, being in France, the Moslems will say that he sleeps within, exhausted by his rebellious plot.

43. "Through the fall of two illegitimate things. The Nephew by blood will occupy the realm. Within Le Torcy will be blows by lances. The Nephew through fear will fold his standard." Through the fall of two illegitimate bastards, or the Moslem and French alliance, because of instigated French rebellions. The Nephew (French being the remaining offspring) will occupy the Italian realm. Within Lectoure (France) being the blows to their pride by Moslem lances retaliating in Italy. The Nephew (French rebels) through fear will fold his standard in defeat.

44. "The natural offspring of Ogmios. From seven to Neuf Pont to turn aside from the road: With the King of long and friend to the Half-man. It behooves Navarre to destroy the fort of Pau." The natural French offspring of Ogmios (Celtic Hercules, symbolizing allied France) From seven (France) to Neuf Pont (spy bridge) to turn aside from the road by French rebellions: With the French king of a long time and friendly to the half-man (moon) or Moslems. It behooves Navarre (France) for the Moslems to destroy the fort of Pau (French rebels.)

45. **"His hand in a sling and his leg bound. Far the younger brother from Calais will be carried. Upon the watchword the death will be delayed. Then he will bleed in the temple at Easter."** French rebels captured with hand in sling and the leg bandaged. Far the younger brother (French rebels) from Calais (France) carried by Moslems. Upon the watchword, indicating conversion to Moslem faith, the death of French captives will be delayed. Then French converts to Islam will bleed from the agony of it in the Moslem temple at Easter.

46. **"He will die at St.-Paul-de-Mausole three leagues from the Rhone. The two fellow beings fled, oppressed by Tarascon: Because Mars will make the most horrible throne. Of Cock and of Eagle of France three brothers."** The French converts will die at St.-Paul-de-Mausole (Moslem temples), three leagues (like end time Protestants) away from the Rhone (Alliance). The two fellow beings (alliance) fled when by Tarascon (Monster rebels) oppressed: Because Mars of retaliation will make the most horrible throne. Of Cock (France) and of Eagle (Empire) of France for three brothers (Moslems like end time Protestants).

47. **"The Lake of Perugia will bear witness to the conspirators locked up within Perugia: A fool will imitate the sage. Killing Tedesque, routed and cut to pieces."** The Lake of < * * > (in Perugia, Italy) similar to the legendary lake at Toulouse, will bear witness from Moslem booty found. Of the French conspirators captured by the Moslems and locked up within Perugia: A fool (variant indicating Moslems) will imitate the Moslem sage. Killing Touquedec (French rebels) routed and cut (Old French) to pieces in retaliation.

48. **"Saturn in Cancer, Jupiter with Mars. In February, Chaldean soothsayer safety of the earth. The Sierra Morena assailed from three sides. Near Serbia what conflict mortal war."** Saturn (France) in Cancer (fourth sign France like Catholic Church resurrected from first four ages). Jupiter (Moslems) with Mars making war. In February (second month indicating after alliance) the Chaldean (Moslem soothsayer thinks safety on earth. The Sierra Morena (Spanish Habsburgs) assailed from three sides by Moslems like Protestants of three ages. Near Serbia (Italy) what conflict.

49. **"Return with beef, Jupiter in the water, Mars with arrow. Six of February will bring mortality: Those of Sardinia to Bruges so great a breach. When the Barberini chief will die at Ponteroso."** Saturn (France) with beef, supplying the food, Jupiter (Moslems) in the water sailing, Mars (warfare) with Moslem arrow. Sceaux (France) of February (two showing alliance) will bring morality by espionage: Habsburgs of Sardinia fleeing to

Bruges (Flanders) so great a breach by Moslems when Habsburgs Barbarini (Old French) chief, spy influenced, will die at Ponterosa (near Geneva).

50.   "The pestilence around Capalledes. Another famine approaches Segunto: The Chevalier bastard from the good old man. With the great son of Tunis will come to lose his head." The pestilence through French spies around Capallades (Spanish Habsburgs). Another famine from espionage approaches Segunto (other Spanish Habsburgs): The chevalier bastard (deceitful French spies with forged credentials) from the good old men (Saturn or France). With the great one of Tunis (Moslems) by alliance, will cause the Spanish Habsburgs in Italy to love his head by defeat.

51.   "The Byzantine making an offering. Afterwards retook Cordoba to himself: His road long peace cut off. Crossing by sea prize taken from the Pillar." The Byzantine (Moslems) making an offering of alliance with France. Afterwards retook Cordoba (Spanish-owned Italy) to himself, France having just before taken and lost Italy: His (Moslem) road long in arriving there, the Habsburg peace is cut off. Moslems crossing by sea, the price of Italian lands taken from the Pillar (Gibraltar) or Spanish defenders there.

52.   "The King of Blois to reign in Avignon. From Amboise and weak he will come the length of the Indre: Claw with Poitiers holy wings to ruin. Ahead Bonjeux he will come to extend the war." The king of Blois (France) to reign in Avignon (on the Rhone symbolizing alliance). From Amboise (France) and weak (Old French) from previous defect, will come the length of the Indre (France) indicating spy participation: Claw (Moslem army) with Poltier (France) to ruin the holy wings (Habsburgs). Ahead Bonjieux ((French spies) will come to extend the war.

53.   "Within Boulogne he will want to wash away his errors. He can not with the temple of the sun: He will fly doing things very mighty. In the hierarchy there was never one to equal him." Within Bologna (Italy), France will want to wash away his errors of defeat. He cannot with the temple of the sun (Habsburg Christianity in Italy): France will fly doing things very mighty through alliance with Moslems and spy activity. In the hierarchy of Christian governments there was never in the burial cask of Italy one France's equal.

54.   "Under the color of the marriage treaty. Magnanimous deed by the great Chyren Selin: Saint-Quentin and Arras recovered through the journey. From the Spanish a second butcher's bench made." Under the color of the marriage or alliance treaty, a magnanimous deed of recapturing Italy from the Habsburgs by the great Chyren Selin (French and Moslems): Saint-Quentin and Arras (France through alliance) recovered through the journey into Italy. From the Spanish Habsburg earlier triumph, a second butcher's bench of allied warfare made to get Italy back again.

55.   "Between two rivers he will find himself encompassed, Touques and Conche joined to overrule: Houtvillers bridges broken the chief run through many times. Perfect children throats being cut with the knife." Between two rivers (French and Moslems) the Habsburgs are encompassed, touques and Canche (French rivers indicating allied France) joined to overrule the Habsburgs defences. Houtvillers (France) bridges indicating the French spy network, begins. The Habsburg chief run through many times due to spies. Perfect Habsburg children throats being cut with the knife (Old French) of French spies.

56.   "The week band will occupy the land. Those of the high place uttering horrible cries: The large herd of the outer corner stirred up. Falls near Dinebro the cries discovered." The weak Moslem band will occupy the Italian land. Those Habsburgs of the high place of government uttering horrible cries from defeat: The large Habsburg herd, from the outer corner (Old French) stirred up by spies, falls near Dinebro (variant Spanish Ebro River), indicating Moslem and Habsburg fighting, the cries (old French) of French influenced defeat discovered.

57.   "From simple soldier he will attain to empire. From short robe he will attain to the long: Valiant in arms Angles at which the very worst. To vex the priests as water does the sponge." From simple soldier, French (similar to Napoleon and Cromwell) will attain to empire capturing Italy. From short robe (consular) he will attain to the long (Imperial) when he rules Italy: Valiant in arms Angles (French spies) causing tumults at which the very worst. To vex the Habsburg priests as water does the sponge, through instigating religious quarrels.

58.   "Realm in quarrel divided between the brothers. Takes the arms and the name Britanny: The Anglican title will be advised too late. Surprised by night by the Gallic air." Realm of the Habsburgs in quarrel, divided by Habsburg brothers from spies instigating trouble. Takes or favors the arms (or Moslems) and the name of Britanny (France): The Anglican title (French spies) will be advised too late to assist. Surprised by night with the Moslems attacking Italy, Habsburgs led to disaster by the Gallic air (French spies).

59.   "By two faiths lead high by two faiths put low. The East also the West will weaken: Their adversary after several battles. By sea chased, will fail in the pinch." By two faiths (Christian and Moslem) high through capture of Italy, by these two faiths Habsburgs put low in defect. The East (Moslems) also the West (French Christians) will together weaken the Habsburg Empire: Their Habsburg adversary after several battles. By sea chased during the Moslem attack, will fail in the pinch through French spies instigating confusion.

60.   "First in Gaul, first in Romania. By land and sea with the Anglois and Paris. Marvelous deeds by that great troop. Violating, the wild beast will lose Lorraine." First ruler governing in Gaul (France) becomes first ruler in Romania (Italy), by land and sea with the Angles and Paris (French rebels) Marvelous deeds through rebellions by the great French troop (old French). Violating the friendship with the Moslems, the wild beast (Greek) indicating Moslems, will lose Lorraine (France) as its partner sharing the Italian lands.

61. **"Never by the discovery of day will he attain to the mark of sceptre-bearing: Until all his sieges are at rest. Bearing to the cock the gift from the armed legion."** Never by the discovery of day (when the cock crows) will France attain to the mark of sceptre-bearing, or being in complete control of Italy: Until all his sieges or rebellion against the Moslems are at rest being victorious. Bearing to the cock (France) the gift (all of Italy) from the armed (Latin) Legion (variant) of Moslems.

62. **"When one visits the holy temple to plunder. The greatest one of the Rhone profaning their sacred things: For them will appear a very copious pestilence. The King escaping injustice not wanting to condemn."** When one (French rebels) visits the holy Moslem temple to plunder. The greatest one (Moslem rulers) of the Rhone (French and Moslem alliance) their sacred Moslem things to profane: Through the French rebels will appear a pertilence so copious. The Moslem king will escape (variant) the injustice, not wanting to quickly condemn the French ally of conspiring.

63. **"When the adulterer wounded without a blow will have murdered his wife and son for spite: Wife knocked down the child strangled: Eight (Houtviller) captives taken, to choke themselves without respite."** When the Moslem adulterer, wounded by the French rebellions without an initial Moslem blow, will have murdered his wife (France) and son (French in Italy) for spite against the Moslem religion: Wife (France) knocked down losing Italian possessions, the child (French rebels) strangled to death: Houtviller (French captives) taken, to choke themselves without respite through forced conversion.

64. **"Within the isles the children transported. Two out of seven will be in despair: Those of the soil being supported by, Montpellier taken, the hope of the leagues flees."** Within the isles near Italy, the children (captured French) transported by the Moslems. Two (French rebels) of the seven (French like the Catholic Church of seven ages) will be in despair: Those French of the Italian soil (Old French), being supported by Montpellier (France), taken, the hope for French control of Italy through the rebel leagues, flees.

65. **"The old one disappointed in his principal hope. He will attain to the head of his empire: Twenty months he will hold the reign with great power. Tyrant, cruel in giving way to one worse."** The old one (France) disappointed in his principal hope to take all of Italy just for himself. He will rise to the head of his empire by chasing out the Moslems: Twenty months (During allied sharing of Italy) Moslems will by election reign with great power, Moslem tyrant cruel giving way to one worse, French rebels.

66. **"When the inscription D.M. is found. And the ancient cave with a lamp is discovered: Law, King and Prince of the Alps tested in the pavilion the Queen and Duke under the covering."** When the inscription D.M. (here lies) is found, where France before was defeated, and the ancient cave or French burial sight with a lamp of new inspiration discovered through alliance to recapture Italy: Law, Habsburg king and prince of the Alps tested, in the pavilion queen and duke under the covering committing adultery, exposed by French spies.

67. **"Paris, Carcassonne, France to ruin in great discord. Neither the one nor the other will be elected: France will have the love and concord of the people. Ferrara, Colonna great protection."** Paris, Carcassonne, France sending spies will ruin the Habsburgs with great discord. Neither the Spanish Habsburgs nor the French will be elected to govern after the Moslems finally capture Italy: France will have the love and concord of the Italian people who prefer Christianity, Ferrara, Colonna being under France's great protection during the allied sharing of Italy.

68. **"The old Cardinal deceived by the young one. Out of his dignity will find himself disarmed: Arles not displayed double is perceived, Both Languedoc and the Prince embalmed."** The old Cardinal (France) deceived by the Moslem young one (variant) in Italy, out of his Christian dignity by instigated French rebellions, will find himself disarmed by Moslem retaliation: Arles (on the Rhone symbolizing alliance) not displayed double, is perceived with France's Italian possessions confiscated. Both Languedoc (France's Italian lands) and the French prince embalmed, indicating loss.

69. **"Near the young one, the old angel to fall. And he will come to rise with him in the end: Dix, years equal in most things, the old one to fall again. From three, two the one Hourtin serephin."** Near the young one (Moslems), the old angel (France) to fall, and the Moslems will come to rise against the French rebels in the end: Dax (France), years equal to the Moslems in most things, the old one (France) to fall again. From three (Moslems), two (allied) making the one Hourtin (French) become seraphin (beggarly like Franciscans).

70. **"He will enter ugly, wicked, infamous. Tyrannizing Mesopotamia: All friends made by the adulterine lady, land horrible black of physiognomy."** The French will enter Italy again, ugly, wicked, infamous after allied victory over Habsburgs, tyrannizing through French rebellions against Mesopotamia (Greek indicating Moslems). All supposed Habsburg and later Moslem friends taken or defeated by the adulterine or untrue lady (France), land of Italy horrible, black or dismal in physiognomy or aspect after French rebels take over completely.

71. **"The number will become very great from astronomers driven out, banished and their books censured: L'an mil six cens and sept with the holy assemblies, such that none will be safe from the holy ones."** The French number in Italy will become very great from astronomers (Moslems) Driven out and banished and their books censured by French rebels: Luneville, Sceaux, Cherente (River), and Septauil (France) with the holy (variant) assemblies (Latinized) or Moslems. Such that none (Moslems) will be safe from the holy ones (French rebels) who want to take over Italy.

72. **"The Perugian field, oh, what an enormous defeat there. And the conflict very near to Ravenna: Holy passage when they will celebrate the feast. Conqueror vanquished, to eat horse's flesh."** The Perugian field

(Italy), oh, what an enormous defeat for the Moslems. And the conflict very near at Ravenna (Italy) as French rebels fight against the Moslems to gain all of Italy: French holy passage (Italy) being completely theirs when French rebels finally celebrate the victory feast, Moslem conqueror now vanquished, to eat horses flesh, showing defeat.

73.   **"A Barbarian soldier will strike the great King. Unjustly not far from death. The covetous reason will be the cause of the deed. Conspirator and realm in great remorse."** A barbarian soldier (French rebels) will strike the great Moslem king. Unjustly attacked by rebellions in Italy, the Moslems are not far from death. The covetous reason of French greed to obtain all of Italy by ousting the Moslems will be the cause of the deed. The Moslem conspirator and realm in great remorse over the rebellions.

74.   **"A King entered very far into the new land. While his subjects come to welcome him: His treachery will have such an engagement that instead of the citizens feast a collection."** A king, Suleiman I, entered very far into the new land (Italy). While his Moslem subjects come to welcome him back after the French rebels tried to possess Italy through rebellions. Moslem treachery will have such an engagement against French rebels. That instead of the Moslem citizens' feast of victory, there is a collection taken for further revenge.

75.   **"The father and son will be murdered together. The count within his pavilion: The mother at Tours will have her belly swelling with a son. Chest green with tiny paper leaves."** The father (Moslem government) and son (Moslem religion) will be murdered together by French rebellions, the Moslem count within his pavilion (Italy): The mother (French government) at Tours will have her belly swelling with a son (possession of all Italy). Chest (variant), indicating Moslem booty, green from tiny paper leaves decorating it, seen in the baby's room.

76.   **"More Butcher than King to Angloterre. Born of obscure place he will have the empire through force: Base without faith without law he will bleed the land. His time approaches so near that I sigh."** More butcher that king to Angloterre (France), through murdering French rebels and religious persecution. Born of obscure place, Moslems, not well known, will have the Italian empire through force: Base without the Christian faith without Christian law. Moslems will bleed Italy to satisfy their greed. The Moslem time of judgment approaches so near that I (Nostradamus) sigh.

77.   **"The third Antichrist very soon annihilated. Seven and twenty years of blood will his war last: The heretics dead, captives exiled, blood of human bodies red rain pockmarks the ground."** The third Antichrist (Moslems like end time Protestants of three ages) very soon annihilated. Seven and twenty years (dissolving of allied French partnership in Italy) with blood will the Moslem war of retaliation last: The Christian heretics dead, captives who convert exiled to slavery. Blood from human bodies will like red rain, poch-mark the ground from Moslem cruelty.

78.   "A broad sword with twisted tongue will come to pillage the sanctuary of the gods: For the heretics he will open the gate. Thus stirring up the Church militant." A broadsword (Old French) indicating French rebels, with twisted tongue speaking against the Moslem religion, will come to pillage (variant) the Moslem sanctuary of the gods in Italy: For the Christian heretics, the Moslems, through trickery, will open the gate by instigating French rebellions. Thus stirring up the militant French Christian church to stage rebellions in Italy.

79.   "He who loses his father by the sword, born in a nunnery. By Gorgon's blood thereupon will be conceiving anew: In foreign land much will he do all to keep silent. He who will burn himself and his child." French government in Italy which loses his father (Moslem government) by the sword, born in a nunnery by religious rebellions. By Gorgon's (Greek) blood, Moslem defeat, thereupon will be conceiving anew, making Italy all Christian. In foreign land, France will do much to keep silent concerning the rebellions. France who will burn himself and his Italian child.

80.   "The blood of innocent ones, of widow and virgin. Much more evils committed by means of himself to the great Red One: Holy images imbued over burning wax. Frightened by terror none will be seen who move." The blood of innocent ones, of Habsburg widow and virgin. Much more evils committed by means of himself (France) to the great (Old French) Red One (Spanish Habsburgs): Holy Christian images imbued over burning wax candles in the temple. By terror frightened, none will be seen to move as Moslems retaliate further, persecuting all Christians in Italy.

81.   "The new empire in desolation will be changed at the northern pole: From Sicily will come the disturbance. To trouble the enterprise tributary to Philip." The new Italian Empire in desolation with Habsburgs under attack from the Moslems will be changed or weakened at the northern pole through French spies instigating Habsburg quarrels. From Sicily will come the disturbance of Moslem invasion. While to trouble the Habsburg defenders the enterprise of French spies will act tributary to Habsburg Philip ruling in Italy.

82.   "Spare, tall, dry playing the good valet. In the end he will have only his leave: Keen poison, and letters in his collar. He will be seized, escaped danger for him." Spare, tall and dry, French spies playing the good valor to the Habsburgs. In the end with Italy lost to the Moslems. French spies will take their leave, abandoning the Habsburgs: Keen poison and letters in his collar, symbolizing influence creating Habsburg confusion, Habsburgs will be siezed by Moslem invaders, danger escaped for the secret French spies.

83.   "The greatest sail out of the port of Zara Near from Bysantium will carry out his enterprise: From the enemy lost and the friend is not. The third upon both will inflict great plunder and capture." The greatest sail (Moslems) out of the port of Zara. Near originating from Bysantium will carry out his enterprise to capture Italy: From the Moslem enemy, Italy lost and their French friend not seen with Habsburgs, the third (Moslems typing end

time Protestants of three ages) will seemingly upon both Habsburgs and French inflict great plunder and capture.

84. **"Paterno will hear from Sicily a cry. All the preparations from the Gulf of Trieste which will be heard how Sicily. From so many sails fled, fled the horrible plague."** Paterno (Habsburg Italy) will hear from the southern Habsburgs in Sicily a cry when Moslems attack there. All being the preparations (Old French) done by French spies through spreading rumors from the Gulf of Trieste which will be heard how that Sicily with the invasion from Moslems, from so many Moslem sails fled, fled the horrible plague.

85. **"Between Bayonne and Saint-Jean-de-Luz will be placed with Mars she who promotes: For the efforts of Aquillon the prostitute will remove the light. Then suffocate in bed without assistance."** Between Bayonne and Saint-Jean-de-Luz (indicating France) will be placed with Mars of Moslem warfare, she who promotes (French spies helping the Moslems): For the efforts (Latin) of Habsburg Aquilon to defend Italy, the prostitute (Latin) or French spies will remove the light. Then suffocate the Habsburg defenses in bed without assistance (Old French) from deceitful spies.

86. **"Through Ernani, Tolosa, and Isle Franca. Infinite band through the Sierra de San Adrian: Passes river, Combat over the plank of the bridge. To enter Bayonne all crying Bichoro."** Through Ernani and Tolosa (France) and the French Isle (variant for spies assistance), infinite Moslem band through the (Italian) mountains of Adrian (Spanish Habsburgs): Passes the (Adour) river, combat (Old French) by Moslems through the plank (Old French) of the Bridge (French spy network) to enter Bayonne (Spanish territory) all crying Bichoro (like when France retook Navarre).

87. **"Death conspired will come into full execution. Charge given and voyage of death: Elected, created, received, defeated by his followers. Blood of innocence before him in remorse."** Death conspired against Habsburgs in Italy will come into full execution. Charge given by the Moslem army invading and voyage of death taken by French spies infiltrating against the Habsburgs: Moslems elected to govern, the created Italian lands received by Frenchmen, Moslems defeated by French rebels. Blood of innocence or Christians before Moslems in remorse of retaliation.

88. **"To Sardinia a noble King will come. Who will hold the kingdom only three years. Several colors will join to himself. He himself after careful slumber afflicts scornfully."** To Sardinia a noble Moslem king will come, who will hold the kingdom (Italian lands) only three years (three indicating the Moslems who type the Protestant churches out of three ages). Several colors (Moslems) will join to himself in alliance with France, France himself after careful sleep pretending innocence, afflicts (Old French) the Habsburgs scornfully through spies.

89. **"In order not to fall into the hands of his uncle who slaughtered his children in order to reign: Arguing from the people putting his foot on Peloncle. Dead and dragged between armoured horses."** In order not to fall into the hands of his Moslem uncle (related by alliance), who slaughtered France's children (Italian Christians) in order to capture Italy: Arguing from the French people through instigated rebellions putting the French foot on Peloncle (Greek) or the Moslem government. Moslems supposedly dead and dragged between armoured horses of the French rebels.

90. **"When one of the crusaders found with his senses troubled, in the place of the holy will see a horned ox: Through the virgin pig its place then will be filled. By the King order will no longer be maintained."** When one of the crusaders (French Christians) is found with his senses troubled. In the Christian holy place one will see a horned ox (Moslem instigators): Through the virgin pig (Christians being greedy) the Moslem place in Italy will be filled with French rebels. By the Moslem king order will no longer be maintained as Moslems retreat.

91. **"Amidst the fields by the Rhone entered where the crusaders being almost united. Mars and Venus met in Pisces. And a great number punished by flood."** Amidst (variant, indicating Moslems) the fields by the Rhone (alliance) the Moslems entered into France where the crusaders (Christian French) will be almost united by friendship forgetting their differences, Mars of war and Venus (Italy) meet with Pisces (allied French and Moslems). And a great number of Habsburgs punished by flood of allied Moslem invasion capturing Italy.

92. **"Far beyond his realm set on a hazardous journey a great army leads to occupy for himself: The king will hold the people captive and hostage. Upon his return the entire country plundered."** Far (variant indicating Moslems) beyond his Moslem realm, set on a hazardous journey of warfare, a great Moslem army (Old French) led (Old French) through French spy assistance, to occupy Italy for themselves: The Moslem king will hold the Habsburg people captive and hostages. Upon France's return to Italy, the entire country plundered by Moslem invaders.

93. **"Seven months, no more he will obtain the prelacy. Through his death a great schism will arise: Seven months will another hold the governorship, near to Venice peace, union arises again."** Seven months (France like end time Catholic Church from seven ages) arrived, no more will Habsburgs obtain the prelacy (ecclesiastic position). Through Habsburg death by Moslem attack a great schism, dividing Italian lands among French and Moslems, will arise: Seven months (with France) another (Moslems) will hold the governorship. Near Venice peace, French union with Italy arises again.

94. **"Before the lake where the dearest one was put down for seven months, and his army routed there will be Spaniards destroyed through those of Alba. Lose through delay is giving battle."** Before Le Luc (east of the Rhone indicating the Moslems) where the Habsburg dearest one was put down (Old French) by seven months (French spies) and his army routed by Moslems. Habsburg Spaniards will be destroyed (Old French) through those French spies of Habsburg Alba (near Rome). Causing loss through delays in giving battle against the Moslem invaders.

95.   "The seducer will be placed in the dungeon. And bound for some time: The scholar joined the chief with his crozier. The sharp right will attract the contented ones." The seducer (French spies) will be placed in the dungeon and bound for some time, keeping the French alliance secret: The scholar (French spies) then joined the Moslem chief with his Christian cross, sharing in the captured Italian lands. The sharp right (or Moslem army-symbolically right of the Rhone) will attract (Old French) the contented French.

96.   "The synagogue sterile without any fruit will be received by the infidels: To Babylon the daughter by persecuting. Miserable and sad to him her wings clipped." The synagogue (French Christian captives like the Jews also helped by Moslems) sterile without any fruit because of earlier French loss to the Habsburgs in Italy will be received by the infidels (Moslems): To Babylon or Moslem thinking, the daughter (French spies) by persecuting from Habsburgs earlier conquest. Miserable and sad, to Moslem thinking, France's wings clipped.

97.   "To the limits of the Var to change the All-powerful. Near the bank the three beautiful children to be born: Ruin to the people of competent age. Influence in the country to change seen growing no more." To the limits of the Var River bordering France the all-powerful (Greek-Latin) Moslems to exchange places with Habsburgs Near the bank the three beautiful childred (Moslems like end time Protestants of three ages) born: Ruin to Habsburg people of competent age in Italy, French influence in the Italian country to change, their Habsburg friendship seen growing no more.

98.   "The blood of the Church people will be poured out. Like water in as great abundance: And for a long time will not be stopped. Woe, woe for the clergy ruin and wailing." The blood of Christian church people will be poured out. Like water in great abundance when Moslems invade: And for a long time will not be stopped as their French ally is tricked. Woe, Woe from the second Antichrist (Moslems like end time Protestants) persecuting the clergy, ruin and wailing for the French like the end time Catholic Church.

99.   "Through the power of the three temporal Kings. For them the Holy Sea will be put in another place: Where the substance of the corporal spirit will be restored and received as the true see." Through the military power of the three kings (Moslems like end time Protestants from three ages). For them the Holy See (Christianity) will be put in another place: Where the substance or doctrines of the corporal spirit (Christian philosophy) will be restored again by the French sharing the Italian lands and received as the true See (true Christianity).

100. "For the abundance of tears shed. From high to low through the low one to the highest: Faith too great, through gambling life lost. To die of thirst through great default." For the abundance of Moslem tears shed, from high to low for Moslems governing Italy by way of the low one (French rebels) switching to the highest ruling position: Faith of the French rebels too great through the gamble, life lost from Moslem retaliation. The French to die of thirst, losing Italian lands through their great default.

Duplicate Fragmentary Centuries
(Century VIII)

1.   **"Being confused, several of them wait. For the inhabitants will not be pardoned: Who thought proper to persist in waiting. But not much spare time will be given them."** Being supposedly confused, several (Moslems like end time Protestants of three ages) of them waiting. For the French inhabitants to stop rebelling in Italy, will not be pardoned by the rebels: The Moslems thought it proper to persist in waiting as though long suffering towards their French ally. But not much time will be given before Moslems retaliate.

2.   **"Several will come, and will speak of peace. Between Monarchs and very powerful lords: But it will not be accorded so soon. Unless they become more obedient than the others."** Several (Moslems, like end time Protestants of three ages) will come and will speak of peace. Between Moslems Monarchs governing Italy and very powerful French Lords sharing Italian lands: But it will not be accorded so soon because of French rebellions. Unless the remaining French become more obedient than the others, even to converting to the Moslem religion.

3.   **"Alas what a fury! Alas what a pity will there be among many of the people: Never did one see such a friendship as the wolves will have, diligent to run."** Alas what a fury from Moslem attackers! Alas what a pity extended to Habsburgs by deceitful French spies! Being there among many of the people in Italy. Never did one see such a friendship (through alliance) As the Moslem and French wolves will have, being diligent to run down the Habsburg prey and capturing Italy from them.

4.   **"Many people will want to come to terms with the great lords who will bring war upon them: They will not want to hear anything of it from them. Alas! If God does not send peace to the earth."** Many Habsburg people under

French spy influence will want to come to terms with the great Moslem Lords who will bring war upon them: The Moslems will not want to hear anything of it from them. Alas or pity to the Habsburgs if God does not send peace to the earth, since the Moslems will invade Italy.

5.   **"Varieties of aid will come from all sides. From distant people who will want to resist: Suddenly they will be much urged on, but not spoiling in order to assist them at that hour."** Varieties of aid will come to the Habsburg defenders from all sides, from distant people (French spies) who will really want to weaken the Habsburg defences: Suddenly, the Habsburgs will be urged on to resist the Moslem invaders. But not spoiling the Moslem enemy in order that French spies will assist the Moslems instead at that hour.

6.   "Alas, what ambition foreign Princes have. Take careful heed lest they come into your country: There should be terrible dangers And in many countries, even in Vienna." Alas, what ambition foreign (French) princes have among the Habsburgs in Italy. Take careful heed lest they (French spies, similar to wickedness in high places) come into your country (like the spiritual promised land of the believer): There should be terrible dangers from the (spiritual) warfare and in many countries (implying many believers) even in Habsburg Vienna.

Nostradamus
Century IX

Nostradamus
Century IX

1.   "In the house of the translator of Bourg. The letters will be found on the table, one-eyed, red-haired, white, hoary-headed will hold from the course, which will change for the new Constable." In the house of the French spy translator of Bourg (France), the coded letters will be found on the table where the spy studies his instructions, one-eyed (double minded), red-haired (Spanish Habsburg), white hoary-headed (French) indicating the French spy, will hold the Spanish defenders from the course, which will change to the new Moslem constable ruling Italy.

2.   "From the top of the Aventine Hill a voice heard, be gone, be gone all of you on both sides: The anger will be appeased by the blood of the red ones, from Rimini and Prato, the Colonna expelled." From the top of the Aventine Hill (Italy) a Habsburg voice heard, "Be gone, Be gone, all of you on both sides (French and Moslems)!" The French anger from earlier defeat will be appeased (Old French) by the blood of the Habsburg red ones, from Rimini, Prato, and Colonna (Italy) expelled (Old French) through French spy assistance.

3.   "The Magnavacca (canal) at Ravenna in great trouble, Canals by fifteen shut up at Fornase: At Rome there will be born two double-headed monsters, blood, fire, flood, the greatest ones in space." The Magnavacca Canal at Ravenna (Italy) in great trouble from espionage, canals, by fifteen French sabateurs (like Catholic Church from five ages), shut up at Fornase (Italy): at Rome there will be born two double-headed monsters (French and Moslems being double minded), blood, fire, flood of war, the Habsburg greatest ones in space, defeated as though hanged.

4.   "The following year discoveries through flood. Two chiefs elected, the first will not hold: By fleeing the shadow, for the one of them, the

refuge, Plundered, the house which the first will defend." The following year, discoveries made from the flood of war, two chiefs (French and Moslems) elected in Italy, the first Habsburg ruler will not hold after their defeat: By fleeing the shadow of advancing Moslems, for the one (French spies) of them, Italy becomes a refuge. Plundered, the Habsburg house which the first Habsburg rulers will defend.

5.   **"The third toe of the foot will seem first to a new monarch from low high, who will possess as tyrant of Pisa and Lucca. His predecessor's fault to correct."** The third (Moslems like end time Protestants of three ages) toe of the foot (allied French and Moslems) will seem first (ruler). To a new French Monarch from low in defeat to high sharing possession of Italy, who Pisa and Lucca the Moslem tyrant will possess, his Habsburg predecessor's fault of earlier Habsburg victory over France, to correct.

6.   **"From Guienne, an infinity of Anglois will settle under the name of Anglaquitaine: In Languedoc, Lapalme, Bordelais, which they will name after Barboxitaine."** From Guienne (France) an infinity of Anglois (French citizens) will settle in Italy under the name of Anglaquitaine, indicating French ownership of some of the captured Italian lands: At Languedoc (in France but symbolizing Moslem lands in Italy) Lapalme (variant) and Bordelais (indicating Moslems) will settle, which place they will name after Barboxitaine, indicating barbarian Moslem leadership.

7.   **"He who will open the tomb discovered, and will not come to close it promptly, evil will come to him, and one will be unable to prove If it would be better to be a Breton or Norman King."** The Moslems who will open the discovered tomb of French sharing Italy and will not come to close it promptly by ousting the French; evil of French rebellions will come to the Moslems, and one will be unable to prove if it would be better to be a Breton or Norman king, symbolizing Moslems and French fighting.

8.   **"The younger son made King will put his father to death, after the conflict of very dishonest death: Inscription found, suspicion will bring remorse, when the wolf driven out lies down on the bedstead."** The younger Moslem son made king in Italy will put his father (allied sharing of Italy) to death. After the conflict of very dishonest (Old French) death caused by French rebellions: Inscription, indicating the French rebel scheme, found, this suspicion will bring French remorse, when the wolf (French) driven out of Italy, lies down on the bedstead.

9.   **"When the lamp burning with inextinguishable fire will be found in the temple of the Vestals: Child found fire, water passing through the sieve: To perish in water Nimes, Toulouse the markets to fall."** When the Christian lamp, burning with inextinguishable rebellion fire, will be found in the temple of the Vestals: Child (French rule for Italy) found in the rebellion fire, water of Moslem retaliation passing through the sieve like a cloud burst: Nimes, indicating shared Italy, to perish in water, the markets to fall in Toulouse, indicating French regret.

10.   **"Monk and nun with child exposed to death. To die through a she-bear, and carried off by a boar, by Foix and Pamiers, the army will be camped, against Toulouse Carcassonne to form the harbinger."** Monk and nun (France and French rebels) with captured child (Italy), exposed to death, to die through a she-bear (Moslem retaliation), and carried off by a Moslem boar (Moon being the half pigman), by Foix and Pamiers (symbolically) the Moslem army will be camped, Against Toulouse and Carcassonne (French rebels) to form the harbinger of Moslem retaliation.

11.   **"The just one they will wrongly come to put to death. In public and in the surroundings extinguished: So great a pestilence in this place will come, that the judges will be forced to flee."** The just one (Moslems) they will wrongly come to put to death by French rebellions. In public and in the surroundings of Italy, the Moslems are extinguished through revolt: So great a pestilence of rebellions in this place of Italy will come to arise that the Moslem judges will be forced to flee the country to safety.

12.   **"So much silver of Diana and Mercury, the images will be found in the lake: The sculptor looking for new clay, He and his followers will be steeped in gold."** So much silver of Diana and Mercury, symbolizing booty taken during French rebellions. The images will be found in the lake like the legendary treasure of Toulouse discovered: The Moslem sculptor looking for new clay, He and his followers will be steeped in gold as they supposedly find the lost treasure as further proof of French plundering.

13.   **"The exiles around Sologne, Led by night to march into Auxois, two of Modena cruel at Bologna, placed, discovered by the fire of Buzancais."** The exiles (French rebels) around Sologne (Westerly in France symbolizing French property in Italy). Led by night to march into Auxios (easterly in France symbolizing Moslem property), two (double strength) with Modena (another French possession) cruel, attacking at Bologna (Moslem possession in Italy), the booty placed, later discovered by the fire of Moslem retaliation at Buzancais (westerly).

14.   **"Put on the flat surface of Dyer's caldrons, wine, honey and oil, and basted over furnaces: Being immersed without evil, pronounced malefactors. Seven, smoke still in the barrel of the executioner."** French Christians put on the flat surface (Old French) of dyer's (Latin) caldrons in Italy, and like wine, honey, and oil, basted over furnaces: Being immersed without evil crimes, Christians are pronounced malefactors. Seven (France like end time Catholic Church out of seven ages) punished, smoke (Old French) still in the barrel of the executioner (variant) or Moslems.

15.   **"Near Perpignan the red ones detained. Those of the surroundings completely ruined, led far off: Three cut in pieces, and five badly supported. On account of the Lord and Prelate of Burgundy."** Near Perpignan (Westerly in France symbolizing French spies) the red ones (Spanish Habsburgs) detained from defending Italy. Those Habsburgs of the surrounding lands completely ruined, led far off in defeat: Three (Moslems) cut them in pieces, and five (French spies) badly supported Habsburg

defenders. On account of the Lord and Prelate of Burgundy (Rhone region indicating alliance).

16. **"From Castille, Franco will bring out the assembly, the ambassador not agreeable will cause a schism: Those of Riviera will be in the squabble, and will refuse entry to the great gulf."** From Castille (Spanish Habsburgs in Italy), Franco (French spies) will bring out the assembly. The ambassador (spy influenced) not agreeable, will cause a schism among Habsburg leadership: Those of Riviera (French spies in Italy) will be in the squabble. And this way will refuse entry of Habsburg ships to the great gulf, weakening defense against Moslem attack.

17. **"The third one foremost does worse than Nero, be gone, how much human blood to flow: He will cause to rebuild the furnace, Golden Age dead, new king great scandal."** The third one (Moslems like Protestants of three ages) foremost, does worse than Nero (French spies) against the Habsburgs in Italy: He will cause to rebuild the furnace, indicating Christian persecution, similar to the scaffolds opposite the Tuileries named after the tile kilns, Golden Age of Christianity dead, caused by the new Moslem king through great scandal.

18. **"The lily of the Dauphin will reach into Nancy, as far as Flanders the elector of the Empire: New confinement for the great Montmorency, Outside proven places delivered to celebrated punishment."** The lily of the Dauphin (French rebels) will reach into Nancy (easterly, symbolizing Moslem regions in Italy). As far as Flanders (westerly, indicating French regions in Italy) the Moslem elector of the Empire retaliates: New confinement for the great Montmorency (French Christians) after Moslems take over, captured outside proven Moslem places, French rebels delivered to celebrated punishment.

19. **"In the middle of the forest of Mayenne, the Sun in Leo. Lightning will fall: The great bastard issued from the great one of Maine, this day Fourgeres tipped with blood will enter."** In the middle of the forest of Mayenne (France), the Sun (France like end time Catholicism) in Leo (Fifth sign indicating grace, like end time opportunity for the Catholic Church): The great bastard (alliance) issued from the great one of Maine (France). This day Fourgeres (France like the dead Catholic Church, resurrected) sword tipped with blood, will enter Italy.

20. **"By night will come through the forest of Reines, Two by roundabout routes, Queen the white stone, the monk dark in gray in Varennes: Elected Capet causes tempest, fire, blood, slice."** By night, indicating secrecy, will come through the forest of Reines (French alliance) two (French and Moslems) by roundabout routes, queen being the white stone (French), the monk (Moslems) dark in gray in uncultivated lands of the east, elected Capetian (absolute) Moslem king to rule in Italy, causes tempest, fire, blood, slice to the French partner there.

21. **"At the tall temple of Saint-Solenne at Blois, Night bridge on the Loire, Prelate, King killing outright: Crushing victory in the marshes of**

the pond. Whence prelacy of whites, destruction." At the tall temple of Saint-Solenne (Moslem temple) at Blois, at night on the bridge on the Loire (alliance), the French king will kill outright the Moslem prelate: Crushing (Old French) victory for French rebels in the marshes of the pond (Provencal) over the Moslems, whence, for the prelacy of whites (French), destruction (Provencal) by Moslem retaliation.

22.   "The King and his court in the place of cunning tongue. Within the temple facing the palace: In the garden the Duke of Mantua and Alba, Alba and Mantua dagger tongue and palace." The Moslem king and his court in the French place in Italy with cunning (Old French) tongue instigating French rebellion, within the Christian temple towards the palace (Moslem run government): In the garden the Duke of Mantua (variant indicating Moslems) and French Duke of Alba, Alba and Mantua with dagger of quarreling in tongue and Moslem palace."

23.   "The younger son playing outdoors under the arbor, the top of the roof in the middle on his head, the father King in the temple of Saint-Solenne, sacrificing he will consecrate festival smoke." The younger son (French) playing outdoors under the arbor (Old French), indicating French possessions in Italy, the top of the roof comes down on the middle of his head, symbolizing instigation of French rebellions. The father (France) and king (Moslem government) in the temple (Italy), sacrificing, will consecrate festival smoke (Old French) of recent capture of Italy.

24.   "Upon the palace from the windows of the balcony, the two little royal ones will be carried off: To pass Orleans, Paris, abbey of Saint-Denis. Nun, apples to swallow green pits." Upon the palace (Italy) from the windows of the balcony, the two little royal ones (French and Moslems sharing Italian lands) will be carried off through rebellions: To pass Orleans Paris (Latinized indicating Italy), abbey of Saint-Denis with Moslem defeat, nun (French rebels like end time Catholic Church) with apples (Moslem enticement) to swallow green pits (Moslem trickery).

25.   "Passing the bridges to come near Rosiers, arrived late sooner than he will believe. The new Spaniards will come to Beziers, so that this chase enterprise will break." Passing the bridges to come near Rosiers (variant), indicating Moslems who share in the Italian possessions, French help arrived late, sooner than France will believe (Old French), the new (Old French) Spaniards indicating French rebels will come to Beziers, over the border, indicating against the Moslems, so that this chase enterprise (Old French) or rebellion will break.

26.   "Departed from Nice under the name with letters later. The great cope will bestow a gift not his own. Near Voltri at the walls of Verese, Carpi. After Plombeno the wind to Benevanto." Departed from Nice (France) under the Habsburg name with letters of secret instruction later. The great cope (Old French) will bestow a gift of Habsburg citizens supposedly not France's own. Near Voltri, at the walls of Verese, Carpi the spies will infiltrate

Italy. After Plombeno, the wind will carry them by ship to Benevento deeper into Italy.

27. **"From Blois, the wind will be close round the bridge. The received one high will strike the Dauphin, the old craftsman will pass the woods in unison, going far beyond the rightful borders of the Duke."** From Blois (On the French Loire, indicating alliance) the wind, taking the Moslems, will close around the bridge (spy network). The received one (French spies), high in influence, will strike the Dauphin (Habsburg prince), the old craftsman (Greek) indicating allied Moslems, will pass the woods in unison, going far beyond the rightful borders of the Habsburg Duke.

28. **"Allied fleet from the port of Marseilles. In the port of Venice to march from Hungary: To leave from the gulf and bay of Illyria. Destruction to Sicily, cannon shots for the Ligurians."** Allied (Greek) Moslem fleet arriving in Italy from the port of Marseilles (France), and In the port of Venice (Italy) to march from Hungary: Moslems also to leave from the gulf and bay of Illyria (Greece) to attack Italy. Destruction to Habsburg ruled Sicily. For the Ligurians (Italy), cannon shots as the Moslems invade at different locations.

29. **"When he who gives place to none will want to abandon a place taken yet not taken: New fire through swamps, bitumen at Charlieu, Saint-Quentin and Calais will be recaptured."** When the Moslems who give place to none, will want to abandon to the French a place taken yet not taken: New fire (variant) through swamps (Old French) and bitumen (Old French) of French rebellions at Charlieu (near the Rhone symbolizing alliance), Saint-Quentin and Calais in northwestern France where Moslems where imprisoned (in Italy) will be recaptured.

30. **"At the port of Pola and of San Nicolo, Norman to perish in the Gulf of Quarnero: Capetian to the streets of Byzantium to cry alas, help from Cadiz and the great Philip."** To the port of Pola and of San-Nicolo (Yugoslavia), Normana or French captives to perish in the Gulf of Quarnero through Moslems retaliating after French rebellions in Italy: Capetian (absolute) French rebel ruler taken to the streets of Byzantium, to cry "Alas, help!" from Cadiz (Spain) and the great Habsburg Philip II because of Christian persecution by Moslems.

31. **"The trembling of land at Mortara, Tin St. George half sunk to the bottom. Drowsy peace the war will awaken, in the temple at Easter abysses opened."** The trembling of land at Mortara (Italy) through French rebellions against the Moslems, Tin St. George, statue representing Christianity, half sunk into the ground, symbolizing Italy's people being half Moslem and half Christian, Peace drowsy at first under shared ownership of Italy, the war will awaken, in the temple at Easter as the abysses of French rebellions opened.

32. **"Of fine porphyry, a deep column found, giving up to the base inscriptions of the Capitol: Bones twisted hair, Roman force proven, Fleet to stir at the port of Mytilene."** Of fine porphyry, a deep column (symbolizing French Christianity) found in Italy, giving up to the base (Greek) inscriptions of the capitol (governing Moslems): Bones, twisted hair like a resurrected corpse, the Roman force (French rebels) show themselves plainly. Fleet (Latinized) of retreating Moslems to agitate at the port of Mytilene (Lesbos in the Aegean) farther east.

33. **"Hercules King of Rome and of Annemark, with Gaul, the triple chief surname, to tremble, Italy and the one with St. Mark. First above all monarchs renowned."** Hercules (Suleiman I) king of Rome (Italy) and of Annemark (Hungary, Bohemia and Moravia), with Gaul (French sharing Italy), the triple chief surname (Moslems like end time Protestants of three church ages). To tremble because of French rebellions against them, and the one of St. Mark (French Christians). First, above all, Francis I becoming monarch renowned by the ousting of Moslems.

34. **"The single part vexed will be mitred. Return conflict passing over the tile: For five hundred one to betray will be titled Narbonne and Salse through knives advanced by oil."** The single (Old French) part, France, vexed, will be mitred, forced to wear the rebel cap, exposed as rebellious. The return conflict of Moslem retaliation passing over the tile (Tuileries) against French rebels: For five hundred (Grace period for sharing Italy), one to betray will be titled Narbonne and Salse (France), through knives advanced by friendship oil.

35. **"And fair Ferdinand will be detached, to abandon the flower, to pursue the Macedonian: In great want his course will fail, and he will march against the Myrmidons."** And fair (indicating French) Ferdinand (like Ferdinand V, a staunch Habsburg Catholic) will be detached rebelling, to abandon the flower (France), to pursue the Macedonian (Greek) symbolizing the Moslems: In great want for a purely Christian populated Italy, the French rebel course will fail France's directions for peace. And rebels will march against the Myrmidons (Greek) indicating Moslems.

36. **"A great King taken by the hands of a young man, not far from Easter confusion knife thrust: Everlasting captives, times, what lightning on the top, when three brothers will wound each other and murder."** A great king (Moslems) taken by the hands of a young man (French rebels), not far from Easter, which inspired the French Christians to cause confusion and knife thrust of rebellions: Everlasting Moslem captives and times, what lightning on the top governing Moslems, when three brothers (Moslems) will wound each other and murder, instigating these French rebellions.

37. **"Bridge and mills overturned in December. The Garonne will rise to a very high place: Walls, edifices, Toulouse overturned, so that none will know his place as much the matron."** Bridge of friendship and mills symbolizing mutual benefit, overturned in December as Christians are inspired while celebrating Christmas, the Garonne (French rebels) will rise to a very high place taking over Italy: Walls, edifices of Moslems, Toulouse (rebels) overturned, so that Moslems will not know their place, as much the same for the matron or Moslem empire.

38. "The entry at Blaye from La Rochelle and the Angles will pass beyond the great Macedonian: Not far from Agen he will wait the Gaul, help for Narbonne beguiled through conversation." The entry at Blaye into the Geronne river from La Rochelle (France sending help), and the Angles (French rebels), will pass beyond the great Macedonian (Greece indicating Moslems) to control Italy: Not far from Agen, the French rebel will wait expecting the Gaul's (French) help for Narbonne (French rebels) farther east, the French rebels deceived through Moslem conversation.

39. "In Albisola to Verona and Carcara. Led by night to seize Savona: The quick Gascon La Turbie and L'Escarene: Behind the wall of the old and new palace to seize." In Albisola (French rebels) to Verona (Moslem instigators) and Carcara (French rebels), led by night during instigated French rebellions to Seize Savona (representing Moslem controled cities): The quick Gascon (Moslem instigators), La Turbie and L'Escarene (both French controled): Behind the wall of the old and new palace (indicating French reclaimed Italian cities) to seize by ousting the Moslems.

40. "Near Saint-Quentin in the forest deceived. In the Abbey the Flemish will be cut up: The two younger sons half-stunned by blows. The suite crushed and the guard all cut up." Near Saint-Quentin (northwest France symbolizing French in Italy) in the forest deceived, in the Abbey the Flamends (northwest France again being French citizens) will be cut up (variant) by Moslem instigators: The two younger sons (French and Moslems) with blows, half stunned by instigators, the French rebel suite crushed the Moslems and the Moslem guard all cut up.

41. "The great Chyren will seize Avignon. From Rome letters in honey full of bitterness: Embassy letter to leave from Chanignon. Carpentras taken by a black duke with a red feather." The great Henry II (son of Francis I, symbolizing French rebels) will seize Avignon (on the Rhone indicating allied Italy) From Rome (Moslem governors) letters in honey desiring friendship, full of bitterness after rebellions: Embassy letter to leave from Chanignon (Henry's Avignon). Carpentras (allied Italy) taken by a black Moslem duke with red plumage (indicating Christians converted to Islam).

42. "From Barcelona, from Genoa and Venice. From Sicily pestilence Monaco joined: Against the Barbarian fleet taking their aim, Barbarian driven 'way back me as far as Tunis." From Barcelona (symbolizing former French spies with Spanish credentials, later living in Italy as French citizens) from Genoa and Venice in Italy. From Sicily too, pestilence with Monaco (French) united causing rebellions: Against the Moslem barbarian fleet, taking their aim to possess all of Italy just for France, barbarian Moslems driven way back as far as Tunis.

43. "Near the descent the Crusader army will be ambushed by the Ishmaelites, from all sides struck by the ship Riviera, Quickly, attacked by ten elite galleys." Near the descent or landing (as though at Tunis), the French Crusader rebel army will be ambushed by the Ishmaelites (Moslems). From all sides with French rebellions struck by the ship Riviera (French rebels).

Quickly, the Moslems attacked in retaliation with ten elite Moslem galleys, which demonstrates how the French rebels were tricked into losing Italian possessions.

44. "Leave, leave from Geneva every last one, Saturn will be changed from gold to iron, Raypoz will exterminate all who oppose him, before the coming the sky will show signs." Leave, leave, from Geneva (Italy) every last one (Old French) of French inhabitants, Saturn (Old France) will be changed from gold of initial success to iron symbolizing loss of Italian lands, Zopyra (tricky Moslems) will exterminate all who oppose the Moslem faith, before the advent of this, the smoking sky will show signs of French rebel defeat.

45. "None will remain to ask, Great Mendosus will obtain his dominion: Far from the court he will cause to countermand Piedmont, Picardy, Paris, Tuscany the worst." None of the Moslems will remain to ask to rule, similar to after Charles IX and Henry III were assassinated, Great Vendome (Henry IV) symbolizing France, will obtain his dominion through French rebellions against the Moslems: Far from the court (Italy) the Moslems will cause to countermand Piedmont, Picardy, Paris, Tuscany (variant) (instigated rebellions in Italy) the worst during retaliation.

46. "Be gone, flee from Toulouse the reds. With sacrifice to make expiation: The chief from evil under the shade of pumpkins: Dead to strangle carnal prognostication." Be gone, Moslems flee from Toulouse the reds, (French in Italy wearing red rebel hats), with sacrifice of initial Moslem defeat, the Moslems to make expiation by later retaliation: The chief (France) from under the shade or disguise of pumpkins (French rebellions): Dead losing Italian possessions, Moslems to strangle the carnal prognostication (fleshly Christianity) by further persecution.

47. "The undersigned with infamous deliverance. And from the multitude having contrary advice: Change Monarch put in danger, thought, shut up in a cage they will see each other face to face." The undersigned (Moslem ally) with infamous deliverance for his people, and from the rebellious French multitude, having contrary advice to oust the Moslems from Italy: Change in Italian ownership, French Monarch put in danger, thought (Old French) the Moslems defeated, shut up in a cage, they will see each other face to face with the Moslems retaliating.

48. "The great city of the maritime Ocean, Surrounded by seas, with crystal: In the winter solstice and the spring. It will be tried by frightful wind." The great city (Italy) of the maritime ocean, surrounded on three sides by seas, with crystal (snow): In the winter (Latin) solstice and the spring (Old French), it will be tried by frightful (Old French) wind symbolizing the French unrest in Italy similar to a stormy winter and spring, with winds of rebellions against the Moslems there.

49. "Ghent and Brussels will march against Antwerp. The Senate of Londres will put to death their King: The Selin and Venice will be to him in the reverse. In order to have them and the realm in confusion." Ghent and Brussels (Netherlands, indicating French rebels will march against Antwerp (symbolizing Moslems in formerly Habsburg Italy), the Senate (rebels) from Londres (France) will put to death their Moslem king through rebellions: The Selin (Moslem moon) and Vin (Venice) will be, to French rebels, inside out. In order to have Moslems and the Italian realm in confusion.

50. "Vendome (Henry IV) will soon come to his high realm, putting behind somewhat the Lorrainers: The pale red one, the male in the interregnum. The youth, fear and terror to Barbarians." Vendome (Henry IV, symbolizing France) will soon come to his high realm with Christians possessing all of Italy. Putting behind, somewhat, the Lorrainers (Strong Catholic Guise family symbolizing Moslems who governed Italy): The pale red one (French rebels) being the male (ruler) in the interregnum. The youth (French rebels) causing fear and terror to the defeated Moslem Barbarians.

51. "Against them red sects conspiring together. Through peace will destroy Champdefeu, Eu, Ferrieres, and Cordes: To the point of dying, those who will plot. Except one who above all the world will ruin." Against the Moslems, red sects (French rebels) will conspire together (Old French). Champdefeu, Eu, Ferrieres, and Cordes (French rebels) through peace acquiring Italian possessions, will destroy (Old French): To the point of dying, the Moslems who will plot (actually instigating the French rebellions). Except one (Moslem reinforcements) who, above all the world, will ruin the rebels in retaliation.

52. "Peace is nigh on one side, and war, never was the pursuit of it so great: To pity men, women innocent blood on the land. And this will be by France to the whole band." Peace is nigh with Italy captured and French and Moslems possessing it together on the one side, and the war of French rebellions, never was the pursuit of it so great against the Moslems: To pity men, women, innocent blood on the land. And this will be by France (French rebels) to the whole band of Moslems.

53. "The young Nero into the three chimneys will have live pages thrown to burn: Happy those who will be far away from such practices. Three by his blood will have him ambushed to death." The young Nero (French rebels) into the three chimneys (against Moslems like end time Protestants from three ages) will have live pages (Moslem teachings) thrown to burn (Old French), indicating French rebellions: Happy those Christians who will be far away from such Moslem practices, three (Moslems) with his blood (Moslem instigators) will have the French ambushed to death.

54. "There will arrive at Porto-Corsini, close to Ravenna, he who will plunder the lady: In the deep sea legate from Lisbon, hidden under a rock they will carry off seventy souls." There will arrive at Porto-Corsini, close to Ravenna in Italy, Moslems who will plunder the lady (French rebels): In the deep sea as indicating French loss is the legate (Former French spy) from Lisbon (Portugal). Hidden under a rock in ambush the Moslems will carry off seventy souls (French rebels like end time Catholic Church from seven ages).

55. **"The horrible war which in the West is prepared, the following year will come the pestilence so very horrible that young, old, nor beast. Blood, fire Mercury, Mars, Jupiter from France."** The horrible war of French rebellions which in the West (France) is seemingly prepared against the Moslems in Italy. The following year will come the rebellion pestilence, so horrible that neither Moslem young, old, nor beast in Italy can escape the blood and fire. Mercury (French rebels) with Mars (war) against Jupiter (Moslems), logically instigated from France.

56. **"The army near from Houdan will pass Goussainville. And by the eager soldiers will leave its mark: Converting in an instant more than a thousand. Looking the two to deliver in fetters and leave."** The Moslem army near from Houdan (French city in Italy) will pass Goussainville (French city in Italy) retaliating against the French rebellions. And by the eager soldiers (Greek indicating Moslems) will leave its mark: Converting Christian captives in an instant more than a thousand, Looking for the two French cities to deliver in fetters and leave defeated.

57. **"In the place of Dreux a king will rest, and will look for a law changing Anathema: While the sky will thunder so very loudly, returned new King will be killed."** In the place of Dreux (symbolizing a French held city in Italy) a French king will rest after French rebellions overthrew the Moslems, and will look for a law changing anathema (Moslem sharing of Italy): While the sky will thunder so very loudly with Moslems. Returned, the new French king will be killed by losing Italian possessions.

58. **"On the awkward side at the spot of Vitry, the three red ones of France will be awaited: All felled red, black one not murdered. By the Bretons restored to safety."** On the awkward side at the spot of Vitry (French city symbolizing French city in Italy), the three (indicating inspired by Moslems like end time Protestants of three ages) red ones of France will be awaited in ambush in Moslem retaliation: All felled red (rebels), black one (Moslems) not already murdered By the Bretons (rebels), restored to safety.

59. **"At La Ferte, Vidame will seize, Nicholas held red who had produced the life: The great Louise to arise who will act secretly. Giving Burgundy to the Bretons through envy."** At La Ferte (relatively easterly, indicating a Moslem city in Italy) Vidame (symbolizing French rebels) will sieze, Nicholas (symbolizing France) held red (as a rebel) who had produced the life of rebel siezed Italy: The great Louise (French rebels) will arise (through Moslem instigation,) who will act secretely. Giving Burgundy (shared Italy) to the Bretons (France) through envy.

60. **"Conflict Barbarian in the black mob-hat, bloodshed, Dalmatia to tremble: Great Ishmael set about his promontory. Rennes to tremble, help to Lusitania."** Conflict of rebellions against the Barbarian (Moslems) in the black mob-hat (emphasizing religious difference of thinking). Bloodshed from fighting, Dalmatia (Moslem in shared Italy) to tremble: Great Ishmael (Moslems) set about their promontory (Italy) retaliating, Rennes (France to tremble because of help to Lusitania (Portugal symbolizing the French rebels who were formerly spies with Habsburg credentials).

61. **"The plunder made upon the marine coast. At Cittanova and relatives brought forward: Several of Malta through the deed of Messina will be closely confined, poorly rewarded."** The plunder (Old French by French rebels upon the marine coast, at Cittanova (Moslem city) and relatives (French who were forced to convert to Islam) brought foreward: Several (Moslems like end time Protestants from three ages) of Malta, through the rebelious deed of Messina (French owned city), will be closely confined, poorly rewarded for their allied friendship.

62. **"To the great one of Ceramon-agora, will the Crusaders all be fastened by rank. The long-lasting Opium and Mandrake. The Rougon on the third of October will be released."** To the great one of Ceramon-agora (Ushak in Turkey, indicating Moslem empire), will the Crusaders (French rebels) all by rank be fastened. The long-lasting (Latinized) Opium (Greek) and Mandrake (Greek) indicating Moslems. The Rougon River (in Turkey the third of October (Moslems like end time Protestants of three ages, now independent - tenth month) will be released to retaliate.

63. **"Complaints and tears, cries and great howls, near by Narbonne with Bayonne and in Foix: Oh, what horrible calamities and changes. Before Mars has made several revolutions."** Complaints and tears, cries, and great howls from the Moslems. Near by Narbonne (easterly indicating Moslems) with Bayonne (westerly indicating French rebels) and in Foix (easterly Moslems, too): Oh, what horrible calamites and changes here in Italy from French rebellions. Before Mars (rebellions) has made several revolutions with Moslems, like Protestants not quite finishing three church ages.

64. **"The Macedonian to pass the Pyrenees Mountains. In March Narbonne will not offer resistance: By land and sea he will carry on very great intrigue. Capetian having no land safe for residence."** The Macedonian (Moslems) to pass the Pyrenees for French alliance. In March (third month indicating Moslems) Narbonne (easterly symbolizing a Moslem city in shared Italy after its capture) will not offer resistance to French rebellions By land and sea carrying on very great intrigue to control Italy, Capetian (absolute Moslem rulers) having no land safe for residence.

65. **"In the wedge with Luna coming to repay, where he will be captured and put in a strange land: The emer's profits will be for great scandal. Great blame to one great praise."** In the wedge (battle formation) with Luna (Moslems) coming back to Italy to repay, where the French rebels will be captured and put in a strange land for slavery: The emir's (Moslem's) profits, or booty from defeating the Habsburgs through French help, will be for great scandal. Great blame against the rebels, for the Moslems great praise.

66. **"There will be peace, union and change, estates, offices, low high and high very low: To prepare a trip, the first offspring torment, war to cease, civil process, debates."** There will be peace after Moslem union of Italy and change, estates, offices which were low, now high for Moslems and high very low for French losing Italian possessions: To prepare a trip into slavery, the first French offspring in torment, war of rebellions to cease, and civil process and debates as only Moslems will be left.

67. "From the height of the mountains around the Isere. One hundred assembled at the haven in the rock Valence: From Chateauneuf, Pierrelatte, in Donzere. Against the Crest, Romans, faith assembled." From the height of the mountains around the Isere (east from the Rhone, indicating Moslems). One hundred Moslems assembled in ambush at the haven in the rock, Valence: From Chateauneuf and Pierrlatte (symbolizing three French cities in Italy) in Donzere, Against Crest (Moslem cities). Romans (symbolizing a French city in Italy) faith assembled by Moslems instigating rebellion.

68. "From Montelimar the noble will be obscure. The evil will come at the junction of the Saone and Rhone: Soldiers hidden in the woods on Lucy's day. That never was there so horrible a throne." From Montelimar (shared Italy) the noble Moslems will be obscure. The evil of retaliation coming at the junction of the Saone and Rhone (turning easterly symbolizing alliance favoring Moslems): Soldiers, like end time Protestants, hidden in the woods on Lucy's day, December 13 (Twelfth judgment hour, thirteenth symbolizing America). That never was there so horrible a Moslem throne.

69. "On the mountain of Sain-Bel and L'Arbresle will be hidden the proud ones of Grenoble: Beyond Lyons and Vienne on them a very great hail. Locust on the land not a third thereof will remain." On the Mountain of Saint-Bel and L'Arbresle will be hidden the proud Moslems of Grenoble (easterly, symbolizing a Moslem city in Italy): Beyond Lyons and Vienne, on those westerly lands symbolic of French possessions in Italy, a very great hail, locust on the land, indicating Moslems retaliating, not a third of French lands in Italy will remain.

70. "Sharp weapons hidden in the torches. In Lyons, the day of the Sacrament. Those of Vienne will all be cut to pieces, by the Latin Cantons Macon does not lie." Sharp weapons hidden in the torches by Moslems. In Lyons (on the Rhone indicating shared Italy), the day of the sacrament when Moslems instigate rebellions. Those French rebels of Vienna will all (Old French) be cut to pieces. By the Latin Cantons (Southeastern Switzerland, indicating Moslems in formerly Habsburg Italy), Macon (formerly French) does not lie, now.

71. "At the holy places animals seen with hair, with him who will not dare the day: At Carcassonne favoring for disgrace will be set for a more ample stay." At the Moslem places animals seen with hair (Old French) as French rebels desecrate the Moslem faith, with Moslem captives who will not dare the day in battle: At Carcassonne (relatively easterly French city symbolizing a Moslem city in Italy) favoring for disgrace of defeat will be set for a more ample stay after Moslem retaliation.

72. "Again will the holy temples be polluted. And plundered by the Senate of Toulouse: Saturn two three cycles completed, in April, May,

people of new leaven." Again will the Moslem holy temples be polluted, and plundered with continued rebellions from the Senate (Roman) Toulouse (French Rebels): Saturn (old man symbolizing France) two (allied) with three (Moslems like end time Protestants of three ages) cycles completed after capturing Italy. In April, May (the time of birth) French Christians of new leaven due to Moslem instigation.

73. **"Into Foix the Blue Turban King entered. And will reign less than an evolution with Saturn: The White Turban King, Byzantium heart banished, Sun, Mars and Mercury near the urn."** Into Foix (relative central in France symbolizing shared Italy) the Blue (variant indicating Moslems) Turban king entered, and will reign less than one evolution (lifetime) with Saturn (old man symbolizing France): The White Turban King (French) banished the Byzantium (Moslem) heart through French rebellions, Sun (Christianity) in Mars (rebellions) and Mercury (French rebels) near the urn (Italy).

74. **"In the city of Fertsod homicide, deed, and deed many oxen plowing no sacrifice: Return again to the honors of Artemis. And to Vulcan dead bodies to bury."** In the city of fertile Sodom (Eastern city, symbolizing a wicked Moslem city in Italy) homicide against Christianity, deed, and deed of heathen practices, many oxen plowing but no sacrifice to God: Return again to Christian honors with Artemis (Greek), and with Vulcan (Greek, symbolizing Moslems and their Italian cities) to bury (Old French) through French rebellions.

75. **"From Arta and the country of Thrace People by sea, evil and help from Gauls: Perpetual in Provence the trace. With vestiges of their custom and laws."** From Arta (west Greece, indicating French cities in Italy) and the country of Thrace (easterly, indicating Moslem possessions in Italy), people coming by sea to Italy, evil from French rebellions and help from the Gauls (symbolizing Moslems): Perpetual in Provence (easterly in France indicating Moslems like early Greek inhabitants), with vestiges of their Greek custom and laws.

76. **"With the black one rapacious and blood-thirsty, issued from the brothel of the inhuman Nero: Between two rivers military left hand will be murdered by Young Baldy."** With the black one (Moslems), rapacious and bloodthirsty retaliating against rebellions, issued from the brothel (ill reputed alliance) of the inhuman Nero (who burned Rome and blamed the Christians similar to Moslem instigators to French rebellions): Between two rivers (alliance), military left hand (From rebels in Italy) will be murdered by young baldy (Moslems acting disgraced by rebels).

77. **"The realm taken the King will conspire. The lady, taken to death sworn by lot: The life of Queen and son they will refuse, and the mistress at the fort of the wife."** The Italian realm taken by French rebels, the Moslem king will conspire (variant indicating Moslems). The lady (France) taken to death losing Italian possessions, sworn by lot indicating fair justice: The life of Queen (France) and son (French rebels) the Moslems will refuse. And the mistress (Christianity) at the Italian fort of the wife (Old French), France.

78. **"The Greek lady with beauty like lais. Made happy by countless suitors: Transferred out of the Spanish realm, captive taken to die a miserable death."** The Greek lady (France which retains some Greek characteristics and sharing Italy with the Moslems) with beauty like Lais (the most beautiful woman of Corinth). Made happy by countless suitors (French rebels ousting Moslems from Italy): Transferred out of the Spanish realm (formerly Habsburg Italy), the captive Moslems taken to die a miserable death through French rebellions.

79. **"The chief of the fleet through deceitful trickery will make the timid ones depart on their galleys: Depart, murdered, the chief renouncer of chrism. Then in the ambush will pay him his wages."** The Moslem chief of the fleet (Latinized, indicating in Italy), through deceitful trickery against French rebels will make the timid ones who convert to Islam, depart on their Moslem galleys: Depart murdered in defeat, the chief renouncer of the chrism (symbolizing Christianity). Then in the ambush will pay the Moslems his wages for rebelling by becoming slaves.

80. **"The Duke will want his followers to exterminate, sending the strongest ones to strange places: Through tyranny Pisa and Lucca to ruin, then the Barbarians without wine will gather the grapes."** The duke (Suleiman I) will want his Moslem followers to exterminate the French rebels, sending the strongest captives to strange places to be slaves: Through French tyranny by rebellions, Pisa and Lucca (French-owned cities) to ruin by Moslem retaliation. Then the Moslem barbarians without wine, will gather the grapes to begin celebrating during this new Moslem peace.

81. **"The crafty King will understand his snares. From three sides enemies to assail: A strange number tears from hoods. Will come the grandeur of the translator to fall."** The crafty Moslem king will understand the French rebel ambushes which Moslems instigated, from three sides (Moslems like end time Protestants of three ages) the Moslem enemies to assail A strange number of French rebels, tears from strange hoods (Christian monks) will come, the grandeur (Greek) of the Moslem translator to fall as Christianity is banned in Italy.

82. **"By the flood and fierce pestilence, the city great for a long time besieged: The sentry and guard at hand dead, suddenly capture but from none wronged."** By the flood and fierce pestilence of instigated French rebellions, the city (Italy) great for a long time with French and Moslems sharing possession of it, now besieged: The Moslem sentry and guard at hand to protect the French and Moslem people, dead, Sudden capture by French rebels, but from none of the Moslems were they wronged.

83. **"Sun twentieth of Taurus the earth will tremble very mightily. The great theater folds, filling: Air, sky and land to darken and trouble, then the infidel God and saints will call."** Sun (Christianity) twenty (allied) in Tournus (France), the earth will tremble very mightily with warfare. The great theater (Italy) folds as from earthquake (from French and Moslem invasion), filling the air, sky, and land, to darken with smoke and trouble with wreckage When the Moslem infidel, God and saints (French Christians) will call to alliance capturing Italy.

84. **"The King exposed will complete the slaughter, after having discovered his origin: Torrent to open the marble and lead tombe, of a great Roman with Medusine device."** The French king exposed by earlier defeat from Habsburgs, will complete the slaughter by defeating them on this second try. After having discovered his Greek origins tying France in alliance with the Moslems: Torrent of Moslem invasion to open the marble and lead to the tombe, of a great Roman (France) in Italy with Medusine (Greek) device of alliance.

85. **"To pass Guienne, Languedoc and the Rhone. From Agen holding from Marmande and La Reole: To open through faith for the king in Marseilles taking his throne, conflict near Saint-Paul with Mausole."** To pass Guienne, Languedoc, and the Rhone from Agen, the French rebels sieze Moslem possessions, coming from Marmande and La Reole (western areas in France symbolizing French possessions in Italy): To open through faith for the French King, Marseilles (Moslem city) taking the Moslem throne to rule Italy. Conflict near Saint-Paul (Christian rebels) with Masseole (variant indicating Moslems).

86. **"From Bourg-la-Reine they will come right to Chartres. And will near at Pont d'Antony pause: Seven through the peace crafty as Martens. Will enter with an army with Paris secured."** From Bourg-la-Reine, Napoleon's army symbolizing the Moslems in Italy will come right to Chartres retreating. And before will near at Pont d'Antony pause after evacuating Paris: Seven (France like Catholic Church of seven ages) through peace (sharing Italy) crafty as Martens, entering with an army (French rebels) against the Moslems, with Paris (Italy) secured as during Napoleon's capitulation.

87. **"In the forest of Torfou cleared. By the hermitage will be placed the temple: The Duke of Etampes through the trick invented From Montlhery the prelate will teach a lesson."** In the forest of Torfou (Moslem possession in Italy), cleared of Moslems by the hermitage (French Christian rebels), will be placed the Christian temple: The duke at Etampes (Napoleon retreating like the Moslems) through the trick (French rebellions) invented from Montlhery near Paris, the prelate (coalition of generals symbolizing French rebels in Italy) will teach a lesson.

88. **"Calais, Arras, help with Therouanne, peace and a semblance of it the spy will simulate: The soldiery at Savoy to descend from Roanne. Deterred people which will end the rout."** Calais (French) and Arras (Moslems) help with Therouanne (midway indicating alliance), peace and a semblance of it the former spy (Old French) will simulate, living in Italy: The French soldiery (Old French) rebelling at Savoy (Moslem possessions), to descend from Roanne (French possessions). Deterred the Moslem people, which will end the rout (Old French) banishing the Moslems.

89. "For seven years fortune will favor Philip, beating down again with the effort of the Arabs: Then in their middle perplexing contrary affair, Young Ogmios will destroy his stronghold." For seven years (France like Catholic Church from seven ages), fortune will favor Philip (Louis Philippe, symbolizing France). Beating the Habsburgs in Italy down again with the effort of the allied Arabs: Then in their middle while sharing Italian lands, a perplexing contrary affair of French rebellions, Young Ogmios (French rebels) will destroy the Moslem stronghold there.

90. "A captain of Great Germany will come to deliver through false help to the King of Kings, support from Hungary. So that his mutiny will cause a great flow of blood." A Habsburg captain of Great Habsburg Germany will come himself to deliver through false help (from French spies acting as friends) to the Habsburg King of Kings, support from Habsburg regions in Hungary, so that in the end Habsburg mutiny will cause a great flow of blood, indicating loss of Habsburg Italy to the Moslem invaders there.

91. "The horrible plague Perinthus and Nicopolis. The Peninsula taken and Macedonia: Thessaly will devastate, Amphipolis, an unknown evil, and the denial from Anthony." The horrible plague of French rebellions with Perinthus (northeast Greece symbolizing Moslems) and Nicopolia (Preveza west symbolizing French possessions), the Peninsula (symbolizing Italy) taken and Macedonia in northeastern Greece (symbolizing Moslem regions in Italy): Thessaly (French rebels) will devastate, Amphipolis (Moslems, farther east), an unknown evil (Henry IV symbolizing French rebels in Italy), and denial from Anthony (France).

92. "The King wanting to enter the new city. Through enemies will come to subdue: Captive free falsely to speak and perpetrate. King to be outside, keeping far from the enemy." The French king, wanting to enter the new city (Italy). Through enemies (Moslems becoming their ally) will come to subdue the Habsburgs there: Captive French spies released, free to live in Italy, falsely to speak against the Moslems and perpetrate rebellions against them, King (Suleiman I) to be outside of Italy, keeping far from the enemy (French rebels)"

93. "The enemies from the fort very far, by wagons passage to the bastion: From about the walls of Bourges crumbled, when Hercules will strike the Macedonian." The enemies (French rebels in Italy) from the fort (France) very far. By French rebel wagons passage to the bastion (strong Moslem defense), from all about in Italy the walls of Bourges (central France symbolizing the strong defense in Italy through French and Moslem cooperation) crumbled, when Hercules (French rebels) will strike the Macedonian (symbolizing the Moslems).

94. "Weak galleys will be joined together. False enemies the strongest on the rampart: Weak ones assailed Bratislava trembles, Lubeck and Meissen will take the barbarian side." Weak Moslem galleys will be joined together by alliance. False enemies (French spies influencing Habsburgs) the strongest on the rampart as they interfere with Habsburg defences: Weak ones

(Habsburgs) assailed, Bratislava (relatively south symbolizing Habsburgs in Italy) trembles as Moslems invade, Lubeck and Meissen (Northernly Habsburgs) will take the barbarian (Moslem) side due to spy instigated quarrels.

95. **"The newly made one leading the army. Almost cut off even to near the shore: Straining for help from the Milanais elite. The Duke deprived of his eyes from Milan an iron cage."** The newly made one (new general after spy influenced shake-ups) leading the Habsburg army. Almost cut off (Greek) by Moslem invaders, even to near the shore: Straining for help from the Milanais elite (Habsburg reinforcements to the west In Italy), the Habsburg duke deprived of his eyes by spy misinformation from Milan, an iron cage indicating defeat.

96. **"To enter the city denied the army. The Duke will enter through persuasion: To the weak gates, the army secretely led. Will put it to fire and death, effusion of blood."** To enter the city (Italy) is denied the Habsburg army because of spy influenced quarrels. The Habsburg Duke himself will enter the city through persuasion from French spies: To the weak gates of the city the Moslem army, led secretly by French spies. Will put to fire and death, effusion of blood as the Habsburgs are defeated.

97. **"By sea the forces of three divided parts. For the second one the supplies failing. Disheartened looking for the range of Elysium. The first one to enter the breach obtaining the victory."** By sea the forces of three (Moslems) divided parts with the allied French spies. For the second one (Habsburg defenders in Italy), their reinforcements failing to show up due to French spy influenced delays. Disheartened looking for the range of Elysium (Greek city symbolizing the Moslems), the first one (Moslems) to enter the breach obtaining the victory.

98. **"Those afflicted through the fault of a single tint, the transgressor from the contrary party: Of Lyons will send word when being constrained from to deliver the great chief of Malta."** The Habsburgs are afflicted through the fault of a single tint (French spy influence). The transgressor (French spy) from the contrary party of Lyons (France) will send word to the Moslem invaders when the Habsburgs will be constrained from effective defense, to deliver the great Habsburg chief of Malta (symbolizing Italy) so the Moslems can become victorious.

99. **"The Aquilon Wind will cause the siege to be raised. Over the walls to drop ashes, lime and dust: Through rain afterwards, which will do them much worse. The utmost help against their frontier."** The Aquilon (north) wind, as it blows a rain storm in their direction, will cause the Moslem siege to be raised. Over the walls to drop ashes, lime and dust upon the Habsburg defenses: Through rain afterwards from the storm, which will do Habsburgs much worse. The utmost help in the siege against the Habsburg Italian frontier.

100. **"Naval Battle night will be overcome. Fire in the ships to the West ruin: New trick, the great ship excused. Anger to the vanquished, and**

victory in a drizzle." Naval battle (Provencal) indicating from Moslem invaders, night will be overcome by fire of torches in the ships, to the West (Habsburg Italy) ruin of defeat: New trick of French spies preventing Habsburg torches from lighting, the great Habsburg ship therefore excused from attacking. Anger to the vanquished Habsburgs over confusion, and Moslem victory in the drizzle.

Nostradamus
Century X

Nostradamus

Century X

1.   "To the enemy, the enemy faith promised will not be kept, the captives retained: Taken near death, and the remainder in their shirts, the remainder damned for being supporters." To the French enemy, the enemy faith promised in the earlier alliance will not be kept, the French rebel captives retained: Taken near (Old French) death during Christian persecution, and the remainder who converted to the Moslem faith, stripped down in their shirts and sent into slavery, the remainder deemed to die for being supporters of Christianity.

2.   "The sail galley the ship's sail will hide, the great fleet will come to go out the lesser: Dax ships near will turn to drive it back, the great one conquered, the united ones to themselves will join." The French sail galley the ship's sail, which distinguished the country of origin, will hide. The great Habsburg fleet will come to go out the lesser in retreat: Dax (French) ships near, the Moslem ships turning to drive the Habsburg fleet back, the great one (Habsburgs) conquered, the united ones to themselves will join, sharing captured Italy.

3.   "While after five the flock not being put out, a fugitive on account of Poland will turn loose: To murmur falsehood, help to come by then, the chief will then abandon the siege." While after five (May, the fifth month), the Habsburg flock in Italy not being put out by the Moslem invaders, a fugitive (French spy), on account of Habsburg Poland earlier victory over France, will turn loose. To murmur falsehood that help from reinforcements to come by then, the Habsburg chief will then abandon the siege in despair.

4.   "At midnight the leader of the army saving himself, suddenly vanished: Seven years later his reputation unblemished, to his return not

ever saying yes." At midnight during cover of darkness the Habsburg leader with the army, saving themselves, suddenly vanish from the fort in Italy as a result of French spy trickery during the Moslem siege: Seven years (France like the end time Catholic Church out of seven ages) later, his reputation unblemished, to Habsburg return to Italy not ever saying yes.

5.   "**Albi and Castres will form a new league, New Arians, Lilly, Voucher and Portugeuse: Carcassonne and Toulouse will end their intrigue. When the new chief will go out from the Lauraguais.**" Albi and Castres (symbolizing French and Moslems) will form a new league, New Arians ancient heretics symbolizing Moslem invaders), Lilly (France), Voucher and Portuguese (Voucher) indicating spies infiltrating the Habsburgs: Carcassonne and Toulouse (French and Moslems) will end their intrigue of sharing captured Italy, when the new chief (French rebels) will go out from Lauraguais (alliance friendship).

6.   "**The Gardon will flood Nimes so high that they will believe Deucalion reborn: From the colossus the greater part will run away, Vesta tomb fire to appear extinguished.**" The Gardon River (symbolizing Moslems capturing Habsburg Italy) will flood Nimes (French city symbolizing a former French possession) so high that they will believe Deucalion was reborn (symbolizing France, saved by the flood): From the colossus of Nimes the greater part of the flood running away. Vesta tomb with fire extinguished, to appear like French sharing of Italy.

7.   "**The great conflict that they are preparing for Nancy, the Macedonian will say I subjugate all: L'Isle Brittany in anxiety over wine and salt. Between Philip two Metz will not hold for long.**" The great conflict which French rebels prepare for Nancy (easterly indicating the Moslems). The Macedonian (Moslems) will say I subjugate all, which antagonizes the rebels: L'Isle (easterly) to Brittany (westerly), indicating all of Italy, in anxiety over wine (force) and salt (wisdom), Between two philips (French and Moslems), Metz (easterly, Moslem ruled) will not hold for long.

8.   "**Forefinger and thumb the forehead will wet. The Count of Senigallia from his own son: There Venus from several of thin forehead. Three in seven days wounded dead.**" Forefinger and thumb the forehead wetting. For the Count of Senigallia (France) from his own son (French rebels): There Venus (Italy) taken from several of thin (Old French) forehead (Moslems showing their embarrassment, like end time Protestants from three ages). Three (Moslems) in seven days (French rebellions, like Catholic Church from seven ages) wounded to death (variant, Moslems).

9.   "**In the Castle of Figueras on a misty day a sovereign prince will be born of an infamous woman: Suleiman I with breeches on the ground, to him posthumous. Never was there a King so very bad in his province.**" In the Castle of Figueras (Spanish city supposedly impregnable, symbolizing a Moslem possession in Italy) on a misty (deceptive) day, from an infamous woman (France), a sovereign prince (French rebels) will be born: Suleiman I

with his breeches on the ground, to French rebels appearing posthumous,
Never was there a Moslem king so very bad in his province.

10. "**Stained with murder and enormous adulteries. Great enemy of the entire human race: One who will be worse than his grandfathers, uncles or fathers, in steel, fire, waters, bloody and inhuman.**" Stained with murder and enormous adulteries even while capturing Italy, the Great Moslem enemy of the entire human race: Who will be worse than his grandfathers, uncles or fathers—centuries earlier when the Moslem faith was unadulterated, with steel (variant, indicating Moslems), fire, waters of capturing Italy, the Moslems (according to French rebels) were bloody and inhuman.

11. "**Below Junquera at the dangerous passage, the posthumous one will have his band cross: To pass the Pyrenees Mountains without his baggage, from Perpignan the duke will hasten to Tende.**" Below Junquera (in Spain symbolizing French rebels in Italy formerly disguised as Spanish) at the dangerous passage. The posthumous one (formerly defeated French) will have his rebel band cross: To pass the Pyrenees Mountains (symbolizing alliance friendship) without his baggage (intending to conquer). From Perpignan (westerly) the rebel duke will hasten to Tende (easterly indicating Moslem possessions).

12. "**Elected to Pope, from election he will be mocked, sudden abrupt affected prompt and timid: through too much goodness and kindness provoked to die, fear extinguished, the night of his death guides.**" Elected to Pope (symbolizing Christian rebels governing Italy), from the election he will be mocked by retaliating Moslems. Sudden, abrupt Moslem retaliation affected against the prompt and timid rebels: Through too much goodness and kindness of tricky Moslems. Provoked to die from French rebellions, then Moslem fear extinguished, the night of his death (retreating) guides Moslem return.

13. "**Beneath the food of ruminating animals, led from them from the market place of the fodder city: Soldiers hidden, their weapons making a noise, Tried not far from the city of Antibes.**" Beneath the food of ruminating animals indicating a hay wagon. Led away from the French rebels, from the market place of the fodder (Latinized) city (Greek) or Moslem city in Italy: Moslem soldiers hidden, their weapons making a noise earlier. Tried not far from the city of Antibes (Easterly in France, symbolizing a Moslem city in Italy).

14. "**Urnel Vaucile without a purpose of his own. Bold, timid, through fear captured, conquered: Accompanied by several pale whores, from the Carthusian convent at Barcelona convinced.**" Urgel (Irratum) valley (Old French) indicating Moslem instigating French without a purpose of their own. Bold rebelling in Italy because timid Christians through fear were captured and conquered: Escorted away by several pale whores (Old French) indicating Frenchmen (three being Moslem religion like three end time Protestant ages). From the Carthusian convent at Barcelona (Easterly, Moslem owned), convinced.

15.   "**Father duke old in years and choked by thirst, on the last day denying the son the jug: Into the well living he will come, plunged lifeless, Senate to the edge, death in the end and trifling.**" Father (Moslem ruler in Italy) old in years and choked by thirst (according to instigated French rebels). On the last day denying his Christian ally, the jug of wine (symbolizing fruit of his labors): Into the well living he will come plunged lifeless, Senate (Moslem governors) to the edge witnessing it, death in the end and trifling.

16.   "**Happy in the realm with France, happy in life, ignorant of blood, death, fury and plunder: From a flattering name will be envied, King concealed, too much faith in the kitchen.**" Happy in the realm of Italy with France as his partner, happy in life as elected ruler. Ignorant of blood, death, fury and plunder to convert Christians to Islam: From a flattering (variant) name the Moslem rule will be envied by the French people, Concealed in a robe, too much faith in the kitchen making Moslems fat.

17.   "**The Queen foreign (variant) seeing her daughter pale: Because of a sorrow locked up in her breast: Lamentable cries will come then from Angouleme, and to the first cousin, marriage impeded.**" The queen (France, like Marie-Antoinette) foreign (variant) to the Moslems, will see her daughter (French in Italian possessions) pale, Because of a sorrow locked up in her breast from misfortunes suffered by France: Lamentable cries will come then from Angouleme (West near Bordeaux indicating French Italian possessions). And to the first cousin (Moslems), marriage (lasting friendship) impeded.

18.   "**The House of Lorraine will make way for Vendome, the high put low, and the low put high: The son of Mammon will be elected in Rome. And the two great ones will be put at default.**" The House of Lorraine (Easterly Moslems) making way for Vendome (westerly French, like Henry IV). The high (Moslems) put low, and the low (French) put high: The son (Moslems) of Hamon (variant indicating Suleiman I) will be elected to govern in Rome (Italy), and the two great ones (French and Moslem) will be put in default after French rebellions.

19.   "**The day that is by the Queen saluted. The day after the benediction the prayer: The reckoning is right and valid, formerly humble never was one so proud.**" The day of French rebel triumph which is by the queen (France, like Elizabeth succeeding bloody Mary) saluted. The day after this victory the benediction and the prayer of Christianity once again dominates in Italy, rebels having ousted the Moslems: The reckoning of the French rebels is right and valid, formerly humble France never was so proud.

20.   "**All the friends who will have belonged to the party. On account of the rude in letters put to death and plundered: Property published at fixed price the great one annihilated. Never were the Roman people so wronged.**" All the friends (French) who will have belonged to the party (alliance). On account of the rude letters sent by instigators, put to death and plundered the Moslems: Property of Moslems published at a fixed price after

the great one (French rebels) annihilated (Old French) them, never were the Roman people (French in Italy) so wronged before.

21. **"Through the spite of the King supporting the lesser one. He will be murdered presenting the jewels to him: The father wishing to appear with nobility to the son does as the Magi did of yore from Persia."** Through the spite for the Moslem king supporting the lesser one (French in Italy). He will be murdered presenting the jewels to the French rebels as their booty after rebellions: The (Moslem) father wishing to appear with nobility to the son or rebel victors, does as the Magi did of yore from Persia, presenting Christ with gifts.

22. **"For not wishing to consent with the divorce, which then afterwards will be recognized as unworthy: The King of the Isles will be driven out by force, with one put in his place who will have no mark of king."** For not wishing to consent with the divorce of Christians converting to Islam, which then afterwards will be recognized as unworthy by the remaining French Christians. The Moslem king of the Isles (Italian lands) will be driven out by force of rebellions, with one put in his place (French rebels) who will have no mark of king.

Extra parallel: For not wishing to consent with the divorce of Mrs. Simpson, which then afterwards marrying King Edward VIII will be recognized as unworthy. The king of the British Isles will be driven out by force of public opinion, with George VI put in his place, who will have no mark of king, abandoning British rule in India during his reign.

23. **"To the ungrateful people the remonstrances made. Thereupon the army will seize Antibes: From the arch of Monaco the complaints will occur. And at Frejus the one will take the shore from the other."** To the ungrateful Moslems (after French spies helped the earlier) the objections made about Moslems converting Christians. Thereupon the army (French rebels) will seize Antibes (Easterly symbolizing a Moslem city in Italy): From the arch of Monaco (Easterly Moslem) the complaints will be placed by rebellions. And at Frejus (Easterly) rebels will take the shore from Moslems.

24. **"The captive prince conquered from Italy will pass Genoa by sea as far as Marseilles: Through great exertion the foreigners overcome, safe from gunshot, barrel of bee's liquor."** The captive Moslem prince conquered by French rebellion in Italy will pass Genoa by sea as far as Marseilles retaking eastern France (Symbolizing Italian possessions lost earlier): Through great exertion by Moslems, the foreigners (Old French) or French rebels are overcome, Moslems being safe from gunshot through tricky strategy, barrel of bee's honey symbolizing conquest like booty.

Extra Parrallel: The captive, Napoleon I, conquered and sent to Elbe, from Italy will pass Genoa by sea as far as Marseilles to retake the throne: Through great exertion the foreigners, Great Britain, Prussia, Austria, and Russia are overcome for 100 days, Napoleon's new army safe from gunshot due to his expertise, barrel of bees honey indicates his short victory.

25. **"Through the Ebro to open the passage of Bezanes, very far away will the Tagus make a demonstration through Pelligouxe will the outrage be committed, with the great lady seated in the orchestra."** Through the Ebro (French with Spanish credentials) to open the passage of Bezanes (Old Spanish invasion route into France). Very far away in Italy will the Tagus (French) make a rebellion demonstration: Through Pollux (rebels) will the outrage be committed. With the great lady (France like Leda, Moslem Jupiter's wife), seated in the orchestra watching the stage play.

26. **"The successor will avenge his handsome brother. To occupy the realm under the shadow of vengeance: Slain obstacle his blood dead, blame for a long time will Brittany hold with France."** The successor (French rebels) will avenge his handsome brother (Christians who were seduced into conversion to Islam). To occupy the Italian realm completely through rebellions against the Moslems under the shadow of vengeance: Slain obstacle to continued friendship, his Christian blood, dead through conversion, blame for a long time will Brittany (French rebels) hold along with France.

27. **"From the fifth one and a great Hercules coming to open the temple by hand of war: One set back Clement, Julius and Ascanius. The sword, key, eagle, never was there such great animosity."** From the fifth (France during grace) and a great Hercules (French rebels) Coming to open the temple (Italy) by hand of war: One (rebels) set back Clement, Julius, and Ascanius (Clement VII symbolizing French and Moslem alliance like Catholics with Protestants of three ages), the Moslem sword, French spy key, empire eagle, never was there such great animosity.

Extra Interpretation

27. From Charles V and a great Hercules (Constable Duke of Bourbon, a renegade French prince commanding an Imperial army of Lutheran Germans): Coming to open the temple, sacking Rome by hand of war: One (Constable) set back Clement, Julius, and Ascanius (Pope Clement VII). The sword of war. Catholic Key and Habsburg eagle, never was there such great animosity.

28. **"Second and third which make prime music through the King being sublimated in honor: Through the fat and the thin nearly half emaciated. Report of Venus false, yield dejected."** Second (Moslem and French allied capture of Italy) and third (Moslems like Protestants from three ages) which make prime music through the Moslem king being sublimated in honor, elected to govern shared Italy: Through the fat (Moslems) and thin nearly half emaciated (French), report from Venus (Italy) about French rebellions false. France yielded dejected, having been tricked.

29. **"From Saint-Paul-de-Mausole in a goats cave hidden and seized pulled out by the beard: Led captive like a mastiff beast by, the Bigorre**

people brought to near Tarbes." From Saint-Paul-de-Mausole (located by the Rhone indicating the shared Italian lands) in a goat's cave the humble Moslems hidden in his home and seized by the French rebels, pulled out by the beard: Led captive like a mastiff beast by the Bigorre people (Westerly French district indicating French rebels) brought to near Tarbes, the chief city there.

30. **"Nephew and blood of the Saint newly created, through the surname will sustain the arches and roof: They will be driven out put to death chased nude, into red and black converting their green."** Nephew (Moslems) and blood (French spies) of the Saint (France) newly created by alliance, through the surname (Christianity) will sustain arches and roof indicating France's portion of Italy: Habsburgs will be driven out, put to death, chased nude in defeat. Into red (French Christianity formerly in Spanish disguise) and Moslem black converting their green (unsaved in Italy).

31. **"The Holy Empire will come into Germany, the Ishmaelites will find places open: The asses will want also Caraman. The supporters all covered by earth."** The Holy Empire (Habsburgs living in Italy) will come retreating into Germany, the Ishmaelites (Moslems) will find places open to them because of allied French spies confusing the Habsburg enemy: The asses (greedy Moslem) will then want Caraman (westerly in France symbolizing France's share of captured Italy). The French supporters all covered by earth from Moslem trickery.

32. **"The great empire, everyone would have, one over the others will come to obtain it: But of short duration will be his realm and existence. Two years in his ships he will be able to maintain himself."** The great empire (Italy), everyone would have, first France and later Habsburgs. One (Moslems allied secretly to France) will come to obtain it: But of short duration will be his realm and existence because of French rebellions. Two years of sharing Italy with the French, then on the sea Moslems will be able to maintain themselves escaping.

33. **"The cruel faction in the long robe coming to hide beneath the sharp daggers: To seize Florence the duke and two tongue place. Its discovery by immature ones and flatterers."** The cruel faction of French rebels in the long robes coming to hide beneath their robes the sharp daggers: To seize Florence (Italy), the Moslem duke, and two tongue place (Italy shared by Moslems and French), its discovery of Italy under just French ownership, made by immature French living there, and Moslem flatterers who instigate the rebellions.

34. **"The Gaul who will hold the empire through war, by his younger brother-in-law will be betrayed: By a fierce, prancing horse, he will be drawn. For the deed the brother for a long time will be hated."** The Gaul (France) who will hold the empire (shared Italy) through war against the Habsburgs. By his younger brother-in-law (Moslem partner), will be betrayed into losing his Italian lands: By a fierce, prancing horse of French rebellions, Moslems will be drawn to retaliate. For the deed the brother-in-law or Moslems for a long time will be hated.

Extra Interpretation: The Gaul (Napoleon Bonaparte) who will hold the empire through war, by his younger brother-in-law (Joachim Murat, King of Naples who married Caroline, Napoleon's younger sister) will be betrayed: By fierce prancing horse indicating revolutionary armies, Joachim will be drawn as leader, for the deed the brother Joachim for a long time will be hated by Napoleon.

35. **"The younger brother of the king flagrant in burning lust to enjoy his first cousin: Female attire in the Temple of Artemis, going to be murdered by the unknown one of Maine."** The younger brother (Moslems sharing Italy) of the king (France) flagrant in burning lust to own all of Italy. To enjoy France's first cousin (French citizens in Italy) by instigating rebellions: Female attire (French rebels) in the Temple of Artemis (Greek, symbolizing Moslem temples). Moslems going to be murdered by the unknown one of Maine (Christian rebels).

36. **"After the King from the stump speaking of wars, the Isle joined together, will hold him in contempt: Some good years gnawing first and pillaging, through tyranny in the isle esteem changing."** After the king (France), from the stump (Italy, growing a new French tree) will speak of wars by French rebellions: The Isle (Italy), joined together by Moslem retaliation (that ousted the French), will hold him in contempt: Some years French rebels gnawing first and then pillaging, through tyranny in the isle (Italy), French esteem (Old French) changing.

37. **"The great assembly near the Lake of Bourget. They will meet near Montmelian: Going beyond the thoughtful ones will draw up a plan, Chambery, Saint-Jean-de-Maurienne, combat Saint-Julien."** The great assembly (French rebels) near the Lake of Bourget (symbolizing the border areas in shared Italy, rallying first near Montmelian (symbolizing deeper inside French areas): Going beyond in reverse direction the thoughtful Moslems in retaliation will draw up a plan, capture of Chambery and Saint-Jean-de-Maurienne (French parts of Italy) for rebels attacking at Saint-Julien (Moslem possessions).

Extra Interpretation: The great assembly under the Duke of Savoy near the Lake of Bourget on the path to invade France, rallying beforehand near Montmelian: Going beyond Montmelian in counter attack, the thoughtful ones (Henry IV of France and his army) will draw up a plan, capture of Chambery and Saint-Jean-de-Maurienne in Savoy in repayment for their attack on Saint-Julien.

38. **"Cheerful love not distant laying the siege, with the saint the barbarian is at the garrisons: The Orsini and Adria will provide a guarantee for the Gauls, for fear delivered by the army of the Grisons."** Cheerful love (allied French spies) not distant, laying the siege, with the saint (Habsburgs) the barbarian (Moslems) is at the garrisons: The Orsini (who favored France, symbolizing French spies) and Adria (east in Italy symbolizing

Moslems) through alliance will provide a guarantee for the Gauls (France). For fear delivered by the army of the Grisons (symbolizing Habsburgs).

39. **"First dues, widow, unfortunate marriage, without any children two Isles in discord: Before eighteen, incompetent age. For the other one, the accord will take place while younger."** First clues the widow (France) unfortunate in marriage (alliance partnership). Without any children (French citizens in Italy) after two Isles (French and Moslem areas in Italy) in discord: Before Dax and Houat (west in France, symbolizing French rebels in Italy) at incompetent age (not thinking clearly), with the other one (Moslems) near, very low is the accord.

40. **"The young heir to the realm of Brittanny, whom his dying father will have recommended: The latter dead, the destroyed will give dispute. And from his son the realm demanded."** The young heir (French citizens) in the Italian realm owned by Brittany (France). Whom his dying father (France, suffering the defeat from Habsburgs, before) will have recommended. The latter (France) dead from that earlier defeat, the Moslems, destroyed later by French rebellions, will give dispute by retaliating, and from his son (French rebels), the Italian realm demanded."

Extra Interpretation: The young heir (Edward VIII) to the British realm, whom his dying father (George V) will have recommended to the throne: The latter (George V) dead. London will give dispute with Edward VIII about his behavior with Mrs. Simpson through public hostility towards her earlier divorce. And from the son (Edward VIII) the realm will be demanded causing his abdication to his brother.

Extra Interpretation: The young heir (James I) to the British realm of Scotland whom his dying father (James VI) will have recommended to the throne: The latter (James VI) dead, Ole Nol (Phonetic pronunciation of Cromwell's nickname) usurping will give dispute, seducing the English people through cunning speeches, and from the son (James I) the realm demanded as he loses his crown and life.

41. **"On the boundary of Gaussade and Caylus. Not at all far from the bottom of the valley: Music from Villefranche to the sound of lutes, Surrounded by cymbals and great stringing."** On the boundary of Causade (symbolizing the Moslem possessions in Italy) and Caylus (French possessions). Not at all far from the bottom of the valley where the Lere River, symbolizing their allied friendship: Music from Villefranche (another French possession in Italy) to the sound of lutes, Surrounded by cymbals (Greek) and great stringing (Greek) indicating Moslem instigators.

42. **"The humane realm of Anglican offspring. Will cause its realm to hold to peace and union: Captive, war, half from its enclosure. For a long time will cause them to maintain the peace."** The humane Italian realm of Angelique (French) offspring will cause its realm of shared Italian lands to hold to peace and union: Captive war (indicating termination of war after defeat of Habsburgs) half from its enclosure (French holdings of shared Italy), for a long time will cause them to maintain the peace next to their Moslem ally.

43. "Too much good times, too much of royal goodness, made and unmade, quick, sudden, neglectful: Lightly will he believe falsely of his loyal wife. He is put to death through his benevolence." Too much good times, too much royal goodness by France made and unmade the Italian realm, quick, sudden French rebellions, France neglectful in controlling its affairs of state: Lightly will France believe falsely or his loyal wife (French in Italy) causing rebellions. France is put to death (losing Italian lands) through his benevolence towards the vengeful Moslems.

Extra Interpretation: Too much good times, too much of royal goodness by Louis XVI Made and unmade is his reign by the quick and sudden revolution because he was neglectful: Lightly will he believe falsely of his loyal wife, putting faith in calamitous reports about her. Louis XVI is put to death through his benevolence making him defenseless before his enemies.

44. "From it being so that a King will be against his people. A native of Blois will subjugate the Ligurians, Memel and Cordoba both the Dalmatians. For seven following the shadow of the King, Christened and broke." From it being so that a Moslem king will be against his people. A native of Blois (French rebels) will subjugate the Ligurians (Italy). Memel (On the Baltic symbolizing French rebels with Habsburg credentials) and Cordoba (rebels carrying Spanish credentials) both the Dalmatians (Italy) for seven (France), following the shadow of the Moslem king, christened and broke.

45. "The shadow of the realm of Navarre untrue. It will make his life one of fate unlawful: The vow made in Cambrai wavering. King Orleans will give a lawful wall." The shadow of total ownership of the Italian realm by Navarre (France), through rebellions in Italy, untrue. It will make France's life, expanding in Italy, one of illegitimate fate: The vow of sharing Italy with Moslems, made in Cambrai (France) wavering from the rebellions, King Orleans (France) will give a lawful wall or boundary supporting the rebels.

46. "Life, fate, and death from the gold, villainous one unworthy. Is not at Saxony the new Elector: At Brunswick he will send a sign of love. The false one, seductive, delivering it to the people." Life through rebellions, destiny becomes death from gold supposedly stolen from Moslems, the villainous one (France) unworthy. Is at Saxony (French lands in shared Italy, French formerly spies carrying Saxony credentials) not the new elector: At Brunswick Moslems will send a sign of love. The false one, seductive, delivering it to the people before Christian persecution begins.

47. "From the town of Burgos to the Garland lady, they will impose a verdict over the treason committed: The great prelate of Leon through Formande, defeated the false pilgrims and ravishers." From the town of Burgos (westerly in Spain, symbolizing French in Italy) to the Garland lady (decorated cathedral symbolizing Christianity), the Moslems will impose a verdict over the treason committed by French rebellions in Italy: The great prelate of Leon (westerly, symbolizing France) through Formande (east, symbolizing biased Moslems). The false pilgrims (Christianity) and ravishers (rebels) defeated.

48. **"From the deepest part of Spain, banners. Coming out from the tip and ends of Europe: Troubles passing near from the bridge of Laignes, its great army will be routed by a band."** From the deepest, most fortified part of Spain (symbolizing in Italy ruled by Spanish Habsburgs), Moslem banners, coming out from the tip and ends of Europe attacking: Troubles for Habsburg defenders passing near, from the bridge (symbolizing French spies) of Laignes (bordering Spain, symbolizing Italian borders). Its great Habsburg army will be routed by a Moslem band.

Extra Interpretation: From the deepest part of Spain, the German Italian, and Russian banners coming from the tip and ends of Europe during the Spanish revolution: Troubles passing near in Spain, from the bridge (alliance) of Laignes (Spanish nationalist rebels), Spain's great army will be routed by a band under Franco out of Morocco with German and Italian help.

49. **"Garden of the world near the new city. In the path of the hollow mountains: It will be seized and plunged into the Tub. Forced to drink waters poisoned by sulfur."** Garden of the world (lava-enriched, fertile campanian plain) near the new city (Naples). In the path of the hollow mountains (vulcanoes symbolizing allied French and Moslems): Italy will be siezed by the Moslem attackers and Habsburg defenders will be plunged into the cystern by French spies. And forced to drink waters poisoned by sulfur of allied vulcanoes.

50. **"The Meuse by day in the land of Luxemburg, will find Saturn and three in the urn: Mountain and plain, town, city and borough. Flood in Lorraine, betrayed in the great urn."** The Meuse River (aligned with the Rhone indicating allied French and Moslems) by day in the land of Luxemburg (Habsburg Italy), uncovering Saturn (France) and three (Moslems) in the urn (Italy, formerly possessed by each): Mountain and plain, town, city and borough from Lorraine flooded (easterly, Moslem attack), and betrayed by French spies in the great urn.

51. **"The lowest places of the land of Lorraine will be united with the Low Germans: Through those by siege Picards, Normans, those of Maine, and will be reunited to the cantons."** The lowest places (made vulnerable to attack) through the land of Lorraine (France, symbolizing French spies) will, by Habsburgs retreating, be united with the low Germans: Through those Moslems by siege, Picards, Normans, those of Maine (French cities symbolizing allied Moslems besides Protestants of three church ages). And Habsburgs retreating will be united to the Swiss Cantons.

Extra Interpretation: The lowest places (vulnerable to flooding or attack) of the land of Lorraine (France) will be united (after French defeat) with the

Low Germans bordering them: Through those Picards, Normans, those of Maine concenting to French defeat from the German siege of Paris in 1871. And it will be reunited to the Habsburg-owned cantons of Switzerland.

52.   "At the place where the Lys and the Scheldt unite. The marriage will be directed for a long time: At the place in Antwerp where the siftings will proceed, Young old age wife undefiled." At the place (Ghent symbolizing Haspsburg Italy) where the Lye (French) and the Scheldt (Moslems) unite. The marriage (alliance) will be directed for a long time: At the place in Antwerp (easterly Moslems) where the siftings (Old French) will proceed (Old French) with French captives released. Young turns to old age with wife (Old French) France undefiled.

53.   "The three concubines will fight each other for a long time, the greatest one the least will remain to listen: The great Selin no longer her patron. Will call him fire shield, white route." The three concubines (Moslems like end time Protestants of three ages) will quarrel with each other for a long time, the greatest concubine being the least will stay in Italy to listen to him (complaining French): The great Selin (Suleiman I), no longer patron (governing) after French rebellions. will call him fire and shield retaliating with white (French) route.

54.   "Born in this world of a furtive concubine, for two raised high from the sad news: Among enemies will be taken captive. And brought to Malines and Brussels." Born in this world (Italy) through a furtive concubine (least of the Moslems), for two concubines who left, Moslems raised high in spirit from the sad news after French rebellions: Among rebel enemies, Moslems will be taken captive, and brought to Malines and Brussels (Habsburg cities symbolizing French. once being spies with Habsburg credentials, controling all Italy).

55.   "The unfortunate nuptials will celebrate in great joy but the end unhappy: Husband and mother will slight the daughter-in-law. The Apollo dead and the daughter-in-law more pitiful." The unfortunate nuptials (French and Moslems) will celebrate alliance. In great Joy later with Habsburgs defeated, but the end unhappy: Husband (French rebels) and Mother (France) will slight the daughter-in-law (Old French) or Moslems who share Italy with France. The Apollo (Moslems governors) dead and the Daughter-in-law (Old French) Moslems remaining, more pitiful under French rebel rule.

Extra Interpretation: The unfortunate nuptials, Francis II and Mary Stuart) will celebrate in great joy first with their marriage and then after Francis II becomes king, but the end unhappy. Mary with Francis II dying after two years of marriage and mother (Catherine de Medici) will slight the daughter-in-law (Mary), calling her a merchant's daughter, the Phi II (Francis II) dead and the daughter-in-law more pitiful.

56. **"The royal prelate his bowing too low, a great flow of blood will come out of his mouth: The Anglican realm by a realm pulled out of danger. For long dead life with Tunis like a stump."** The royal prelate (Moslems governing Italy) his bowing too low, by sharing Italian lands, a great flow of blood will come out of his mouth as French rebellions beheaded him: The Angelican (variant) shared realm by a French rebel realm pulled out of danger, for long dead and now life with Tunis (Moslems) becoming like a stump.

57. **"The revolting one will not know his sceptre, the young children of the greatest ones disgracing: Never was there a more filthy and cruel being, for their wives to death the King will banish."** The revolting one (France) will not know the Moslem sceptre before ruling in Italy, the young children of the Moslem greatest ones disgracing to the new French rebel government: Never was there a more filthy (Old French) and cruel being as French rebels, for their Moslem wives, to death the Moslem (black) king the rebels will banish.

58. **"In the time of mourning when the feline monarch will make war, the young Macedonian: To shake Gaul, the bark to be in Jeopardy, Marseilles to be tried in the West a talk."** In the time of mourning over Moslem losses due to French rebellions, when the feline (catlike) Moslem monarch will make war in retaliation, the young Macedonian (Moslems who temporarily retreated from the rebels): To shake Gaul (France), the bark (French Christians in Italy) to be in jeopardy, Moslems to try Marseilles (France), in the west peace talk.

Extra Interpretation: In the time of mourning, the death of Louis XIII when the feline monarch (Philip IV of Spain) will make war, the young Aemathien (Louis XIV) and Gaul (France) to shake in civil war (the fronde) the bark (Christianity) in Rome from nascent Jansenism, to be in jeopardy. Marseilles breached by Louis XIV, to be tried, returns to allegiance, in the west in France at the Isle of the Conference, a talk concluding the Peace of the Pyrenees with Philip IV.

59. **"Within Lyon twenty-five of one mind, five citizens, Germans, Bressans, Latins: Above a noble one leading a long train, and discovered by barks of mastiffs."** Within Lyon (on the Rhone symbolizing shared Italy) twenty-five (French and Moslems in friendship) of one mind, five (grace) friendly citizens, Germans, Bressans (France), Ladins (SE Switzerland), symbolizing Moslems (three cities) and French who before had used various credentials: Above governing, a Moslem noble one leading a long train, and discovered by barks of mastiffs (Moslem instigators).

60. **"I weep for Nice, Monaco, Pisa, Genoa, Savona, Siena, Capua, Modena, Malta: For the top blood and sword for New Year's gifts, fire. The earth to tremble, water, unhappy reluctance."** I weep for Nice, Monaco, Pisa, Genoa, Savona, Siena, Capua, Modena, Malta, representing

Italy shared by the victorious French and Moslems: For the top (Moslems who are elected to govern the captured possessions) blood and sword of French rebellions for New Year's gifts, fire, the earth to tremble, tears shed as the Moslems with unhappy reluctance retreat.

61. **"Guadalquivir, Vienna, Mirida, Sopron, will want to deliver Hungary from the Barbarians: Through pike and fire, enormous violence, the conspirators discovered by a matron."** Guadalquivir (Spain), Vienna (Austria), Merida (Spain), and Sopron (Hungary but possessed by Habsburgs) all symbolizing French in Italy who were once spies carrying Habsburg credentials, will want to deliver Hungary (Moslems in Italy) to the Barbarians (French rebels): Through pike and fire enormous violence of rebellions, the French rebel conspirators discovered by a matron (Moslems governing Italy).

62. **"Near from Saxony to assail Hungary, the herald from Buda coming to warn them: Byzantine chief, Salona of Slavonia, to the law of the Arabs will come to convert them."** Near from Saxony (westerly indicating French owned Italian lands) French rebels to assail Hungary (easterly indicating Moslem possessions in Italy). The herald (Moslem instigator) from Budapest (farther east symbolizing Moslem origins) coming to warn them of rebellions: Byzantine chief, Salona (Suleiman I) of Slavonia (easterly). To the law of the Arabs will come to convert them in retaliation.

63. **"Cydonia, Ragusa, the city of St. Jerome, will grow green again with healing help: The king's son dead because of the death of two heroes, Him Araby and Hungary will take the same course."** Cydonia (Crete), Ragusa (Dubrovnic in Dalmatia), the city of St. Jerome (Aquillia in Italy) indicate Moslems will grow green again with healing help from Moslem reinforcements: The king's (Francis I) son, French rebels, dead (defeated) because of the death of two heroes (French and Moslem friendship), Him, Araby and Hungary (Moslems) will take on the same course in retaliation.

64. **"Weep Milan, weep Lucca and Florence, as your great Duke climbs into the chariot: To change the see, near from Venice he advances, when Colonna at Rome will change."** Weep Milan, weep Lucca and Florence (westerly in Italy, symbolizing French possessions under restored Moslem rule), as your great Duke (Moslem governor) climbs into the chariot for further retaliating: To change the see (Christian church), near from Venice (easterly Moslem stronghold) he advances, when Colonna (Italian family protecting Christianity symbolizing French citizens) at Rome (Italy) will change.

65. **"O vast Rome, thy ruin approaches. Not of thy walls, of thy blood and substance: The harsh one through letters will make a horrible notch, pointed steel driven into all up to the hilt."** Oh, vast Rome, under French rebels, thy ruin approaches! Not of thy walls as Moslems reclaim possessions, but of thy blood and substance with retaliation after French rebellions: The harsh Moslems, through letters of new laws, will make a horrible notch gaining advantage. Pointed steel driven into all up to the hilt as they murder any objectors.

66. **"The chief of Landes through the realm of Merignac, the Isle of Corsica will be tried by frost: King and Reb will face an Antichrist so false. That he will place them in the conflict all together."** The chief of Landes (Francis I) through the Italian realm taken over by Merignac (French rebels), the Isle of Corsica (symbolizing Italy) tried by frost (rebellions): King (Francis I) and rebel will face a very false Antichrist (Moslems like end time Protestant churches against the Catholic Church) who will place them in the conflict together (Old French) as for blame.

67. **"A very mighty trembling in the month of May, Saturn in Capricorn, Jupiter, and Mercury in Taurus: Venus also, Cancer, Mars in Virgo, then hail will fall larger than an egg."** Trembling very great in the month of May (Like fifth age reformation) Saturn (France) Capricorn (tenth sign, independent), Jupiter (Moslems) and Mercury (French in Italy) Taurus (second sign, together): Venus (Italy) also, Cancer (forth sign, France like Catholic Church from four ages), Mars (war) from Virgo (French rebels), falling hail (Moslem retaliation) then larger than an egg.

68. **"The army of the sea will stand before the city, then will leave without making a long passage: A great flock of citizens with land seized, Fleet to return to seize, great robbery."** The Moslem army of the sea will stand before the city (Italy) governing French and Moslem possessions, then will leave, after French rebellions, without making a long passage: A great flock (Old French) of French citizens with Italian land siezed, Moslem fleet to return to seize back Italy in retaliation for great robbery (Old French) from rebellions.

69. **"The shining deed of the new old one exalted, will be very great through the South and Aquilon: By his own sister great crowds raised, fleeing, murdered in the thicket of Belledonne."** The shining deed of the new old one (French who returned) exalted through rebellions, will be very great through South and North in Italy: By the Moslem own sister (French partner) great crowds (Old French) of French rebels raised against Moslems, Fleeing, murdered in the thicket of Belledonne (east of the Rhone indicating Moslem possessions in Italy).

70. **"The eye from an object will swell such a one, burning both so much until he will fall in the snow: The fields sprinkled, will come to melt. When the primate will succumb at Reggio."** The eye, from an object striking the Moslems during rebellions, will swell such a one, Burning both eyes so much, until he will fall in the snow: The fields sprinkled by snow will come to melt. When the primate (highest ranking Moslem government) will succumb at Reggio (Italy) as they tried to flee from the French rebels.

71. **"The earth and air will freeze a very great sea, when they will come to venerate for Thursday: That which will be never being so fair, from the four parts coming to honor them."** The earth and air (French rebels as when cold weather blows down) will freeze a very great sea, (Moslems in Italy), when rebels will come to venerate for Thursday (fifth, day of grace): Success which will be never, being so fair now, from four parts (France like end time Catholic Church from four ages) coming to honor them.

72. **"The year 1999, seventh month, from the sky will come a great King of Terror: To bring back to life the great King of the Mongols, before and after Mars to reign by good luck."** The year 1999 (indicating allied sharing of Italy) and seventh mouth (indicating after French rebels take over Italy), from the sky, as by divine judgment, will come a great king of terror (Moslems retaliating): To revive the great King of the Mongols (Moslems in Italy), before and after Mars of rebellions, to reign again by good luck.

73. **"The present time with the past will be judged by the great Jovialist: The world late will be tired of him. And disloyal through the oath taking clergy."** The present time (after retaliation against French rebellions) with the past (while sharing Italy with the French) will be judged by the great Jovialist (Moslems) who begin pursecuting the Christians: The world (French living in Italy) late, being tired of the Moslems sharing in Italian lands, and disloyal through the oathtaking Christian clergy causing the French rebellions.

74. **"The year accomplished with the great seventh number, will appear at the time of the games of slaughter: Not far from the great millennial age, when the entered will go out from their tombs."** The year accomplished with the great seventh number (France like end time Catholic Church from seven ages). Appearing allied at the time of the games of slaughter, recapturing Italy: Not far from the great millennial (alone) age (defeated in Italy earlier by the Habsburgs), when the entered (French buried by former defeat) will go out from their tombs.

75. **"Long awaited never returning, in Europe, and in Asia he will appear: One of the league born from the great Hermes, and towards all the Kings of the East will increase."** Long awaited French never returning to Italy after Habsburgs defeated France, in Europe and in Asia the allied French and Moslems will appear sharing Italy after its recapture: One (French in Italy) of the allied league, born from the great Hermes (France), and towards all the kings of the East (Moslems) will increase the empire, sharing Italy.

76. **"The great Senate will ordain the triumph with one who afterwards will be vanquished, driven out For the adherents there will be at the sound of the trumpet put up for sale their possessions, enemies expelled."** The great Senate (French and Moslem alliance) will ordain the parade in Italy, with one (Habsburgs), who after the Moslem invasion, will be vanquished, driven out: For the French and Moslem adherents of the alliance at the sound of the trumpet capturing Italy, there will be properties for sale, Habsburg enemies expelled (Old French) with French help.

77. **"Thirty adherents of the order of Quirites Banished. Their possessions given their adversaries: All their benefits will be taken as**

misdeeds, fleet dispersed, delivered to the Corsairs." Thirty adherents (Moslem ally like end time Protestants from three church ages) of the order of citizens (variant indicating Moslems) in Italy banished by French rebellions, their possessions given to their French adversaries: All their benefits as an ally against the Habsburgs will be taken as misdeeds, Moslem fleet dispersed (Old French), delivered to the Corsairs (French pirates).

78.   **"Sudden joy to sudden sadness, occurring at Rome for the graces embraced: Grief, cries, tears, weeping, blood, excellent mirth, Contrary bands surprised and trussed up."** Sudden joy over the French and Moslem capture of Italy, changed to Sudden Moslem sadness after French rebellions, Occurring at Rome (Italy) in poor repayment for the graces friendly Moslems embraced: Grief, cries, tears, weeping, blood for the Moslem victims, excellent mirth for the French victors, contrary bands of rebellions surprised and trussed up the Moslem partner.

79.   **"The old roads will all be improved, one will proceed on them to similar Memphis suddenly escaped: The great Mercury of Hercules fleur-de-lys, Causing to tremble land, sea and country."** The old roads in Italy will all be improved for easy use, Moslems will proceed on them to similar (Greek) Moslem Memphis in Greece, suddenly escaped: The great Mercury (messenger god symbolizing French rebels) from Hercules fleur-de-lys (both symbolizing expanded condition of France), causing to tremble land, sea, and country in order to sieze all of Italy.

80.   **"In the realm the great one of the great realm reigning. Through force of arms the great gates of brass He will cause to open, the King and Duke joining. Fort demolished, ship to the bottom, day serene."** In the Italian realm the great one (allied French and Moslems) in the great (shared) Italian realm reining, through force of arms the great (shared) gates of brass French rebels will cause to open, the French king and Moslem duke joining protecting Italy, fort (variant) of Moslems demolished, ship to the bottom, day serene for French victors.

81.   **"A treasure placed in a temple by Hesperian citizens. By them withdrawn to a secret place: The temple to open the chains with starvelings. Retaken, ravished, a horrible prey in the midst."** A treasure of Moslem booty placed in a temple by Hesperian citizens (French rebels formerly spies using Spanish credentials), by them later withdrawn to a secret place (supposedly): The temple to open after Moslem retaliation, the chains with starvelings (French rebels) Retaken, looking ravished, a horrible prey in the midst where the treasure was supposed to be.

82.   **"Cries, weeping, tears will come with knives, seeming to flee, they will deliver a final attack, around the parks they will set up high platforms. The living pushed back and murdered instantly."** Cries, weeping, tears from the Moslems, will come with knives of French rebellions, Moslems seeming to flee, the French rebels will deliver to final attack, around the parks French rebels will set up high platforms surrounding the

unsuspecting Moslems there, the living (Moslems) pushed back and murdered instantly (Old French) by French rebels, indicating an easy victory.

83. **"The signal to battle will not be given, from the park being constrained from going out: The banner from around Ghent will be recognized, which will cause all his followers to be put to death."** The signal to do battle will not be given by the Moslems now surrounded, from the park being constrained by French rebels from going out: The banner from around Ghent (indicating French rebels, formerly spies with Spanish Neitherlands credentials) will be recognized, which will cause all of his Moslem followers to be put to death indicating defeat.

84. **"The artless girl so high, high, not low, the late return will make the grieved ones contented: The Reconciled One will not be without debates. From employing and losing all his time."** The artless girl (French rebels) so high through rebellions to obtain all of Italy, high Moslems not low in true defeat, however, the late return of Moslem reinforcements will make the grieved ones (Moslem victims) contented: The reconciled Moslem will not be without debates against the French, from employing and losing his time during rebellions against them.

85. **"The old tribune to the point of trembling will be pressed not to deliver the captive: The will, non-will, evil speaking timidly, for the legitimate to his friends to deliver."** The old tribune (Moslem governors of Italy) to the point of trembling (Latinized), will be pressed not to deliver the captive Moslem during French rebellions: The will (Old French) of the French in Italy being Non-will (Old French), evil Moslem instigators speaking timidly for the legitimate (French citizens in Italy) to his Moslem friends to deliver captive.

86. **"Like a griffin will come the King of Europe, accompanied by those of Aquilon: Of red and white ones leading a great troop, and going against the King of Babylon."** Like a griffin (bird of prey) will come the King of Europe (Francis I, supposedly), accompanied by those of Aquilon (French living in Italy, formerly spies with northerly Habsburg credentials). Of red ones (French formerly having Spanish credentials) and white ones (French), leading a great troop, and going against the King of Babylon (Moslems sharing Italy with them).

87. **"A Great King will come to take port near by Nice, the great empire from the death thus completed: In Antibes will he place his heifer, by sea the plunder all will vanish."** A great king (Francis I) will come to take port near by Nice, the great French empire from the death or defeat of Moslems, completed: In Antibes (easterly in France, symbolizing Moslem possessions in Italy) will Francis I place his heifer (French rebels), by sea the plunder against the Moslems, all of whom will vanish from Italy in defeat.

88. **"Feet and Horse at the second watch, will make an entry devastating all by sea: Within the port he will enter Marseilles, Tears, cries, and blood, never times so bitter."** Feet of soldiers and horse (French rebellion) at the second watch (during allied sharing of Italy), will make an entry devastating (variant) all the Moslems by sea: Within the port French rebels will enter Marseilles (on the Rhone symbolizing alliance) dishonoring agreement to share Italy, Tears, cries, and blood, never times so bitter for the Moslem partner.

89. **"From brick to marble the walls will be converted, seven and fifty peaceful years: Joy to mortals, the aqueduct renewed, Health, abundance of fruits, joy and mellifluous times."** From brick to more extravigant marble will the walls of France's enlarged empire be converted as they share Italy with the Moslems, seven (France like end time Catholic Church from seven ages) and fifty (grace) peaceful years with the Moslems: Joy to mortals, the aqueduct, indicating trade, with Italy renewed, health, abundance of fruits, joy and melifluous times.

90. **"A hundred times will the inhuman tyrant die, in his place put one learned and mild. The entire Senate will be under his hand. He being vexed by a rash scoundrel."** A hundred times (indicating broken alliance agreement) will the inhuman tyrant (Moslem rulers) die, indicating defeat from French rebellions, in his place running the Italian government, put one (French rebels), learned and mild, the entire Senate (Italian government) will be under his (French) hand through rebellions, the French being vexed by a rash scoundrel (their Moslem partner).

Extra Interpretation: A hundred times, from English abuses during his exile at St. Helena, will the inhuman tyrant (Napoleon) die, in his place put one (Louis XVIII), learned and mild, the entire Senate, giving him full support, will be under his hand, Louis XVIII being vexed by a rash scoundrel named Louvel who murdered Duke-de-Berry who was in line for the throne.

91. **"Roman clergy in the year 1609, at the beginning of the year will hold an election: Of one gray and black issued from Campania, Never was there one so wicked as he."** Roman clergy in the year 1609 (Catholic grace ended during Reformation, similar with France), at the beginning of the year for sharing Italy, will hold an election: Of alliance gray (French, Catholic during death from Satan riding the gray horse) and Black (Moslem) issued (elected) from Campania, westerly French, Never was there one so wicked as Moslems.

92. **"In front of his father the child will be killed. The father afterwards between ropes of rushes: The people of Geneva will be exerted, the chief lying in the middle like a log."** In front of his father (France) the child (French in Italy) will be killed in retaliation for rebellions. The father (France) afterwards between ropes and rushes being helpless: The people of Geneva (French rebels with Geneva credentials from former spy activity) having exerted themselves during rebellions, the chief (France) will lie in their midst like a log.

93. **"The new bark will conduct the voyages, there and near by, transfering the Empire: Beaucaire, Arles will retain the hostages, near,**

two columns found of Porphyry." The new bark (allied France, like the end time Catholic Church) will conduct voyages, there (spies in Italy) and nearby (spies in Spain and Austria), transfering the Italian Empire away from Habsburgs: Beaucaire and Arles on the Rhone, indicating the allies, retaining Habsburg hostages, near from them two columns, allied French spies, found of Porphyry (France's grave stone).

94.   **"From Nimes, from Arles and Vienne to scorn, not to obey the Hesperian edict: To the tormented in order to condemn the great one, Six escaped in seraphic garb."** From Nimes (symbolizing French in Italy) from Arles (east side of Rhone symbolizing Moslem instigators) and then later Vienne (French rebels only) to scorn, not to obey the Hesperian (French) edict of friendship: With the tormented (Old French) French in order to condemn the Moslem great one, Six (Moslem instigators working) later escaped in seraphic (Christian) garb.

95.   **"From the Spains will come a very powerful King, by land and sea subjugating the South: This evil will cause, lowering again for the crescent, clipping the wings of those of Friday."** From the Spains (including Spanish possessions in Europe), symbolizing French rebels who used Spanish credentials while spying against Habsburgs, will come a very powerful King (France), By land and sea subjugating the South (Italy): This evil of rebellions will cause lowering again for the crescent (moon symbolizing Moslems), clipping the wings of those of Friday (Moslem Sabbath).

96.   **"The Religion of the name of the seas will win out against the sect the sons attached to: Sect made stubborn and lamented will be afraid of two wounded by A and A."** The Moslem religion with the name of the seas (Arabian Gulf) will win out against the sect (allied sharing of Italy) the sons (French and Moslems) attached themselves to: Sect made stubborn by French rebellions and lamented by Moslems retreating, will be afraid of two sons wounded by A (Arab instigated rebels) and A (Arab reinforcements retaliating).

97.   **"Triemes full of captives of every age, good times for bad, the sweet for the bitter: Prey to the Barbarians hasty they will be too soon, anxious to see the plume wail in the wind."**
Triremes (of Moslems like end time Protestants of three ages) full of French captives of every age, good times for bad, the sweet for the bitter for the Moslems retaliating: Prey to the Moslem barbarians making religious converts, hasty French rebels will be too soon, anxious to see the plume (of smoke) wail in the wind during rebellions.

98.   **"For the merry maid the bright splendor will shine no longer, for long will she be without salt: With mercenaries, bullies, odious wolves. All confusion, monster universal."** For the merry maid (French rebels) the bright splender of initial success against their Moslem partner will shine no longer, for a long time being without salt (symbolizing wisdom) while the Moslems instigated the rebellions: With Moslem mercenary soldiers, bullies,

and odious wolves returning, all the French living in Italy in confusion, monster of Moslem retaliation universal.

99. **"The end of wolf, lion, ox and ass, timid deer they will be with mastiffs: No longer will the sweet manna fall upon them, more vigilance and watch from the mastiffs."** The end the Moslem wolf and lion prevail over French ox and ass, French in Italy like timid deer will be with mastiffs (Moslem guards) after the French rebellions are stopped: No longer will the sweet manna, prosperity in shared Italian lands, fall upon the French, more vigilance and watch from the mastiffs (Moslem guards) will begin.

100. **"The great empire will be for Angleterre, the all-powerful one for more than three hundred years: Great forces to pass by sea and land, the Lusitanians will not be satisfied thereby."** The great Italian Empire will be (taken) from Angleterre (France), the all-powerful (Greek) indicating Moslems possessing for more than (variant) three hundred years (symbolizing Moslem owned like end time temporarily victorious Protestants out of three ages): Great Moslem forces to pass by sea and land retaliating, the Portuguese (French, formerly spies imitating Habsburgs) will not be satisfied thereby.

Duplicate and Fragmentary Centuries

X 100. **"When the fork will be supported by two Pau's, with six Corps, half, and six Sceaux open: The very powerful Lord, heir of the toads, then will subject the entire world to himself."** Fork will be supported by two in Pau (westerly in France symbolizing French Italian possessions). With six of corps (east symbolizing Moslem instigators), half, and six of Sceaux (westerly symbolizing French) opened: The very powerful Moslem lord, heir of the toads (first Merovingian insignia symbolizing France) then will subject the entire world (Italy) to himself. (Work-6 of claiming conquered Italy with Moslems half hearted in order to have an occasion against French).

XI 91. **"Meysnier, Manthi and the third one that will come, plague and new affront, to trouble the enclosure: The fury will bite Aix and the places thereabout, then those of Marseilles will want to double their evil."** Meusnes and Manthelan (symbolizing French possessions in Italy with moissonneus—French harvester and Manteline—Moslem instigator) and the third (Moslem retaliation) that will come, plague and new affront, to trouble the enclosure (Italy): The fury will bite Aix (easterly Moslems) and the places thereabout, then those Moslems of Marseilles (easterly) will want to double their evil, retaliating.

97. **"By Villefranche, Macon in disorder, soldiers will be hidden in the bundles: To change the times of Spring for the King, in Chalon and Moulins all cut to pieces."** By Villefranche and Macon (on the Rhone indicating shared Italy), in disorder from French rebellions, Moslem Soldiers will be hidden in bundles: To change the times (Old French) of Spring (revival of French control) for the king (Francis I), in Chalon (on the Rhone) and

Moulins (westerly), indicating French rebels, all cut to pieces by the retaliating Moslems.

XII 4. **"Fire, flame, hunger, robber, wild smoke, will cause to fail, striking hard, to destroy faith: Arrow of Dente all Provence sucked in, Driven out of the realm, enraged blood to spurt."** Fire, flame, hunger when the French robber (Old French) with wild smoke of rebellions, will cause Moslem governed Italy to fail, striking hard to destroy the Moslem faith: Arrow (Old French) of Dante (symbolizing French rebellions) and all Provence (France) sucked in by Moslem trickery, driven out of the realm the enraged Moslems, without, to spurt blood.

24.   **"The great relief come from Guienne, will halt quite near Poitiers: Lyons surrendered through Montluel and Vienne, and tradesmen plundered everywhere."** The great relief (French army) come from Guienne (symbolizing France) will halt quite near Poitiers (in France) on their way to help the French rebels in Italy: Lyons (east on the Rhone) symbolizing Moslem owned Italian lands had already surrendered with Montluel and Vienne, too, and the Moslem tradesmen everywhere plundered by the supposedly successful French rebels.

36.   **"Ferocious attack being prepared in Cyprus, tear in the eye, for thy imminent ruin: Byzantine fleet moorish very great loss, Two different ones, the great devastation by the rock."** Ferocious attack by French rebels being prepared in Cyprus by Moslem instigators against their own possessions in Italy, tear in the eye indicating Moslem grief, for thy imminent ruin through rebellions: Byzantine fleet. Moorish with very great loss, for two different ones (French and Moslem allied sharing of Italy) the great devastation by the rock of rebellions.

52.   **"Two bodies, one head, fields divided in two, and then to reply to four unheard ones: Little for great, clear evil for them, lightning at the tower of Aiguesmortes, worse for Eussouis."** Two bodies (French and Moslem), one Moslem head, fields divided in two, and then to reply to four (France like end time Catholic Church revived from first four ages) unheard ones (not actually participating): Small (French) for great (Moslems), clear evil for Moslems, lightning at the tower of Aiguesmortes (France losing Italian possessions) worse for Essoyes (French rebels).

55.   **"Sad counsels, disloyal, cunning, wicked advice, the Law will be betrayed: The people stirred, wild, quarrelsome, in borough as in town, the entire peace hated."** Sad acting Moslem counsels because of French rebellions, counsels disloyal to their own Moslem faith using cunning trickery against their French partner living in Italy, wicked advice given, the allied Moslem Law will be betrayed by French rebels: The French citizens stirred, wild, quarrelsome, in borough as in town, the entire peace hated due to Moslem instigation.

56.   **"King against King and the Duke against Prince, Hatred between them, horrible dissension: Rage and fury throughout every province, in France great war and horrible change."** King Francis I against King

Suleiman I and French duke against Moslem prince while sharing Italian lands. Hatred between them, horrible dissension brought about by Moslem instigation using the differing religious beliefs: Rage and fury throughout every province, France (French rebels), great war of rebellions, and horrible change as the Moslems quickly retreat and rebels take over Italian government.

59.   **"The accord and peace will be broken everywhere: Friendships polluted by discord: Hatred awakened, all faith corrupted, and hope, Marseilles without concord."** The accord and peace (Old French) between French and Moslems will be broken everywhere throughout the shared Italian lands: Friendships at first established becoming polluted by discord: Hatred awakened by Moslem instigators, all the Christian faith and the hope for a lasting peace corrupted by Moslems seeking new converts. Marseilles (French in Italy) without concord begin their rebellions.

62.   **"Wars, debates, at Blois war and tumult, diverse watches, unexpected avowals: To enter into Chateau Trompete, affront, Chateau du Ha, those who will be to blame for it."** Wars, debates among the French concerning Christianity, at Blois (westerly in France symbolizing French possessions in Italy) war and tumult from Diverse watches or ministers overlooking the Christian faith, unexpected (Old French) avowals by French citizens converting to Islam: To enter into Chateau Trompete, affront to Christianity. Chateau du Ha, where those French converts will be worthy of blame.

65.   **"To hold the fort through fury restrained, every heart to tremble. At Langon a terrible arrival: The kick becomes a thousand kicks, Gironde, Garonne, never more horrible."** To hold the fort (Chateau Trompete) through fury restrained as long as possible, every French heart to tremble. At Langon (westerly in France, symbolizing a French possession in Italy), a terrible arrival of a French convert to Islam: The kick will become a thousand kicks to Christianity, Gironde, Garonne in their flooding never more horrible in comparison.

69. **"Savoy near to Lake of Geneve to avert, very great preparations, return, confusion: Far from the nephews of the late great super inhabitant, all of their following."** Savoy (French rebels) near Lake of Geneve (symbolizing other French Christians in Italy) to avert, very great preparations for rebellious, return unsuccessful, confusion among French citizens: Far from the nephews (France, who once possessed all of Italy until the Habsburgs defeated them), all of France's following on army.

71. **"Rivers, streams with evil will be obstacles. The old flame of anger unappeased: To run in France; this as if oracles. Houses, manors, palace, shaven sect."** Rivers, streams (Gironde and Garonne earlier described) with evil, as during floods, will be obstacles, symbolizing quarreling among French Christians in Italy. The old flame of anger concerning Moslem converts unappeased. To run in France (symbolizing French possessions in Italy), this as of oracles (Moslem instigators causing it), houses, manors, palace, shaven Christian sect, indicating shame.

Preface of M. Nostradamus
To His Prophecies

24.   And also that I find letters (written Word of God) will suffer a very great and incomparable loss (as less of truth is preached in churches). I find also that before the universal conflagration (total destruction when Jesus in His Word is fully revealed), the world will be deluged by many floods (prejudgments) to such heights that there will remain scarcely any land not covered by water, and this will last for so long that cultures and topographies will be put out that everything will not perish. Furthermore, before and after these inundations, in many countries the rains will have been so slight (droughts), and there will have fallen from the sky such a great abundance of fire, and of burning stones (prejudgments compared to Sodom and Gomorrah or maybe wartime bombings) that nothing will remain unconsumed. And this will occur a short time before the final conflagration.

25.   For although the planet Mars (symbolizing war) will finish its cycle, at the end of its last period, it will start again. Some will assemble in Aquarius (eleventh sign of the Zodiac, indicating just before the twelfth judgment hour) for several years, indicating the last three church ages in the Protestant Churches, others in Cancer (forth Zodiac sign, indicating the Catholic Church resurrected back to respect again in the end time as during their time of grace in the first four church ages) for an even longer time (extra time of emerging prior to judgment becomes final). By means of the supreme power of God, we are led by the Moon (the Moslem faith, which symbolizes the Protestant churches), before Mars of war has completed her entire circuit at the final conflagration, but first the Sun (Habsburgs, symbolizing the end time believer in the partial glory of God's Word partially revealed) will come and then Saturn (France symbolizing the revived Catholic Church) will try to lead the world. For according to the signs in the heavens, the reign of Saturn (Catholic

Church) will return, so that, all told (Protestant later takeover included), the world is drawing near an anarigonic (destruction-engendering) revolution, as predicted by Anaxagoras, due to sovereign mob (church) dominance.

26. From this moment before 1977 with Catholic Church dominance and after 1977 for three months and eleven days have passed (symbolizing Protestant dominance, Protestants from out of three end time church ages just at the eleventh hour before their twelfth or final judgment hour begins, by pestilence, long famine, wars, and most of all, floods, the world will be so diminished by these prejudgments, with so few remaining, that no one will be found willing to work the fields (of perverted religion) which will remain wild for as long a period as they had been tilled, indicating judgment upon the churches.

27. This according to the visible judgment (prophecy) from the stars, for although we are now in the seventh millenary since Adam, which finishes all at Christ's return through revelation of His Word, we are approaching the eighth (one thousand years where the saints return and rule through God's Word over the heathen who also return), wherein is located the firmament (higher realm of God's glory) of the eighth sphere (renewed earth). This is in the latitudinary (full extent) dimension of God's Word, whence the great eternal God will come to complete the revolution (mysteries revealed), and the heavenly bodies (saints) will return to their origins (truths of God), and the upper motion (rapturing into higher knowledge of God) will render the earth stable and fixed for us, not deviating from age to age as did former church ages during changes in doctrines.

28. How much which by ambiguous opinions beyond all natural reason (indicating interpretation), by Mahometan dreams (methods similar to the dream origins of the Koran) and even sometimes through the flaming missives (inspired written messages) brought by the angels of fire (describing the symbolic characteristics of the angels) of God the Creator, there come before exterior senses of man, even our eyes, predictions of future events or things significant to a future happening.

29. These ought to manifest themselves to one who presages (prophesies). For the presage (prophecy) which is made by the exterior light (supernatural inspiration) comes infallible to judge partly with it (God's Word brings judgment in part, and when fully revealed, brings full judgement) and by means of the exterior light (God's judgment). Truly, the part which seems to come by the eye of the understanding (without God's inspiration) comes only by the lesion of the imaginative sense (human reasonings, like the historical interpretations of these prophecies of Nostradamus).

30. The reason is very evident. All is predicted through divine inspiration, and by means of the angelic spirit with which the man prophesying is inspired, rendering him anointed with prophecies, illuminating him, moving him before his fantasy (imagination) through diverse nocturnal apparitions (visions) with astronomic calculation (comparing these visions with God's known truths)

certifying the prophecy in the daytime (when awake), there is nothing more to the holiest future prediction than free courage (just to believe).

31.   You must see how, my son, that I find by my calculations (checking with God's Word), which are according to revealed inspiration, that the sword of death is now approaching us, in the shape of pestilence and war more horrible than has been known, how much for the life of three men (three reformation church ages), not in summer, and famine which will fall upon the earth, and return there often, according to the words (in the Bible) "I will visit their iniquities with a rod of iron, and will strike them with blows."

32.   For the mercy of the Lord, my son, shall not be extended at all for a long time (until the Millennium), not until most of my prophecies will have been accomplished (with the Lord's return through mysteries of His Word being revealed) and will by accomplishment have become resolved (revealed). Then several times (previous three Reformation church ages) during the sinister tempests of God's wrath, the Lord will say, "I will trample them and break them, and not show pity."

33.   And thousands of other events will come to pass, because of floods and continual rains (of God's judgments), as I have set forth more fully in writing my other *Prophecies* (*Ten Centuries*) which are drawn out in length, in prose at their time of interpretation, setting forth the places and times so that men coming after may see them, knowing the events to have occurred infallible. This we have noted in connection with the others, speaking more clearly. For although they are written under a cloud (ten centuries written in riddles), the meanings will be understood. When the time comes for the removal of ignorance, the event will be cleared up still more.

Nostradamus and His Prophesies by Edger Leoni, 1982 Edition

This book contains the supplementary prophecies, along with the *Ten Centuries*, which most other authors have.

In memory of my mother, Alverna Jones, who was tolerant and friendly to me during this ministry of interpretation.

A. Sixains (1605)
Other Prophecies of M Nostradamus

LV.

Shortly before otherwise after a very great Lady, Her soul to Heaven, and her body under the blade, She will be regretted by many people, all her relatives will be in great sadness, tears and sighs for a Lady in her youth, and by two great ones, the mourning will be abandoned.

Shortly before the sickness was first recognized and after (her death), a very great Lady (Alverna Jones). Her soul to Heaven, and her body under the blade (through the angel of death). She will be regreted by many people. All her relatives will be in great sadness, tears end sighs for a lady in her youth (new believer), and by two great ones (believers united in the double annointing of God's fullness), the mourning will be abandoned, according to God's direction.

Presages drawn from those made by
M. Nostradamus in the years
1555 and subsequent ones
up to 1567
1555

From a presage on the said year

1.   **"From the divine spirit the soul by pressage touched, trouble, famine, plague, war to follow: Floods, droughts, land and sea stained with blood. Peace, truce, prelates to be born, princes to die."** From the divine spirit of French spy influence the soul of Habsburgs in Italy by presage touched. Trouble famine, plague, war to follow with the Habsburgs unprepared: Floods, droughts, land and sea stained with blood from Moslems invading, peace, truce afterwards, French prelates (bishops) to be born, Habsburg princes to die by defeat with Moslems replacing them.

From the luminary Epistle on the said year

2.   **"The Tyrrhenian Sea, the Ocean through the care of the great Neptune and his trident soldiers: Provence safe in the hand of the great Tende, more Mars from Narbonne the heroic de Villars."** The Tyrrhenian Sea, the Ocean through the care of the great Neptune (allied French and Moslems sharing Italy) and his trident (Moslem) soldiers: Provence (east of the Rhone indicating Moslem possessions in Italy) safe in the hand of the great Tende (Moslems). More Mars (war) from Narbonne (westerly, indicating French), the heroic French rebels from Villars (westerly).

January

3.   **"The large brazen one which decrees the hours, upon the death of the Tyrant it will wear out: Tears, laments and cries, waters, ice bread does not give V.S.C. peace, the army will pass."** The large brazen one (Moslem government) which decrees the hours. Upon the death or defeat of

the Habsburg tyrant, will wear out as the French rebel: Tears, laments and cries due to Moslems, waters of friendship changing to ice, bread of sharing Italy does not give Charles V's successor (Moslem government) peace, the Moslem army will pass, retreating.

February

4. **"Near the Lake of Geneva the terror will be great. From the counsel, that cannot fail: The new King has his band to prepare, the young one dies, famine, fear will cause failure."** Near the Lake of Geneva (east of the Rhone, symbolizing Moslem possessions in Italy) the terror of rebellions will be great. From the French allied counsel that cannot fail: The new French king has his rebel band to prepare for takeover, the Moslem young one before elected by alliance, dies, famine, and fear will cause Moslem failure.

On March

5. **"O cruel Mars, how thou art to be feared, more is the Scythe conjoined with the Silver: Fleet, forces, water, wind the shadow to fear, truce by land and sea. The friend has joined L.U."** O cruel Mars of war, how thou art to be feared. More is the Scythe (Saturn symbolizing France) conjoined with the Silver (Moon symbolizing Moslems): Fleet, forces invading Italy by water and wind, the shadow of fleeing Habsburgs to fear, truce by land and sea after Moslem victory. The French friend has joined Luther (Protestants, symbolizing Moslems).

April

6. **"From not having care, he will injure more, the weak strong, the uneasy peaceful: They will cry famine, the people are oppressed, the sea reddens, the Tall One proud and unjust."** From not having care who they befriended, France will injure the Habsburgs more with the Moslems capturing Italy, the weak French becoming strong, the uneasy French (from earlier loss) peaceful concerning Habsburg defeat: Habsburgs will cry famine, the people are oppressed (due to French spies), the sea reddens from battles, the Tall One (Moslems) proud and unjust.

May

7. **"The five, six, fifteen, late and soon they remain, the heir without end: the cities revolted: The herald of peace twenty and three returns, the opened five locked up, news invented."** The five (allied peace), then six (work of French rebellions), fifteen (rebel peace), late after rebellions and soon during allied sharing, the French remain, the heir without end: the French cities revolted: The herald of rebel peace, twenty (shared Italy) and three (Moslem rule) returns, the opened five (rebel peace) locked up, news of rebel acts invented.

June

8. **"Far near by the Urn the wicked one turns back, so that for the great Mars fire will provide an obstacle: Towards the North to the south the great proud female, Flower will hold the gate from thought."** Far from France, near by the Urn (Italy, where France was earlier defeated) the wicked one (France) turns back the Habsburgs, so that aiding the great Mars

(Moslem invasion) French spies will provide an obstacle: Towards the north to the south the great proud Flower (France) will hold the gate of Habsburg defense from thought, causing confusion.

July

9. **"Eight, fifteen and five what disloyalty will come to be allowed the wicked spy: Fire from the sky lightning, fear, Papal terror, the West trembles, too much pressing the wine salty."** Houat (westerly indicating rebel victory), fifteen (rebel government) and five (former allied sharing) what disloyalty will come to be allowed the wicked French spies. Fire from the sky, lightning, fear, papal (French like end time Catholic takeover) terror, the West (French rebel government) trembles during Moslem retaliation, too much pressing by rebellions, the wind of victory becoming salty.

August

10. **"Six, twelve, thirteen, twenty to speak to the Lady, the older one will be by the woman corrupted: Dijen, Guienne hail, lightning cuts it, the insatiable with blood and wine satiated."** Six (rebellion work), twelve (Moslem and loyal French retaliation work), thirteen (Moslem total ownership), twenty (sharing) to speak to the Lady (France), that the older one (France) is by the woman (rebels) corrupted: Dijon (shared Italy) by Guienne (westerly, French rebellions) hail, lightning cuts the sharing agreement, the insatiable Moslems with blood (retaliation) and wine (victory) satiated.

September

11. **"The sky to weep for him made to do that, the sea is being prepared, Hannibal performs his tricks: With Nice soaked, fleet delays, does not keep silent, has not known the secret, and at which you are amused."** The sky to weep for Moslems, made to retreat from rebellions, the sea with Moslem reinforcements is being prepared, Hannibal performs his tricks against France: With Nice (east of the Rhone symbolizing Moslem possessions in Italy) soaked, the Moslem fleet delays but does not keep silent. Not knowing the secret defeat, and at which France is amused.

October

12. **"Venus Neptune will pursue the enterprise, reflective ones confined, those in opposition troubled: Fleet in the Adriatic, cities towards La Tamise, the fourth noise wounded them reposing by night."** Venus (Italy) Neptune (Moslems) will pursue, the enterprise for complete ownership, reflective French rebels confined, the Christian opposition troubled: Moslem fleet in the Adriatic retaliating against cities towards La Tamise (western border town in Flanders symbolizing France's Italian possessions), the fourth (French like Catholic Church resurrected from its first four ages) rebel noise wounded Moslems reposing by night.

November

13. **"The great one from the sky under the cloak will give aid, Adriatic makes an offer to the Porte: He who can will save himself from the dangers, by night the Great One wounded, pursues the chest."** The great one (Moslems), from the sky weeping, under the cloak of reinforcements will give aid to retreating Moslems, Adriatic Moslem fleet makes an offer to the Port (rebel held Italy): He who can convert to Islam will save himself from dangers of retaliation, by night the Great one (Moslems) wounded by rebellions, pursues the stolen chest.

December

14. "The Porte cries out too fraudulent and false, the mouth open, condition of peace: Rhone in ice, rain, snow, ice stained, the death, death, wind, through rain burden broken." The Port (French rebel held Italy) cries out too fraudulent and false converting to Islam, Moslem reinforcements with mouth open giving condition of peace: Rhone (allied sharing of Italy) in ice because of French rebellions, rain, snow and ice stained with the death (Moslem retreat), death by Moslem retaliation wind through the rain, burden of rebellions broken.

1557

January

15. "The unworthy one embellished will fear the great furnace, the elected one first, not returning the captives: Great bottom of the world, the Angry Female not at ease, Barb. Danube, Malta. And the empty one does not return." The unworthy (French rebels) embellished will fear the great furnace of Moslem retaliation, the Moslem elected one first again, not returning the French captives: Great bottom of the world for the "angry" (Old French) "female" (France), not at ease, barbarian Moslems control Danube (north) to Malta (south). And the empty (Old French) one, France, does not return.

May

16. "Conjoined now, in the sky despatch manifest, taken, abandoned, mortality uncertain: Little rain, entry, the sky the earth dries, in fact, death, taken, arrived at a bad hour." Conjoined now with Moslem reinforcements, in the sky smoke of battle, despatch of French rebellions manifest, taken captives are abandoned by French rebels, mortality uncertain according to French knowledge: Little rain (drought) makes entry for remaining French, the sky and the earth dries from Christian persecution, indeed death, taken by Moslems who arrived at a bad hour.

June

17. "Naval victor at Hoek, at Antwerp divorce, Great heir, fire from the sky, trembling, high burning: Sardinia woods, Malta, Palermo, Corsica, Prelate to die, the one who strikes on the Mule." Naval victor at Hoek (symbolizing French, formerly spies with Habsburg credentials, who rebel in Italy), at Antwerp rebels divorce from Moslem friendship, Great French heir then with fire from the sky, trembling, high burning from Moslem retaliation: Sardinia woods, Malta, Palermo, Corsica (Italian lands), French Prelate to die, the Moslem retaliation strikes on the Mule (French rebels).

July

18. **"The wandering herald turns from the dog to the Lion, fire will burn a town, pillage, new capture: To discover foists, Princes captured, they return, Spy captive Gaul joined the maiden to the great one."** The wandering Moslem herald turns from defeated dog to formadable Lion, fire of retaliation will burn a town, pillage, new capture: To discover Moslem foists in the harbor, French princes captured, Moslems return to Italy, French spy who turned rebel against Moslems, now captive, Gaul (France) forced to join the maiden (Italy) to the Moslem great one.

August

19. **"Banished from the great court, conflict, wounded, elected, surrendered, accused, cunning rebels: And fire from the Pyrenees city, waters, venoms, pressed not to sail the wave, not to vex the Latins."** Moslems banished from the great court where they governed in Italy, conflict from French rebellions, wounded, the elected Moslems surrendered, accused by cunning rebels of religious evils: And fire from the Pyrenees city (French possessions in Italy), waters, venoms from rebels pressed the Moslems not to sail the wave, not to vex the Latins (French in Italy).

September

20. "Sea, land to go, faith, loyalty broken, pillage, shipwreck, in the city tumult: Proud, cruel act, ambition stinks again, weak one injured, the author of the deed unpunished." Sea travel and land possessions for the Moslems to go, faith, loyalty broken by the French rebels, pillage, shipwreck, in the Moslem city tumult from French rebellions: Proud, cruel act of the French, ambition to own all of Italy stinks again, weak one (Moslems) injured, the author (French rebels) of the deed unpunished up to this point.

October

21. **"Cold, great flood, expelled from the realm, Nephew, discord, Bear East consumes: Poison, siege laid, driven out of the City, Happy return, new sect in ruins."** Cold, great flood from French rebellions in Italy with Moslems expelled (Old French) from the realm, Nephew (Old French indicating French) in discord, Bear (Moslems) from the East consumes in retaliation: Poison of Moslem instigation and French rebel siege laid, Moslems driven out of the city, then Happy Moslems return with the new Christian sect in ruins.

November

22. **"Sea closed, world opened, city surrendered, the Great One to fail, newly elected great mist: Florence to open, army to enter, faith broken, a severe effort will be made by the white feather."** Sea closed for the Moslems, world (Italy) opened by French rebellions, Moslem city surrendered, the Moslem Great One to fail, newly elected Moslems to govern Italy, in a great mist of confusion: Florence (Italy) to open for the French, rebels to enter, the Moslem faith broken, a severe effort will be made by the white (French) feather.

December

23. **"Guardianship for Vesta, war dies, transferred, Naval combat, honor, death, prelacy: Entry death, France greatly augmented, Elected one passed, come to a bad end."** Guardianship of Italy for Vesta (French Christians) when war of rebellions dies (or ends), transferred (Old French) to France, Naval battle by French rebels for Christian honor, death to the Moslems, prelacy (like Biships) symbolizing Christian takeover: Entry death by rebellions, France greatly augmented gaining more Italian possessions, Moslem elected one passed, come to a bad end.

1558

January

24. **"The Younger King makes a mournful wedding song, Holy one stirred up feasts, games, Mars quieted: By night to arms they cry, they lead the Lady outside, the arrest and peace broken on all sides."** The younger (French) king makes a mournful wedding song because Italian lands are shared, Moslem Holy one (dominating) stirred up feasts and games to celebrate after Mars of war capturing Italy: By night (Indicating conspiracy), to arms French rebels cry, they lead the Moslem lady outside, the Moslem arrest and French peace on all sides (Old French).

March

25. **"Vain rumor in the hierarchy, Genoa to rebel: flights, offenses, tumults: The monarchy will be for the greater King, election, conflict, coverings, burials."** Vain rumor spread by Moslem instigation in the French hierarchy, Genoa (westerly, indicating French possessions) to rebel: flights of Christians converting to Islam, offenses against the French, tumults result: The monarchy (Italian government) will be for the greater French king in the end, election of Moslem government, conflict of French rebellions, coverings and burials indicating Moslem defeat.

April

26. **"Through discord to fail in the absence, one suddenly will put him back on top: Towards the North the noises will be very loud, injuries, points across, above."** Through discord of French rebellions, the Moslems to fail in the absence (retreat), one (French rebels) suddenly will put France back on top to rule all of Italy: Towards the North (More into French areas of shared Italy) the noises of rebellions will be very loud, injuries to the Moslems, points stabbing across, hacking above at them.

May

27. **"On the Tyrrhenian Sea, with different sail, on the Ocean there will be diverse assaults: Plague, poison, blood in the house of cloth, Prefects, Legates stirred up to advance on the high seas."** On the Tyrrhenian Sea (west of Italy indicating French possessions) with different rebel sail, on the Ocean there will be diverse assaults (including scattered throughout Italy): Plague, poison from Moslems seeking after converts, blood of desecration to the Christian house of cloth, French Prefects and church Legates stirred up to advance on the high seas through rebellions.

June
28. **"There where the faith was it will be broken, the enemies will feed upon the enemies: The sky to rain fire, it will burn, interrupted, enterprise by night. Chiefs will make quarrels."** There where the Christian faith was in Italy, through Christians converting to Islam the Christian faith will be broken, the Moslem enemies will feed upon the French enemies, having opposing religions, making converts: The sky to rain fire through French rebellions, it will burn, Moslems interrupted, enterprise by night secretely seducing Christians. Moslem chiefs will make quarrels.

July
29. **"War, thunder, many fields depopulated, terror and noise, assault on the frontier: The Great Great One fallen, pardon for the exiles, Germans, Spaniards, by sea the Barbarian banner."** War, thunder from French rebellions, many fields depopulated as Moslems flee, terror and noise where rebels assault on the Moslem frontier areas: The Great Great One (allied sharing of Italy) fallen, pardon for the Christian exiles freed, Germans and Spaniards (French who formerly used Habsburg credentials during spy work), by sea fleeing is the Moslem barbarian banner.

August
30. **"The noise will be vain, the faltering ones trussed up, the Shaven Ones taken: the All-powerful One elected: The two Red Ones and four true crusaders to fail, rain inconvenient for the powerful Monarch."** Rebellion noise will be vain, the faltering rebels trussed up, the Shaven Ones (embarrassed French) taken: elected the All-powerful Moslems again: The two Red Ones (takeover by former spies with Habsburg credentials) and four true crusaders (end time Catholic Church back from first four church ages) to fail, rebellion rain inconvenient (Old French) to the powerful Moslem Monarch.

October
31. **"Rain, wind, Barbarian fleet, Danube, Tyrrhenian Sea, to pass holcades, Ceres, soldiers furnished: Retreats well executed by the Flower, Siena crossed, the two will be dead, friendships joined."** Rain, wind (retaliation), Barbarian Moslem fleet Danube, Tyrrhenian Sea, to pass holcades (easterly in Spain, symbolizing Moslem possessions controled by rebels, former spies with Spanish credentials). Ceres (goddes of grain) furnished the Moslem soldiers this time: Retreats well executed by the Flower (French rebels), Siena (Italy) crossed, the two (rebel takeover) will be dead, friendships united again.

November
32. "Venus the beautiful will enter in the Flower. The secret exiles will abandon the place: Many widows death of a Great One will lament, to remove from the realm, the Great Great One does not threaten." Venice (easterly Moslem lands) will enter within the Flower (French ownership). The secret exiles (disfavored Christians) will abandon (Old French) the Moslem place to advancing rebels: Many Moslem widows death of a Great One (Moslem

government) will lament, to remove from the realm, the Great Great One (Moslems and loyal French sympathizers) does not threaten the rebels.

December

33.   "Games, feasts, nuptials, Prelate of renown dead, noise, peace by truce while the enemy undermines: Noise on sea, land and sky, deed by the great Brennus, cries gold, silver, the enemy they ruin." Games, feasts, nuptials after the prelate (Moslem government) of renown dead, noise of French rebellions, peace by truce while the rebel enemy undermines: Noise (rebellions) on sea, land and sky, deed by the great Brennus (Celtic chief who conquered Rome, symbolizing French rebels), cries by rebels over gold and silver supposedly captured, the Moslem enemy they ruin.

1559

On the said year

34.   "Fear, knell, great pillage, to pass the sea, realm to grow, sects, holy ones beyond the sea more polite: Plague, heat, fire, banner of the King of Aquilon, to prepare as a trophy, city of Henripolis." Fear, knell, great pillage of rebellions to pass the sea, France's Italian realm to grow, Moslem sects, holy ones beyond the sea retreating are more polite (unable to harrass): Plague, heat, fire of rebellions, banner of the Moslem king of the north, to prepare as a trophy the city of Henripolis (Francis I's son, symbolizing captured Moslem cities).

January

35.   "The Great One to be no longer, rain, in the chariot, the crystal. Tumult stirred up, abundance of all goods: Shaven Ones, Holy Ones, new ones, old ones, frightful, ingrate elected, dead, lament, joy, alliance." The Great One (Moslems) to be no longer, rain (harrassment) in the chariot (leadership), the crystal (Moslem instigators prophecy). Tumult stirred up, abundance of all goods supposedly captured by rebels: French Shaven Ones, Holy Ones become new ones (governing), Old ones (Moslems) frightful retreating, Moslem ingrate elected now dead, French lament, but finally joy over the alliance.

February

36.   "Grain spoiled, air pestilent, locusts, Suddenly will fall, new pasturage to arise: Captives put in irons, light ones, high low, burdened, through his evil bones which the King did not wish to be." Grain spoiled, air pestilent, locusts (rebellion plague), suddenly will fall upon the Moslems, new pasturage to arise for rebel victors: Moslem captives put in irons, Moslem light (gay) ones, high governing shared Italy now low, burdened under rebel rule, through the Moslem evil bones (bothering French Christianity) which the rebel king did not wish to be anymore.

March

37.   "Seized in the temple, through sects diffuse intrigue, elected ravished in the woods forms a quarrel: Seventy pairs new league to be born, from there their death, King appeased by the news." Christians seized in the temple by Moslem sects in diffuse intrigue simulating conversions, elected Moslems then ravished in the woods by French rebellions, form a quarrel against France: Seventy pairs (Old French), new league to be born of French rebels and France in agreement, from there (French rebellions) Moslem death (defeat), French king appeased by the news.

April

38. **"King hailed as conqueror and Master, faith broken, the royal deed known: Macedonian blood, King made conqueror of a proud people become humble through tears."** King Francis I hailed by French rebels as conqueror and master in Italy with the Moslem faith broken and the royal deed of French rebellions known by Francis I to be for France's full ownership of Italy: Macedonia (Moslem) blood from rebellions, Francis I made conqueror of a proud Moslem people now become humble through tears of lost French friendship.

May

39. **"Through spite wedding, wedding song, for the three parts Red Ones, Shaven Ones parted: For the young King, by fire the soul restored, Ogmios changed from the great Neptune."** Through spite against Habsburgs, wedding (alliance), wedding song, for the three parts (Moslems like end time Protestants of three ages) and Red Ones (French spies using Habsburg credentials), Shaven Ones (France) parted afterwards: For the young king (Francis I), by fire of rebellions the soul (French dignity) restored, Ogmios (France) changed from the great Neptune (French and Moslem partnership).

June

40. **"From the house seven with death mortal pursuit, hail, tempest, pestilent evil, furies: King of the East of the West all in flight, He will subjugate his former conquerors."** From the house (Italy) seven (French spies like end time Catholic Church from seven ages) with Habsburg death their mortal pursuit, hail, tempest of Moslem invasion, pestilent evil and furies from spies: Moslem king of the East and French king of the West in alliance, all Habsburgs in flight, France will this way subjugate his former Habsburg conquerors.

July

41. **"Plunderers pillaged heat, great drought, through too much not being, event unseen, unheard of: For the foreigner the too great affection, new country King, the East dazzled."** Plunderers (Moslems) pillaged Habsburg Italy like a plague of heat and great drought, through too much not being, event unseen, unheard of as French spies caused Habsburg confusion: For the foreigner (French spy) Habsburgs had the too great affection, allowing themselves to be influenced, new country of Italy now with Moslem king, the East dazzled the world.

August

42. **"The Urn found, the city tributary, fields divided, new deceit: Spain wounded famine, plague, military, mockery obstinate, confused, evil, reverie."** The Urn (Italy) found back in French possession, the French city tributary to the Moslems there, fields divided as they share Italy, then deceit by French rebels: Spain (Spanish Habsburgs) wounded by famine, plague, military from French and Moslems capturing Italy, mockery (Old French) by obstinate French, Moslems confused, evil of French rebellions, reverie of French success.

September

43. "Virgins and widows, your good time approaches, It will not at all be that which they pretend: Distant it will be necessary that the approach for it be new, the very comfortable ones taken, completely restored, it will hold worse." Virgins (rebels) and widows (France once defeated), your good time approaches, it will not at all be that which the Moslems pretend for themselves: Distant Italy, it will be necessary that the approach for it be new through French ownership, the very comfortable Moslems taken, Italy completely restored to France, it will hold worse through Moslem retaliation.

October

44. "Here within it will be completed, the three Great Ones outside the Bourbon will be far: Against them one of them will conspire, at the end of the month they will see the need." Here within Italy French rebellions will be completed, the three Great Ones (Moslems symbolized by end time Protestants from three ages) outside, the Bourbon (rebels) will be far from them: Against them (Moslems) one of them (French rebels) will conspire, at the end of the month after Moslem retaliation, they (Moslems) will see the need for stricter laws.

November

45. "Talks held, nuptials begun again, the Great Great female will go out from France: Voice in Romagna not weary of crying out, receives the peace through too false assurance." Talks held by France and Moslems, nuptials (alliance) begun again with new limitations, the Great Great female (allied French) will go out from France now instead of Italy which was before shared: Voice in Romagna (French captives in Italy), not weary of crying out against the Moslems, receives the peace through too false assurance from the Moslems.

December

46. "The joy in tears, Mars will come to captivate, before the Great One will be stirred up, the Divine ones: Without saying a word will enter through three sides, Mars quieted, wines run on ice." The joy of rebel success in tears, Mars of Moslem retaliation will come to captivate, before the Moslem Great One will be stirred up, the Divine Ones (French rebels): Without saying a word of warning, will enter through three sides (Possessions of Moslems, like end time Protestants of three ages), Mars of rebellions quieted, wines run on ice.

1560

January

47. "Day, regimen, interim, no council, the year peace is being prepared, plague, famine schismatic: Put outside inside, sky to change,

domicile, end of the holiday, revolt against the hierarchy." Day of regimen during the interim of sharing Italy, no council for the French, the year peace is being prepared for the allies to live together, plague, famine from schismatic French rebellions: Moslems inside Italy put outside, sky to change with French domicile in Italy, end of the holiday for Moslem celebrations, revolt against the Moslem hierarchy.

February

48. "Regimen to break up, the ancient holy one to recover, under the two, fire through pardon to follow: Consecration without arms: the tall Red One will want to have, Peace of neglect, the Elected One Widower to live." Regimen sharing Italy to break up, the ancient holy one (France) to recover Italy, under the two allys fire of warfare against Habsburgs through pardon to follow for French spies: Consecration of living together without arms: the tall Red One (French, formerly spies) will want to have peace of neglect, the elected Moslem Widower to live (governing).

March

49. "To be made to appear elected from newness, place a day's journey to go beyond the boundaries: The feigned goodness with change to cruelty, from the suspect place they will all go out quickly." Moslems to be made to appear elected from newness, having just captured Italy, place of Moslem possessions a day's journey across, Moslems to go beyond their boundaries to gain Islam converts: The feigned goodness at first with change to cruelty against Christianity, from the suspect place Moslems will all (Old French) go out quickly during French rebellions.

April

50. "From the place the elected shaven ones will not be satisfied, by the Lake of Geneva led unproven: They will cause the old times to be renewed. They will frighten the plot so well hatched." From the place (Italy) chased, the Moslem Shaven Ones (defeated) will not be satisfied, by the Lake of Geneva (westerly from Italy indicating French strongholds) Moslems led unproven (not fighting): French rebels will cause the old times to be renewed with all Italy French owned, they will frighten (Old French) the Moslems, the plot so well hatched.

May

51. "Peace of Savoy will be broken, the last hand will cause a strong levy: The great conspirator will not be corrupted, and the new alliance approved." The peace of Savoy (from French rebels in Italy, formerly spies disguised as Spanish) will be broken by Moslems retaliating, the last hand of the Moslems will cause a strong levy upon Christianity in Italy: The great Moslem conspirator (originally instigating the French rebellions) will not be corrupted by rebellions, and the new alliance (outlawing Christianity) approved.

July

52. "A long comet to injure the Governor, Hunger, burning fever, fire and reek of blood: To all estates Jovial ones in great honor, sedition by

Shaven Ones stirred up." A long comet (Jesus' return in end time prophecy) to injure the governor (Habsburgs symbolizing end time saints shaken by chastizement), hunger, burning fever, fire and reek of blood from losing Italy: To all estates the Jovial Ones (French and Moslems allied like followers of Jupiter) in great honor possessing Italy, sedition later by Shaven Ones (French) stirred up.

August

53. **"Plague, famine, fire and intense heat incessant, lightning, great hail, temple struck from the sky: The edict, arrest, and grievous law broken, the chief author he and his people caught."** Plague, famine, fire and intense heat not ceased after Moslem retaliation against French rebels and Christianity in Italy, lightning, great hail, Moslem temple struck from the sky with Habsburgs battling again (like end time saints in God's fullness): The Moslem edict, arrest of Christians, and grievous Moslem law broken. The Moslem chief author, he and his people caught.

September

54. **"The Shaven Ones will be deprived of their arms. It will increase their quarrel much more: Father wine deceived lightning Albanians, Sects will be gnawed to the marrow."** The Shaven Ones (French) will be deprived of their arms after rebellions, It will increase much more the quarrel for Moslem defenders against renewed Habsburg attacks: Father (Moslems) with wine deceived the French causing lightning of rebellions by Albanians (westerly symbolizing French), sects (French and Moslems, symbolizing end time Catholics and Protestants) will be gnawed to the marrow.

October

55. **"The modest petition will be received, they will be driven out and then restored on top: The Great Great female will be found content, blind ones, deaf ones will be put uppermost."** The modest petition (French rebel claim over possessing all of Italy) will be received, Moslems will be driven out and then restored on top by Moslem retaliation: The Great Great female (France still allied to Moslems) will be found content, though losing Italian possessions, blind ones, deaf ones (Moslems who ignore Christian rights) will be put uppermost.

November

56. **"He will not be placed, the New Ones expelled. Black One and of Lyons and the Great One will grasp: To have recourse to arms. Further exiles driven out, to sing of victory, not free, consolation."** Moslems will not be placed in government, expelled (Old French) by the New Ones (French rebels). Black One of Lyons (east on the Rhone, symbolizing Moslems in Italy) and the Great One (French rebels) will grasp: Moslems to have recourse to arms. Further exiles (rebels) driven out, Moslems to sing of victory, French not free, Moslem consolation.

December

57. **"The mourning abandoned, supreme alliances, Great Shaven One dead, refusal given to the entry: Upon return to be benefit in oblivion,**

the death of the just one at a banquet perpetrated." The Moslem mourning abandoned after retaliating against French rebels, supreme alliances with France with changes made after French rebellions, Great Shaven One (France) dead, refusal given to French entry into Italy because of rebellions: Upon Moslem return to be benefit in French oblivion. The death of the just one (French) at a banquet perpetrated by Moslem instigators.

1561

On the said year

58. "The King King not to be, for the Clement One calamity, the year pestilent, the stirred up beclouded: Every man for himself, for the great ones no joy: And the term of jeerers will pass." The King (rebel rule) King not to be, for the Clement One (rebel, doux) calamity, the year pestilent with Christians persecuted in further retaliation, the stirred up (rebels) beclouded (fooled): Every man for himself according to instigators, for the great ones (French) no joy sharing Italy: And the term of Moslem jeerers will pass if French rebel.

March

59. "At the foot of the wall the ashy Franciscan. The enclosure delivered the cavalry trampling: By the temple outside Mars and carrying a scythe, outside, appointed, dismissed, and upon the daydream." At the foot of the wall the ashy Franciscan (French rebels desiring pure Christianity in Italy). The enclosure with the Moslems delivered, the French cavalry trampling them in defeat: By the Moslem temple outside Mars of rebellions and the French carrying a scythe, rebels outside against the appointed and now dismissed Moslems, and upon this French daydream.

April

60. "The times purged, pestilential tempest, Barbarian insult, fury, invasion: Infinite evils for this month prepared for us, and the Greatest Ones, two less, from mockery." The times of sharing Italy purged, pestilential tempest of French rebellions, because of barbarian insult to Christianity, fury and invasion by Moslems retaliating: Infinite evils for this month prepared for us (French remaining in Italy), and the Greatest Ones (French) two (sharing Italy) less in number as Moslems murder and persecute Christians, from mockery to Moslem laws.

May

61. "Joy not long, abandoned by his followers, the year pestilent, the Greatest One assailed: The good Lady in the Elysian Fields, and the greater part of the good things cold unpicked." Joy not long for Moslems living in Italy, abandoned by his French friends, the year pestilent as the Greatest One (French partner) assailed during French rebellions: The good lady (supposedly innocent Moslems) in the Elysian fields (heaven) of shared Italy enjoying themselves, and the greater part of the good things (crops) cold and unpicked, indicating Moslem laziness.

June

62. **"Courses of Lyon, not to prepare for conflicts. Sad enterprise, the air pestilential, hideous: From all sides the Great Ones will be afflicted, and ten and seven to assail twenty and two."** Courses of Lyon (east side of Rhone symbolizing Moslem possessions in shared Italy), not to prepare for conflicts (French rebellions), sad enterprise of Moslem loss, the air pestilential, hideous as rebels defeat them: From all sides the Great Ones (Moslems) will be afflicted (Old French), and ten and seven, French rebels, to assail twenty and two Moslems.

July

63. **"Retaken, surrendered, frightened by the evil, the blood far and near, and the faces hideous: To the most learned ones the ignorant one frightful, gate, hatred, horror, the pitiful to fall low."** Italy retaken by French rebels and then surrendered back to Moslems, the French frightened by the evil, the blood of Moslem retaliation far and near, and the Moslem faces hideous, seeking revenge: To the most learned ones (French), the ignorant one (retaliating Moslems) frightful, at the gate entering Italy, hatred, horror, the pitiful French to fall low.

August

64. **"Dead and seized, the change of the careless ones, who will go far away in approaching much more: Close united ones in the ruin, grange, through long help the hardiest one astonished."** Dead and seized in defeat, the change of the careless Moslems who will go far away retreating as a trick, in approaching much more by returning and retaliating: Close united ones (alliance) in ruin, grange together sharing in Italy's prosperity. Through long help to each other before, the hardiest one (French rebels) astonished when Moslems begin retaliating.

October

65. **"Gray, white, and black ones, hidden and broken, will be replaced, dismissed, put in their seats: The ravishers will find themselves mocked, and the Vestals confined behind strong bars."** Gray (Moslem instigators), white (French) and black ones (Moslems), hidden (Old French) French rebels secretely ready to fight and Moslems broken (Provencal), will be replaced and dismissed, French rebels put in their seats in Italy: The French ravishers will then find themselves mocked by Moslem retaliation, and the Vestals (French Christians) confined behind strong Moslem bars (Provencal).

1562

On the said year

66. **"Season of winter, good spring healthy, bad summer, destructive autumn, dry, wheat rare: Of wine enough, bad eyes, deeds, molested, war, sedition, seditious waste."** Season of winter from France's earlier defeat, good spring (Old French) with allied recapture, healthy existance sharing Italy, bad summer from rebellions, destructive autumn with Moslem retaliation, dry, wheat rare indicating Christians persecuted: French with wine enough, bad eyes against Moslems from deeds of Christians molested, war and sedition through rebellions, seditious waste due to Moslem retaliation.

January

67. "Hidden desire for the good will succeed, Religion, peace, love, and concord: The wedding song will not be in accord entirely, the high ones who were low, and high put to the rope." Hidden desire of France for the good (recapture of Italy from Habsburgs) will succeed through allied help, Christian religion, peace, love and concord together with the Moslems: The wedding song (alliance) will not be in accord entirely after French rebellions, the French high ones, who were low and then high, put to the rope by Moslem retaliation.

February

68. "For the Shaven Ones the Chief will not reach the end, edicts changed, the confined ones set at large: Great One found dead, less of faith, standing low. Dissimulated, chilled struck in a heap." For the Shaven Ones (France) the chief (Francis I) will not reach the end (full management of Italy), edicts changed by retaliating Moslems, the confined Moslems set at large following captivity, Great One (France) found dead, less of faith (Christianity), standing low during persecution. Dissimulated by rebellions, chilled by retaliation, French rebels struck in a heap (Old French).

March

69. "Moved by Lyon, near Lyon he will undermine, taken, captive, pacified by a woman: He will not hold as well as they will hesitate, Placed unpassed, to remove the soul from rage." Moved (instigated) by Lyon (east side of Rhone symbolizing allied Moslems in Italy), near Lyon ousted Moslems will undermine, taken, French captive pacified by a woman (Moslem religion) through conversion: French rebels will hold as well as Moslems will hesitate in their retreat, Rebels placed but Moslems unpassed, to remove the Moslem soul from rage by retaliating.

April

70. "From Lyon he will come to arouse in order to move, vain discovery against infinite people: Known by none the evil through the exercise, in the kitchen found dead and finished." From Lyon (symbolizing Moslem owned possessions) instigators will come to arouse in order to move French rebels, vain discovery by French rebels against infinite Moslems who finally retaliate: Known by none of the French is the evil through the exercise of Moslem trickery, in the kitchen (as though poisoned) France found dead and finished from sharing Italy.

May

71. "Nothing in accord, trouble worse and more severe, as it was, land and sea to quiet: All stopped it will not be worth a double, the wicked one will speak, counsel of destruction." Nothing in accord during rebellions, trouble worse and more severe from Moslem retaliation, as it was on land and sea, Moslems to quiet (Old French) the rebels: All stopped, Moslems feel it will not be worth a double (second opportunity), the Moslem wicked one will speak laws and counsel of French destruction (Old French) out of Italy.

June

72. "Portentous deed, horrible and unbelievable, the Bold One will cause the wicked ones to be stirred up: Those who then afterwards supported by the rope, and the greater part exiled on the fields." Portentous deed of French rebellions, horrible and unbelievable to the Moslems (pretending astonishment), the Bold Ones (French rebels) will cause the Moslem wicked ones to be stirred up into retaliation: Those rebels who then afterwards supported by the rope (hung to death in punishment), and the greater part of Christian captives exiled on the fields into slavery.

July

73. "Right enthroned come from the sky into France, the Universe pacified by virtue: Wiser to scatter, soon change to come, through the birds, through fire, and not through men." Right enthroned (for Christianity to dominate) come from the sky (by Moslem instigation) into France (French partners who share Italian possessions), the universe (all Italy) pacified by Christian virtue through rebellions: Wiser Moslems to scatter, soon change to come again in Italy. Through the birds (instigators), through fire of Moslem retaliation, and not through French men rebelling.

August

74. "The colored ones discontented the Holy Ones, then suddenly through the gay Hermaphrodites: From the greater part to see, the time not come, several amongst them will make their soups weak." The colored ones (Moslems) discontented the Holy Ones (French Christians sharing Italy with them), then all the French to strike through the gay hermaphrodites (disguised Moslems) instigating French rebellions: From the greater part (Moslems who also govern Italy) the French to see, the time of prosperity not come, several (Moslems) amongst them will make their soups weak.

September

75. "They will be restored to their full power, conjoined at one point of accord, not in accord: All defied, more by the Shaven Ones betrothed, several amongst them in a band outflanked." The French will be restored to their full power, conjoined with Moslems at one point of allied accord, not in accord now: All the Habsburgs defied by allied capture of Italy, more Italian lands captured by the Shaven Ones (French) betrothed in alliance but now rebelling, Several (Moslem partners) amongst them in a band outflanked by rebels.

October

76. "For the legate of land and sea, the great Capet will accommodate himself to all: Silent Lorraine to be listening, but to his advice will not want to agree with." For the Moslem legate of land and sea governing in shared Italy, the great Capet (French partner) to all the laws laid down by the Moslems will accomodate himself: Silent (pretending humbleness) Lorraine (eastern France symbolizing Moslem owned Italian lands) to be listening to his French partner, but to French advice will not want to agree with.

November

77.   "The wind will impede the enemy troop, for the greatest one difficult to advance at all: Wine with poison will be put in the cup, the great gun to pass without horse-power." The wind of rebellions will impede the enemy Moslem troop, for the greatest one (Moslems) it is difficult to advance at all against the rebels (supposedly): Wine with poison (Moslem instigation) will be put in the cup of French partners sharing Italy with them, the great gun of French rebellions to pass without horse-power (indicating poor planning).

December

78.   "From the ice the enterprise broken. Games and feasts with Lyons to be established again: No longer will he take his meal near the Great Ones, sudden catarrh the water consecrated to wash." From the ice (symbolizing French rebellions), the enterprise of sharing Italy broken, French games and feasts, Lyons (east of Rhone indicating Moslem owned lands) to be established again under French rule: No longer will the French take their meal (Old French) near the Moslem Great Ones, sudden catarrh (rebellions), the water consecrated to wash indicating Christianity reestablished.

1563

On the said year

79.   "To restore health, blood, but stirred up, nothing in accord, infinite murders, captives, deaths, warned: So much water and plague, little at all, horns sounded, Taken, deaths, flights, to become great, they come." To restore health and French blood in shared Italy, but stirred up by Moslem instigators, nothing in accord for the French, infinite murders, captives, deaths for Christianity the instigators warned: So much water and plague, little at all benefit to France, horns sounded rebellions, Moslems taken, death and flights for them, to become great the rebels come.

January

80.   "So much water, so many deaths, so many arms to stir up. Nothing in accord, the Great one takes captive: When blood, rage, fury has not, Late repentant, plague, war the cause." So much water (indicating Moslem encroachments), so many deaths from Moslems gaining converts, so many arms available to stir. Nothing in accord as rebellions begin, the Moslem Great One takes the rebels captive: When blood, rage and fury of rebellions has not (indicating rebel failure), late the French repentant of rebellion plague and war being the cause.

February

81.   "The bite of the enemy's tongue approaches, the Good-natured One in peace will want to subjugate: The obstinate ones will want to ruin the close, surprised, captives, and suspects passion to injure." The bite (Old French) of the rebel enemy's tongue (against Moslem citizens) approaches after initial rebellion success, the Good-natured One (new French government) in peace will want to subjugate Moslems in revenge: The obstinate ones (French rebels) will want to ruin the close Moslem partner, Moslems surprised, become captives and suspects because of passion to injure Christianity.

March

82. "Fathers and mothers dead from infinite sorrows, women in mourning, the pestilent monster: The Great One to be no more, all the world to end, under peace, repose yet all in opposition." Fathers and Mothers (Moslems) dead from infinite sorrows, Moslem women in mourning from the pestilent monster (French rebellions): The Great One (Moslems who governed shared Italy) to be no more, all the world (Italy) to end for the Moslems, under peace, repose (after allied French and Moslems captured Italy), yet all (Old French) the French in opposition.

April

83. "From debates Princes and Christendom stirred up, foreign nobles siege on Christians molested: Become very evil, much good, mortal appearance. The East death, plague, famine, bad treaty." From debates started by Moslems seeking religious converts, French princes and Christendom stirred up, for foreign nobles (Old French) indicating French living in Italy, siege on Christians who are molested by Moslems: Moslem partner become very evil, much good by helping capture Italy, now a mortal appearance, from the East (Moslems) death, plague, famine to Christianity, bad treaty.

May

84. "Land to tremble, prodigy killed, monster, numberless captives, to do, undone, done: To go by sea mishap will occur, proud against proud, evil done in disguise." Land (Italy) to tremble, prodigy (Moslems formerly helped by France) killed by the monster of French rebellions, numberless Moslem captives (supposedly), Moslems to do in Italy, undone by rebellions, done again after retaliation: Moslems to go by sea to Italy, mishap of rebellions will occur, Proud French against proud Moslems, evil of Moslem instigation done in disguise.

June

85. "The unjust inferior, they will molest terribly, Hail, to inundate, treasure, yet marble engraved: Chief of Persuasion people mortally will kill, and the swordsman will be attached to the tree." The unjust Moslems inferior, French rebels will molest terribly, hail of rebellions to inundate, treasure of booty supposedly taken, yet marble engraved French grave stone (captured Italy) persisted: Chief of persuasion people (or Suardones of Germany), both indicating former French spies with German credentials, mortally will kill, and the Moslem swordsman will be attached to the tree.

July

86. "Of what not evil? Inexcusable consequence, the fire not double, the Legate outside confused: Against the worse wounded the struggle will not be waged, the end of June the thread cut by fire." Of what not evil? (witnessing) Inexcusable consequence for Moslems, the fire (fighting) not double as the allys disagree, the Legate (Moslem governors) outside acting confused: Against the worse wounded (originally weaker French ally) the struggle will not be waged by retreating Moslems, the end of June (early) the thread of resistance cut by rebellion fire (Old French).

August

87. **"Good ones acutely weakened by agreements, Mars and Prelates united will not stop: The Great Ones confused by gifts bodies cut open, worthy ones unworthy ones undue goods will seize."** Moslem good ones acutely weakened by agreements with their French partners, Mars of French rebellions and prelates (Moslems governing Italy) will not stop so the two can live together peacefully: The Moslem great ones confused by gifts of initial cooperation ending in Moslem bodies cut open, from worthy Moslems the unworthy French rebels will sieze undue goods.

September

88. **"From good to evil the times will change, the peace of Austria, hope of the greatest ones: The Great Ones grieving Louis VI too much more will blunder, Shaven Ones recognized neither power nor recognition."** From good to evil, times will change in Italy, the peace (Old French) of Austria (symbolizing French before spying as Austrians), hope of the Moslem greatest ones for defeating the Habsburgs: The Moslem great ones grieving Louis VI (symbolizing French rebels) too much more, will blunder, French Shaven ones recognized neither Moslem power nor Moslem recognition of friendship. **Extra Interpretation:** Also describes the reign of Louis VI, who routed the robber barons, symbolic of routed Moslems.

October

89. **"Here is the month for evils as many to fear, deaths, all to bleed from plague, famine, to quarrel: Those on the reverse from exile will come to observe, Great Ones, secrets, deaths, not to be critical of."** Here is the month of rebellion evils as many Moslems to fear, deaths, all to bleed from plague as French rebels to quarrel: French on the reverse from exile (sharing Italy) will come to observe, the Moslem great ones with secrets of Moslem faith at work, deaths to opposers, Moslems then not to criticize the Christian faith.

November

90. **"Through death death to bite, a device of plunder, pestiferous, they will not dare to attack seamen: Deucalion a final trouble to cause, few new people: half-dead to wince."** Through death upon Christians who shared Italy, death by French rebellions to bite, advice from secret Moslem instigators result in rebel plunder (Old French), pestiferous against Moslems, who will not dare to attack French seamen due to inadequate strength: Deucalion (the rebel flood) to cause a final trouble, Few new Moslems in Italy: half-dead to wince.

91. **"The dead through spite will cause the others to shine, and in a high place some great evils to occur: Sad concepts will come to harm each one, the temporal worthy, the Mass to succeed."** The dead (ousted Moslems) through rebel spite, will cause the others (French) to shine, and in a high place (governing) some great evils against Moslems to occur: Sad concepts by both sides will come to harm each other through quarrelling Like Temporal ideas of men appearing worthy, the Mass or French forces to succeed over the lesser.

1564

On the said year

92. **"The year sixty degrees rains wheat to abound, hatreds, for men joy, Princes and Kings divorced: Flock to perish, mutations of humans, people oppressed: and from poison under the crust."** The year sixty degrees (springtime) with rains, wheat to abound, hatreds between French and Moslems, for French men joy, Moslem princes and kings divorced from Italy: Moslem Flock to perish, mutations of humans as French replace Moslems, people oppressed (Old French) by French Christians: and from poison under the crust as they did before against the Habsburgs.

January

93. **"Times very diverse, discord discovered, counsel of war, alteration made, exchanged: The Great one not to be, conspirators in the water in ruin, great hatred, all by the Greater One put in order."** Times very diverse, discord discovered in Italy, counsel of war by the French, alteration made with rebels fighting, exchanged the Moslem government: The Great One (Moslem rule) not to be, Moslem conspirators (who instigated French rebellions) in the water as if in ruin, great hatred against Moslems, all by the greater one (French rebels) put in order.

February

94. **"Great flood, noise of death conspired, age renewed, three Great Ones in great discord: Through incendiaries the concord aggravated, Rain impeding, wicked counsel of agreement."** Great flood of French rebellions, noise of Moslem death (defeat) conspired by tricky Moslems, age renewed for total French ownership of Italy, three (Moslems symbolizing end time Protestants from three church ages) Great Ones in great discord: Through incendiaries (Moslem instigators) the concord of sharing Italy aggravated. Rain of quarrels impeding, friendship becomes a wicked counsel of agreement.

March

95. **"Between Kings one will see hatreds appear, dissensions and wars to begin: Great Change, new tumult to grow, the plebeian order they will come to injure."** Among kings (Charles V. Suleiman I, and Francis I) one will see hatreds appear, dissensions in the Habsburg Empire caused by French spies, and wars to begin with Moslems invading Italy and later French rebellions against Moslems: Great change at first with Moslems ruling, then new tumult to grow, the plebeian (common) order, French citizens rebelling, will come to injure.

April

96. **"Secret conspiracy, rabble to conspire, the discovery with the device to move: Against the Great Ones.... Then slaughtered and put without power."** Secret conspiracy (Old French) by French rebels in Italy, rabble to conspire against the elected Moslems, the discovery of this the Moslems learned (supposedly) with the gimmick to move out of the way at first, feigning a defeat: Against the Moslem great ones, the French rebels, like the end time Catholic Church, then slaughtered and put without power.

May

97. **"Times inconstant, fevers, plague, weaknesses, wars, debate, times desolated without pretending: Submersions, Princes to minors severities, happy kings and Great Ones, another death to fear."** Times inconstant with French and Moslems together sharing Italian lands, fevers, plague, weaknesses in the friendship of opposing religions, wars from French rebellions, debates over religion, times desolated without pretending as the Moslem religion is banned: Submersions for Moslem princes lowered to minors, severeties of Christianity, happy kings (rebels) and great ones (Moslems), another death to fear.

June

98. **"In the place fire placed the plague and flight will arise, times variant, wind, the death of three Great Ones: From the Sky great thunderbolts, to feed upon the estate of Shaven Ones, Old One near death wood scarce in twigs."** In the place (Italy) where Moslem fire placed, French spy plague and Habsburg flight will arise, times variant, rebellion wind, the death of three Great Ones (Moslems symbolizing end time Protestants): From the sky great thunderbolts (Moslem retaliation) estate of the Shaven Ones (rebels) to feed upon, Old one (France) near death, wood scarce in twigs (Old French).

July

99. **"The world in peril and Kings to rejoice in participation, Shaven Ones stirred up by counsel that which was The Church Kings for the sake of themselves to irritate people, one will show afterwards what he was not."** The world (Italy) in peril from attack and kings (Francis I and Suleiman I) to rejoice in allied participation, shaven ones (French rebels) stirred up by counsel (from Moslem instigators) about that which was the Church Kings' for the sake of themselves to irritate the people to rebellion, Moslems retreating will show afterwards what they are not (still defeated).